Finding God in the Basement

"Dr. Carlier's new book is a wonderful addition to pastoral care and systematic theology. By appealing to the lived experiences of addicts, she provides a much-needed corrective to models of addiction that focus on blame. She offers a fierce indictment of the way some atonement theories have exacerbated the suffering of addicts and proposes a refreshing antidote. The news from the 'basement' makes available life-giving insight into the human condition and theology's role in addressing human suffering."

—Wendy Farley, Rice Family Chair of Spirituality,
San Francisco Theological Seminary

"At once theologically acute and pastorally wise, Jennifer Carlier's *Finding God in the Basement* merits a place at the center of conversations about how church communities can better respond to persons with addictions. The chapters on the impact of atonement theories on persons' ability to recover from addiction alone are worth the read. Carlier, however, follows up these chapters with deeply informed recommendations for how church communities can alter their own practices in order to become more hospitable to all, including their own members. In the United States 48.5 million people have addictions; churches cannot *be* churches without following the many insights that Carlier offers."

—Todd Whitmore, Associate Professor of Theology
and Anthropology, University of Notre Dame

"There is no shortage of books on addiction, or even on addiction and the church, but none of them provides the kind of sustained reflection on Christian faith and practice found in *Finding God in the Basement*. Carlier's argument, at once existentially gripping and theologically astute, offers a vision of salvation for those living with addiction that is as realistic in its analysis as it is uncompromising in its hope."

—Ian A. McFarland, Robert W. Woodruff Professor of Theology,
Emory University; *Quondam* Regius Professor
of Divinity, University of Cambridge

"Theological treatments of addiction are limited, especially ones that single out a particular doctrine as a culprit. But Jennifer Carlier does just this, asserting that the 'penal-substitutionary' view of the atonement (that God needs recompense for our sin in order to forgive us) is the very thing that keeps people with addiction mired in shame and guilt. She suggests that only the 'bondage of the will' aspect of original sin makes sense for sufferers. Replete with her own and others' personal stories, this book makes a good case for a more liberative theology."

—Linda Mercadante, Distinguished Research Professor Emerita,
Methodist Theological School in Ohio, founder of HealthyBeliefs.org

"There are two kinds of people in the United States: those who feel the crushing crisis of addiction and those who will soon. Jennifer Carlier provides a much-needed resource for Christians of all kinds, offering a medical and scientific understanding of addiction, a theological grounding for the challenge, and a framework of hope for recovery. This book will undoubtedly find its way out of the basement and into seminaries, as well as into the hands of church leaders across the country. The story told is about more than addiction and recovery, but about the journey everyone must make from a place of bondage to a new life of freedom."

—Timothy McMahan King, author of *Addiction Nation: What the Opioid Crisis Reveals about Us*

"Filled with beautiful writing, insightful critique, and concrete suggestions, *Finding God in the Basement* represents the very best of constructive theology oriented toward liberation and healing. Dr. Carlier offers crucial theological analyses of beliefs and practices that exacerbate shame and undermine recovery. In their stead, she highlights models and metaphors that sustain practices of healing. *Finding God in the Basement* is a gift to all who struggle with addiction and to the loved ones and church communities journeying with them."

—Ellen Ott Marshall, Professor of Christian Ethics and Conflict Transformation, Candler School of Theology

Finding God in the Basement

*Reimagining a Theology
of Addiction and Recovery*

JENNIFER CARLIER

© 2026 Jennifer Carlier

First edition
Published by Westminster John Knox Press
Louisville, Kentucky

26 27 28 29 30 31 32 33 34 35—10 9 8 7 6 5 4 3 2 1

All rights reserved. No part of this book may be reproduced or transmitted in any form or by any means, electronic or mechanical, including photocopying, recording, or by any information storage or retrieval system, without permission in writing from the publisher. For information, address Westminster John Knox Press, 100 Witherspoon Street, Louisville, Kentucky 40202-1396. Or contact us online at www.wjkbooks.com.

Unless otherwise indicated, Scripture quotations are taken from the New Revised Standard Version Updated Edition. Copyright © 2021 National Council of Churches of Christ in the United States of America. Used by permission. All rights reserved worldwide.

Bible quotations marked NIV are from THE HOLY BIBLE, NEW INTERNATIONAL VERSION®, NIV® Copyright © 1973, 1978, 1984, 2011 by Biblica, Inc.® Used by permission. All rights reserved worldwide.

Excerpt(s) from BROKEN: MY STORY OF ADDICTION AND REDEMPTION by William Cope Moyers with Katherine Ketcham, copyright © 2006 by William Cope Moyers and Katherine Ketcham. Used by permission of Viking Books, an imprint of Penguin Publishing Group, a division of Penguin Random House LLC. All rights reserved.

Excerpt(s) from *Parched* by Heather King. Reprinted by permission of SLL/Sterling Lord Literalistic, Inc. Copyright by Heather King 2005.

Excerpt(s) from DRINKING: A LOVE STORY by Caroline Knapp, copyright © 1995 by Caroline Knapp. Used by permission of The Dial Press, an imprint of Random House, a division of Penguin Random House LLC. All rights reserved.

Excerpts from *Lit* by Mary Karr. Copyright © 2009 by Mary Karr. Used by permission of HarperCollins Publishers.

Portions of chapters 3, 4, and 5 were previously published in Jennifer Carlier, "Penal Substitutionary Atonement and the Problem of Shame in Addiction," *Pastoral Psychology* 72, no. 5 (17 July, 2023), 659–73, https://doi.org/10.1007/s11089-023-01089-5, Springer Nature. Used with permission.

Book design by Sharon Adams
Cover design by Luisa Dias

Library of Congress Cataloging-in-Publication Data is on file at the Library of Congress, Washington, DC.

ISBN: 978-0-664-26858-9

Most Westminster John Knox Press books are available at special quantity discounts when purchased in bulk by corporations, organizations, and special-interest groups. For more information, please email SpecialSales@wjkbooks.com.

In memory of T.S.
For my fellow R12 unicorns and all those in the basement.
I wouldn't be here were it not for you.

Contents

List of Illustrations	viii
Acknowledgments	ix
Introduction	1
Chapter 1: What Is Addiction?	9
Chapter 2: Addiction: Sin or Disease? A Theological Account of Addiction	35
Chapter 3: The Bondage of the Will and Pastoral Responses to Addiction	58
Chapter 4: Penal-Substitutionary Atonement and the Problem of Shame in Addiction	72
Chapter 5: Penal-Substitutionary Atonement and the Making of a Criminal	89
Chapter 6: Salvation Is a Journey through No-Man's-Land	105
Chapter 7: Finding God in the Basement	137
Chapter 8: Basement Practices for the Sanctuary	154
Conclusion	170
Bibliography	175
Index	185

List of Illustrations

Chapter 1

Figure 1.1: Freedom–Compulsion Spectrum   11

Figure 1.2: Freedom–Compulsion—Blame–Blamelessness Spectrum   11

Figure 1.3: Synapse and Neuron Cells Sending Electrical Chemical Signals   22

Figure 1.4: Ski Track for Cross Country   27

Chapter 2

Figure 2.1: Sin–Disease Spectrum   36

Figure 2.2: Pelagian–Manichean Spectrum   41

Figure 2.3: Calvin on Freedom–Compulsion Spectrum   48

Acknowledgments

I am deeply grateful to Wendy Farley and Ellen Ott Marshall, whom I rarely quote in this book and yet are on every page. Their scholarship, teaching, mentorship, and friendship have profoundly shaped both my theology and my writing. They helped me find my voice and fostered in me a commitment to clarity, authenticity, and vulnerability, even in academic settings where that is not always the norm.

I'm grateful also to Pam Hall and Don Saliers who read an early draft of this work and whose insights helped shape this book. I am indebted to the Louisville Institute for their generous support through their fellowship programs, which gave me the financial breathing space to do this work. I'm thankful for all my peers in the Graduate Division of Religion (and beyond) at Emory for the many ways they have shaped me. I am especially grateful to Callie Tabor, Norah Elmagraby, Michael Yandell, Isaac Horwedel, and Katie Givens Kime, who have all been meaningful conversation partners at different stages in the process of studying, writing, and vocational transitions. I'm grateful to Kim Long for helpful conversations about the last chapters of the book. I'm thankful for Ryan Bonfiglio and the Candler Foundry for taking a chance on me with the TheoEd Talk, which allowed me to distill the essence of what I most wanted to say about addiction and recovery.

Further, I'm grateful to my current colleagues at Columbia Theological Seminary who offer their support, encouragement, and friendship in so many ways. I'm especially grateful to my direct colleagues in the Office of Academic Affairs who bore the brunt of my sleep-deprived grumpiness and picked up more than their share in the final stretch of this project. I'm thankful to the John Bulow Library staff, especially Emily Peterson and Liz Miller, who helped me access all the resources I needed and kept an eye out for any new resources I might need.

I'm grateful to faculty colleagues at both Candler School of Theology and Columbia Theological Seminary who offered guidance in this process and helped me to let go of the manuscript when it was time to do so (or closely thereafter, in any case). I'm grateful to Lucy Baum for her help, especially in the proposal-writing stage of this project. Deep thanks to Mark Douglas and

Martha Moore-Keish for their careful reading of the draft of this manuscript. Their feedback, questions, encouragement, and mentorship have had a deep impact on me. I am also very thankful for Christine Roy Yoder, who read the chapter on Exodus and offered much needed guidance. More than that, however, I'm grateful for her partnership in the work we do, for her wisdom and mentorship, and for her continual support for me in my vocation as an administrator, scholar, and teacher. I feel lucky to have the colleagues that I do at Columbia Theological Seminary.

I'm grateful to Westminster John Knox, and especially to my editor, Stacy Davis, who reads manuscripts and answers emails faster than anyone I know. I'm grateful for her patience, encouragement, thoughtful edits, and belief in this project.

My gratitude extends also to the many people who kept me sane along the way: to Elizabeth Edge, without whom this book would simply not exist; to Kathryn Threadgill and Alex Zareth for their endless hospitality and to Kathryn especially for sharing her passion (and space!) for woodworking with me (in many ways, the title of the book applies to her basement woodshop as well); to Sue Maschinot and my many pickleball friends who help me remember that I'm more than what goes on in my head; to Matt and Lucy Baum for knowing me deeply and loving me still; to L'Anni Hill for being my family and leaving an indelible mark on who I am as a person.

I am grateful to my parents, Rein and Kathy Carlier; my brother and sister-in-law, Timo Carlier and Vanessa McCulloch; and my sister and brother-in-law, Jamie Carlier-Lewis and Phil Lewis: all have supported me on this journey from afar. I am most especially thankful for Hannah McCulloch, Robin and Astrid Carlier-McCulloch, and Zoë and Noah Lewis, who remind me to meet the world with wonder and a good dose of humor (and a stash of Lego). The five of them have made my life richer than I could ever have imagined. Thank you.

Introduction

I began the long journey of recovery from addiction fifteen years ago when I went to rehab. At the time, I told everyone at church that I was going on a lengthy silent retreat and thus wouldn't have access to my phone or email for a month. The idea of telling anyone at church that I was suffering from addiction, much less going to rehab, was simply unthinkable. Church was, after all, where everyone showed up in their Sunday best, a subtle but clear hint about the kind of person you were expected to be at church.

I felt a profound sense of failure and shame. To most people who knew me at church and elsewhere, I was a decently smart, ambitious, somewhat successful, well-loved person. From the outside I looked like a perfectly functional, happy person. Not wanting to disavow anyone, including myself, of that image, I went away on a "silent retreat," thinking I would fix myself in twenty-eight days and then come back to join regular society, never to speak of it again. I have since learned that while I certainly needed help with addiction, what I really needed more than anything was freedom from the crushing shame that kept me trapped in addiction and affected so many other parts of my life as well.

This introduction includes material previously presented as a TheoEd Talk (Jennifer Carlier, "Finding God in the Basement," TheoEd, filmed Sept. 2022, https://www.theoed.com/jennifercarlier).

In rehab, I learned that addiction affects all sorts of people from all sectors of society and that it is far more common than I thought. It turns out that approximately 17 percent of US adults suffered from some kind of substance use disorder (SUDs) in 2023, whether that be an addiction to alcohol, illicit drugs, prescription medications, or legal drugs (depending on what state you live in) such as marijuana.[1] That percentage doesn't include the millions of people suffering from what are often called process or behavioral addictions, such as gambling, gaming, compulsive internet use, and compulsive sexual activities, to name a few. Addiction is an enormous problem in the United States; a few statistics help paint the picture.[2] Drug overdose deaths have increased rapidly in the last twenty years. In 2021, more than one hundred thousand people died of drug overdoses.[3] The sharpest rise (a 50 percent increase) occurred, not surprisingly, between 2019 and 2022. Nora Volkow, director of the National Institute of Drug Addiction (NIDA), said in a 2022 interview that the COVID-19 pandemic significantly impacted drug use and abuse.[4] Encouragingly, the latest findings indicate that drug overdose deaths have decreased in 2023–2024 for the first time

---

1. "Key Substance Use and Mental Health Indicators in the United States: Result from the 2023 National Survey on Drug Use and Health," Substance Abuse and Mental Health Services Administration (SAMHSA), July 2024, https://www.samhsa.gov/data/sites/default/files/reports/rpt47095 /National%20Report/National%20Report/2023-nsduh-annual-national.pdf, p. 26, fig. 28.

While "Substance Use Disorders" (SUDs) and "Substance-Related Disorders" are the technical terms that the *Diagnostic and Statistical Manual of Mental Disorders,* more commonly known as the DSM-V (American Psychiatric Association, *Diagnostic and Statistical Manual of Mental Disorders: Fifth Edition, Text Revision (DSM-5-TR)* [American Psychiatric Publishing, 2022]) uses to talk about addiction, I mostly use the term "addiction" in this book because this term is more expansive (see below). I use the term SUDs when I am referring specifically to addiction to substances (e.g., alcohol, methamphetamines, opioids, etc.).

Further, while most of the addiction literature and memoirs I rely on focus primarily on substance use, I include the so-called behavioral or process addictions (e.g., addictions to food, sex, pornography, gambling, gaming, etc.) in the category of addiction, because people suffering from these addictions show many of the same symptoms as those suffering from SUDs, and much of what I write about applies to these addictions as well.

Finally, while I take a people-first approach in principle, there are moments when I use the word "addict" instead of "person suffering from addiction" or "person with addiction" to refer to a person with addiction. I do this primarily when I'm referring to someone who refers to themselves in this way. Many people with addiction (myself included) refer to themselves as "addict."

2. Statistics on SUDs and drug overdose deaths change rapidly. The statistics named here are the latest available as of 2025. Most definitive reports in 2025 refer to the years 2023 and 2024. These numbers may be different at the time of publication and will almost certainly be different at the time of reading. I use them here to paint a picture of the problem. While the numbers have changed over the last ten years (i.e., 2015–2025—with numbers largely increasing), and the last couple of years, in particular, show some encouraging trends with regard to a decline in drug overdose deaths (see note 3), the problem remains significant.

3. "Drug Overdose Deaths in the U.S. Top 100,000 Annually," Centers for Disease Control and Prevention (CDC), November 17, 2021, https://www.cdc.gov/nchs/pressroom/nchs_press_releases/2021 /20211117.htm. For a comparison of drug overdose death rates from 1999 through 2023, see "Drug Overdose Deaths: Facts and Figures," National Institute of Drug Abuse (NIDA), August 2024, https://nida.nih.gov/research-topics/trends-statistics/overdose-death-rates.

4. Kevin Kunzmann, "Nora D. Volkow, MD: Combating COVID-Era Issues in Substance Use Disorder," May 23, 2022, https://www.hcplive.com/view/nora-volkow-md-covid-era-issues-substance -use-disorder.

in years, though these numbers are still significantly higher than pre-COVID-19. As the CDC indicates, "While this national decline is encouraging news, overdose remains the leading cause of death of Americans aged 18–44."[5] These statistics, while staggering, are just the tip of the iceberg, because behind these thousands upon thousands of annual deaths in the United States are the more than 46 million people in the United States who suffer daily from substance use disorders, not counting the many who suffer from other addictions along with the millions who are impacted by the addictions of a close friend or family member.[6]

Each one of these 46 million people represents a complex and often heartbreaking story if we are willing to listen. I have been a part of recovery communities for well over a decade and in those years have met hundreds upon hundreds of people and listened to thousands of stories. At times, I have been overwhelmed by the anguish and tragedy I have witnessed. At the same time, I have seen in these stories a strength, beauty, and resilience that I have seen nowhere else. I have seen many people released from the bondage of addiction after years of use and witnessed the slow but sure resurrection of their lives after it seemed all hope was gone. I have, sadly, also lost friends in these communities to overdoses and suicides despite their best efforts to recover.

When I first started going to Twelve-Step meetings in the basements of churches, they asked of me something the churches I had been a part of had never asked of me—they asked me to show up fully and completely as *me*.[7] Here

---

5. "CDC Reports Nearly 24% Decline in U.S. Drug Overdose Deaths," CDC, February 25, 2025, https://www.cdc.gov/media/releases/2025/2025-cdc-reports-decline-in-us-drug-overdose-deaths.html#:~:text=New%20provisional%20data%20from%20CDC%27s,steep%20decline%20in%20overdose%20deaths. This decrease in drug overdose deaths is promising. It is hard to know, however, whether these decreases are due to diminished drug use, the restarting of services and less isolation post-COVID-related interruptions, or greater availability of Naloxone. Further, while the 2023/2024 numbers are not yet available, previous years demonstrate that these decreases tend to show up more in White communities than BIPOC (Black, Indigenous, [and] People of Color) communities (Matthew Garnett and Arialdi M. Miniño, "Drug Overdose Deaths in the United States, 2003–2023," NCHS Data Brief, no. 522, National Center for Health Statistics, December 2024, https://dx.doi.org/10.15620/cdc/170565).

6. "Key Substance Use and Mental Health Indicators," p. 26, fig. 28. In 2023 this number was 48.5 million. NIDA puts that number at over 46 million in 2025 ("NIDA IC Fact Sheet 2025," National Institute on Drug Abuse [NIDA], March 7, 2024, https://nida.nih.gov/about-nida/legislative-activities/budget-information/fiscal-year-2025-budget-information-congressional-justification-national-institute-drug-abuse/ic-fact-sheet-2025#:~:text=46.3-million%20people%20in%20the%20United%20States%20had%20an%20SUD%20in%202021.&text=In%202021%2C%20only%206.3%20percent%20of%20people%20with%20SUD%20received%20treatment.&text=In%202022%2C%20about%20110%2C000%20people%20died%20of%20drug%20overdoses). Note that the 2025 numbers cited by NIDA (above) are part of a budget justification.

These statistics only reflect what is happening in the United States, so the problem is much larger than I talk about here.

7. Twelve-Step groups include groups such as Alcoholics Anonymous (AA), Narcotics Anonymous (NA), and many others (e.g., Gamblers Anonymous [GA], Crystal Meth Anonymous [CMA], Overeaters Anonymous [OA], and Sex and Love Addicts Anonymous [SLAA], etc.). I talk about Twelve-Step groups in this book because they are among the most popular addiction recovery groups worldwide and happen to be the groups I'm most familiar with. While I talk most about these groups in this book, it is not my purpose to exclusively endorse these groups over others, or to claim that this is the only way to recovery. Other groups include Refuge Recovery, SMART Recovery,

was a community that wanted nothing more than my honesty and authenticity, and in response to my many relapses, sloppy failures, and moments of deep shame offered me grace and unconditional acceptance. I didn't trust it at first, but slowly I began to retrieve things from the recesses of myself and showed them to this group of people, as if asking—can you love me even now? And no matter what I brought back from the depths, they loved and accepted me. In fact, the more I showed of myself, the more they seemed to love me—not in spite of my relapses and moments of shame, but *with* all my messiness. This notion of being loved with all my flaws was different from any concept of grace I had experienced growing up in the sanctuary.

While I wouldn't have been able to name it as such at the time, I can see in hindsight that my concept of grace, growing up, was very much influenced by the doctrine of penal-substitutionary atonement. This particular interpretation of the cross and salvation was central to my community's faith. To put it very simply, I was taught in the Christian school I attended and in Sunday school that our sin incites God's wrath and necessitates eternal punishment. Out of God's deep love for us, however, God places the punishment on Jesus instead of humans, thereby fulfilling the demand for punishment, saving us from hell, and allowing for an eternal relationship with God. This judicial metaphor for atonement infused not only conversations and teachings about salvation but also many of the hymns and liturgies I participated in, such as the hymn "My Hope Is Built."

> My hope is built on nothing less
> than Jesus' blood and righteousness
> ....
> Dressed in his righteousness alone
> faultless to stand before the throne![8]

Similarly, I remember singing "O Sacred Head Now Wounded" on Good Friday every year, the whole congregation mournfully singing the words as the lights were dimmed in the sanctuary:

> What Thou, my Lord, hast suffered
>   Was all for sinners' gain:
> Mine, mine was the transgression,
>   But Thine the deadly pain.
> Lo, here I fall, my Savior!
>   'Tis I deserve Thy place;

Secular Organizations for Sobriety, Women for Recovery, Celebrate Recovery, and Moderation Management. Beyond these, people recover in a variety of ways (therapy, medication, rehab, on their own, etc.), and some never make use of these support groups. Further, recovery means different things to different people. Where a lot of people in addiction recovery adhere to total abstinence, others successfully implement harm reduction methods. Again, it is not my intention to endorse one method over the other, as I have seen both used successfully by friends in recovery. While I adhere to abstinence in my own recovery, I am not invested in telling other people what healthy recovery looks like for them.

8. *United Methodist Hymnal* (United Methodist Publishing House, 1989), #368, vss. 1 and 4.

> Look on me with Thy favor,
> And grant to me Thy grace.[9]

The themes of sin, punishment, and substitution permeated much of the language in the teachings, liturgies, hymns, and prayers I grew up with.[10]

The notion that my sin made God so angry that someone had to be punished with a death sentence for it generated in me a sense that God could only love me in spite of who I am, not because of who I am. That is, I was taught that even though I am a worthless sinner, God could, through the death of Christ on the cross, love me in spite of who I am.[11] Of course, being gay, and being told, in so many words, that the church could love me but not my "sin," didn't help. All these things compounded the sense that I was loved in spite of myself. The experience of being loved *with* all of my messiness, while still being held responsible for taking steps toward health, in these basement communities, therefore, instilled a profound sense of grace in me that I had not yet experienced in the sanctuary.

I have found that many Christians, without being fully aware of it, tend toward an understanding of atonement that aligns with penal-substitutionary atonement. Scholars such as Leanne Van Dyk, Mark Baker and Joel Green, and Sonia Waters make similar observations.[12] Van Dyk, for instance, says that "many Christians simply assume that this version of the cross [i.e., penal-substitutionary atonement], which sounds so familiar to them, is the best—perhaps even the only—understanding of the cross."[13] While many more progressive churches do not adhere to this understanding of salvation, the language of the liturgies often still evokes this understanding of the cross. Penal-substitutionary atonement is pervasive in churches, and I would argue in American culture as a whole, with its fondness for punishment and retributive justice.[14]

While my understanding of salvation grew more complex over time, it wasn't until I went to seminary that I learned that there are multiple ways to think about salvation and that each of these, far from being a literal description of what happens in salvation, is a metaphor. Thus, at seminary, well into adulthood, I finally learned that my specific understanding of salvation was called penal-substitutionary atonement and that this is one among several theories of atonement including, for instance, *Christus Victor* (including ransom theory),

---

9. *Glory to God* (Westminster John Knox, 2013), #221.

10. Because ransom theory and penal-substitutionary atonement both rely on the language of substitution, it is hard to tell in these hymns what version of atonement they are referencing.

11. I am grateful to Sallie McFague for naming this reality in *Models of God: Theology for an Ecological, Nuclear Age* (Fortress, 1987), 102. Her recognition of the importance of being valued not in spite of who we are but because of who we are helped me name this tension in my own life.

12. Leanne Van Dyk, *Believing in Jesus Christ* (Geneva Press, 2002). Mark D. Baker and Joel B. Green, *Recovering the Scandal of the Cross: Atonement in New Testament and Contemporary Contexts*, 2nd ed. (IVP Academic, 2011), 161. Sonia E. Waters, "Punishing the Immoral Other: Penal Substitutionary Logic in the War on Drugs," *Pastoral Psychology* 68, no. 5 (October 1, 2019): 534, https://doi.org/10.1007/s11089-018-0836-y, 539.

13. Van Dyk, *Believing in Jesus Christ*, 87.

14. See, for instance, Waters, "Punishing the Immoral Other," 541.

satisfaction theory, and moral influence.[15] Theoretically, I understood and bought into the fact that there are many metaphors for atonement and began to explore others that are more freeing. However, at this point in my life, I had been unintentionally (and intentionally) spoon-fed penal-substitutionary atonement for so many years that it was infused into my very being. Even though I very much wanted to believe otherwise, I could not simply shed this notion of atonement and all the incumbent notions of God and grace attached to it.

Having a healthy dose of my own shame to contend with, it was easy to imagine God as being perennially angry at and disappointed in me. Thus, when I began to suffer from addiction, the combination of feeling doomed to continually engage in behaviors that caused me a deep sense of shame with the belief in an angry and disappointed God generated a guilt and shame in me that I can only describe as hellish. Where my faith should have been a source of comfort and help in the midst of the suffering of addiction, I found it to be an obstacle to my recovery. Ironically, the theological concept that should have offered me the most hope to free me from the bondage of addiction (i.e., salvation) ended up miring me further in the hell of addiction.

I found God and redemption in a different place than I was taught to look. I found the God of love and redemption not in the sanctuary among the saints but in the basement among the so-called sinners—among the drunks, tweakers, and junkies. And in that basement, I found liberation not just from the bondage of addiction but also from the bondage of toxic theologies, like penal-substitutionary atonement, which offered me a God who could only love me in spite of myself. I have since also seen glimpses in the sanctuary of this God who loves me fully, but I am indebted to these groups that meet in the basement for my first introduction to the God of grace, acceptance, love, and redemption.

---

15. Broadly, *Christus Victor* refers to the notion that Jesus Christ conquers the forces of evil. This theory usually includes ransom theory, in which Jesus Christ offers himself as ransom to free humans from the clutches of the devil. Note that in this case, our giving of ourselves to the forces of evil means that God must negotiate with the devil to free us. In some versions of this theory, Jesus tricks the devil into accepting his death as a ransom (e.g., see Gregory of Nyssa, "The Great Catechism" in *Nicene and Post-Nicene Fathers: Second Series, Vol. 5 — Gregory of Nyssa: Dogmatic Treatises*, ed. Philip Schaff and Henry Wallace, trans. William Moore and Henry Austin Wilson [Christian Literature Publishing, 1893], I.24). Theologians, such as Anselm, find this line of reasoning unacceptable because everything, including Satan and humankind, already belongs to God. He therefore expressly denies the idea that God has to strike a deal or trick the devil in order to free humankind. God does not owe the devil anything, because Satan belongs to God. (Anselm, *Cur Deus Homo*, in *Anselm: Basic Writings*, ed. and trans. Thomas Williams [Hackett, 2007], 1.7) Anselm, thus, offers the satisfaction theory of atonement where Jesus Christ pays the debt we owe to God on our behalf. Penal-substitutionary atonement, while having many of the same features as satisfaction theory, is a specific interpretation of substitutionary atonement that moves the metaphor from the marketplace (the language of debt) to the justice system. Moral influence theory focuses on Jesus Christ as example. Jesus's death is seen as an example of God's deep love for us, which then transforms humans. This theory is most closely associated with Peter Abelard. (Peter Abelard, *Commentary on the Epistle to the Romans*, trans. Steven R. Cartwright [CUA Press, 2011], esp. sections on the latter part of Romans 3.)

Over the years I've come across many people in addiction recovery who've shared similar stories and talk about the fact that they somehow encountered God in these recovery communities in ways they hadn't in the churches they had been a part of.[16] Some even say that these basement communities have become their church, because in these communities they discovered the grace they longed for yet often could not find in the sanctuary. Kent Dunnington names a similar tension, noting that the "prevalence of such [i.e., recovery] communities can be seen as an indictment of the church." He goes on to say, "The massive growth of twelve-step groups has exposed the church's inability or failure to deal honestly and adequately with the brokenness of persons."[17] Given the fact that Jesus' ministry is centered around broken persons, this inability on the church's part seems profoundly sad. As a theologian who is deeply committed to the church, this concerns me.

In this book, I seek to retrieve theological concepts that attend with compassion to the brokenness of persons, especially those suffering from addiction, and ask what we, as the church, might offer those suffering to help free them from the bondage of addiction. Many churches already offer spaces for recovery communities to meet in, and some offer programs and Bible studies specifically geared toward those with addiction, or meals for those experiencing houselessness as a result of addiction. These are crucial works. Equally important to these programs, however, are the theological constructs that undergird these efforts. What do we have to offer theologically that can bear the weight of the realities of addiction while also offering a sense of hope for recovery? These are the questions that drive this book.

Before diving into these theological waters, however, it is important to get a sense of what exactly it is that we are dealing with. Thus, chapter 1 begins with a general overview of what addiction is, relying on models of addiction from the social sciences and experiences of addiction as described in memoirs on addiction and recovery. In chapters 2 and 3 I explore what addiction is from a theological perspective, taking into account the models and experiences of addiction described in chapter 1. Here I present a modified version of the bondage of the will as an effective model for thinking about addiction that both bears the weight of the suffering of those with addiction while limiting the shame that is often associated with it.

Where the first three chapters focus on the problem of addiction and human brokenness, chapter 4 begins engaging the themes of recovery, hope, and salvation. In this chapter I explain why penal-substitutionary atonement, a predominant model for thinking about salvation, is especially harmful for those with addiction

---

16. E.g., in *Why Can't Church Be More Like an AA Meeting?* Stephen Haynes explores his own journey in recovery and his (and others') longing for church to be "more like AA meetings." (Stephen Haynes, *Why Can't Church Be More Like an AA Meeting? And Other Questions Christians Ask About Recovery* [Eerdmans, 2021], 9).

17. Kent Dunnington, *Addiction and Virtue: Beyond the Models of Disease and Choice* (IVP Academic, 2011), 170, 179.

and, by extension, for anyone struggling with brokenness and shame. Where chapter 4 focuses on the harm that the logic of penal-substitutionary atonement does to individuals, chapter 5, by examining the war on drugs, focuses on the devastation that the logic of this model causes in communities. In chapter 6 I turn to an alternative way of thinking about salvation that offers hope for those with addiction while validating the realities of the difficulty of recovery. Here I demonstrate that the exodus story offers a more hopeful and grounded way of thinking about what redemption from bondage looks like in practice. Throughout these chapters, I analyze theological constructs through the lens of experiences of addiction and recovery to find both resonances and places of tension. My aim in these chapters is to offer liberative theologies that decrease the shame and stigma often associated with addiction and attend with compassion and care to those suffering.

In chapter 7 I turn from thinking about what churches might offer theologically to those with addiction to thinking about what the sanctuary might learn from the basement. Thus, I offer the journey of recovery as a helpful metaphor for thinking about salvation as this metaphor recognizes the importance of seeing both justification and sanctification as integral to salvation. Salvation doesn't just happen *to* us but must also happen *with* us and *in* us. Finally, in chapter 8, I offer several "basement practices" the sanctuary might adopt that, while helpful for those with addiction, are liberative for everyone in the church. Specifically, I focus on what it means to build community and what it looks like to become a community of authenticity and vulnerability that allows everyone to show up as themselves.

Through its mix of storytelling and robust theological engagement, this book offers a glimpse of the God of grace I have seen reflected in the many faces of the people I have met in the basement. I am profoundly grateful to their witness. It is my hope that this book may give those of us in the sanctuary theological language to speak with compassion about what it means to be caught in the bondage of brokenness and imagine anew what it looks like to journey together toward the hope of the promised land, even while walking through no-man's-land.

Chapter 1

What Is Addiction?

In 2013, Elizabeth Vargas, successful host of ABC's *20/20*, came home from her third stay in rehab for alcoholism. And sadly, within four days of coming home, she relapsed. In her memoir she describes this moment by saying, "I came home, and I drank. Again. I hurt my children, whom I adore, again. I hurt and enraged Marc yet again. Why on earth would I do this? Why would I risk everything, undoing all I had accomplished?" She goes on, "I hated myself so much for what I was doing," and felt "guilt and shame . . . crowding around me," yet could not stop.[1]

Given everything she had to lose—her job at ABC, her marriage, her children—why, indeed, would she allow herself to continue drinking? Her many painful attempts at recovery and her deep shame over every failure indicate that she wanted to stop drinking, and yet time after time she seemed to do precisely what she, paradoxically, did not actually want to do. As someone in long-term recovery, I know this struggle well.

---

1. Elizabeth Vargas, *Between Breaths: A Memoir of Panic and Addiction* (Grand Central, 2016), 197, 198, 199.

Addiction was baffling to me. I wanted sobriety. I was desperate for it. I spent hundreds of hours in recovery meetings, thousands of dollars on therapy and rehab. I journaled, did the Twelve Steps, and did the work that was asked of me, and yet, time and time again I would find myself doing the very thing I did not want to do. One of the most terrifying things about addiction for me was that it called into question everything I thought I knew about my will. I, like most of us, experience myself as having the capacity to make free choices, yet I would find myself making choices against my own will. How is that possible? Addiction is terrifying because what is disordered is not an organ (e.g., the heart, lungs, kidneys) but our very capacity to make choices. How do we come to understand this obsession of the mind that slavishly compels people to continue to engage in behaviors that have obvious negative and often fatal consequences?

Despite the significant number of people suffering from addiction, it remains a notoriously difficult problem to define. The *Diagnostic and Statistical Manual of Mental Disorders* (DSM-V) recognizes four main clusters of symptoms: those related to "impaired control over substance use" (e.g., a desire to stop, yet unable to); "social impairment" (e.g., interpersonal problems due to persistent use); "risky use" (e.g., putting oneself in danger in order to use); and "pharmacological criteria" (e.g., drug tolerance and withdrawal).[2] The symptoms that make up addiction are not as contested as the etiology (causes) of addiction, which are captured in the various models (theories) of addiction.

Models of addiction can illuminate how addiction works and why it occurs. Scientific and psychological theories of addiction have tremendous explanatory power. These theories further addiction research and help provide much-needed funding for addiction treatment. To understand what an addiction is, however, also requires an understanding of the experience. Without the complementary knowledge of experience, we have an incomplete picture of what addiction is. For instance, a person who gets drunk on a regular basis and does harmful things as a result is not necessarily an addict. On the outside an excessive drinker and an alcoholic may look quite similar. The difference lies in the experience of compulsion, in the inability to stop despite negative consequences. Thus, while theories have tremendous explanatory power, only stories can describe how an addiction is actually experienced by the person suffering from it. As such, I will be using memoirs of addiction and recovery, as well as the personal stories recorded in *Alcoholics Anonymous: The Big Book* and *Narcotics Anonymous* alongside descriptions of models of addiction to give a fuller picture of what addiction is and what it feels like to those in its grip.[3] Beyond offering a fuller picture, the stories of people's experiences also remind us that addiction is not an object to be studied and fixed but rather a profoundly painful human experience.

---

2. American Psychiatric Association, *Diagnostic and Statistical Manual of Mental Disorders: Fifth Edition, Text Revision (DSM-5-TR)* (American Psychiatric Association, 2022), 544–46.

3. *Alcoholics Anonymous: The Big Book*, 4th ed. (Alcoholics Anonymous World Services, 2002). *Narcotics Anonymous*, 6th ed. (World Service Office, 2008).

MODELS OF ADDICTION

Addiction has been variously characterized as a choice, an effort to self-medicate or cope, a brain disease, a kind of accelerated learning, and a syndrome. Each of these models is an attempt to explain how it is possible for people to keep making choices, seemingly, against their own will. In that sense each model for addiction falls somewhere along the spectrum between freedom and compulsion.

Characterizing addiction as a moral failure, for instance, assumes a lot of freedom. After all, it only makes sense to name addiction a moral failure if the person has the capacity to choose otherwise. Thus, a moral failure model of addiction would fall on the "freedom" side of the spectrum. The other extreme would be the brain disease model of addiction (BDMA) where, in its purest form, addiction is seen as a disease affecting the brain. This model would fall on the "compulsion" side of the spectrum. Most models of addiction fall somewhere in between these two extremes, and even proponents within each model fall on different points along this spectrum.

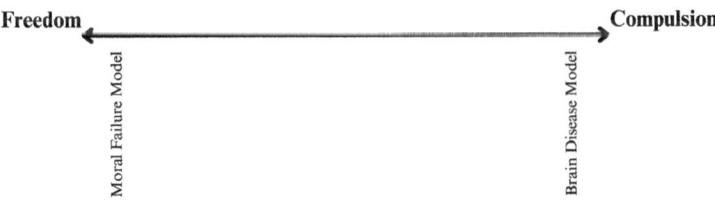

Figure. 1.1. Freedom–Compulsion Spectrum

A parallel spectrum that runs alongside the freedom and compulsion spectrum is that of blame and blamelessness. Seeing addiction as a moral failure assumes a tremendous amount of freedom on the part of the person using, which in turn allows us to see the person as blameworthy. This is the logic of the "war on drugs." It only makes sense to blame someone for possession of cocaine if we assume the person had the freedom to choose otherwise. Conversely, seeing addiction as purely a brain disease that compels a person to keep using despite negative consequences allows us to see the person as blameless.

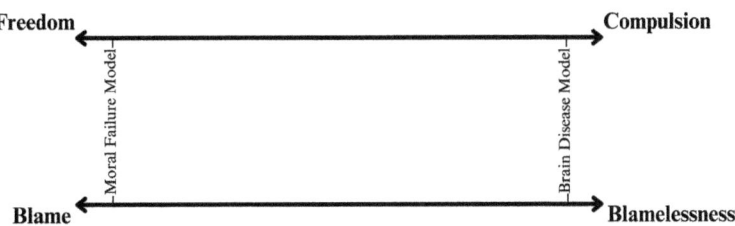

Figure. 1.2. Freedom–Compulsion—Blame–Blamelessness Spectrum

An example that may help illuminate the difference is to think about a disease like Alzheimer's disease. Having a family member who has Alzheimer's can be exceedingly painful. The person with Alzheimer's may forget her spouse or children's names or yell at them in anger. Despite the pain that family members experience, most do not blame the person with Alzheimer's for the behaviors exhibited as a result of the disease. The reason we do not tend to blame people who have Alzheimer's for actions that would in any other circumstance be blameworthy is because we recognize it as a disease and, therefore, understand that the person suffering cannot help but behave the way they are behaving. They are, in a sense, compelled. If they had the freedom to act otherwise, then we would hold the person responsible for their actions and perhaps assign blame.

Addictions are complex precisely because addictions tend to wreak havoc on those closest to the person suffering, and we do not quite know where to place them on the freedom/compulsion continuum. William Moyers describes this well in his memoir, *Broken*. When Moyers first sought help for his addiction at a hospital, he told the admissions counselor about his addiction to alcohol and cocaine. The counselor noted that his wife, Mary, thought Moyers was merely dealing with a temporary problem with alcohol and said, "'I think you'd better go out to the waiting room and tell her the truth.'"[4] Moyers finally tells Mary that he is "a junkie and a drunk" and says, "All these years later I can still see the look on her face—the blood vessels in her eyes, the way her lips twisted open and then closed, the sudden intake of breath and then the stillness, as if she had stopped breathing completely."[5] He describes that she "nearly collapsed in the foyer" on the way out "and had to lean up against the wall to steady herself."[6] Years later, Moyers recalls, "a family friend, a doctor at St. Vincent's, confronted me in my room at the psych ward," saying, "'How could you have done this to Mary? Why did you do this to her?'"[7] Moyers recognizes that the doctor, whose tone was "angry and incredulous," was really saying, "*What's wrong with you?*"[8] He says, "that sentiment was secretly shared by everyone, including me. What was wrong with me that I would willfully choose to use drugs and destroy my marriage and my life? How could I be so weak, so thoughtless, so self-centered?"[9]

There is no doubt that Moyers harmed his wife, Mary, in his addiction. Months after his admittance to St. Vincent's, she writes him a letter which begins, "'My heart is broken,'" and continues, "'I remember when my heart used to feel joy, and I don't know how I'll ever get back there again.'"[10] Moyers says that "the person she had trusted and believed the most had deceived her the

---

4. William Cope Moyers, *Broken: My Story of Addiction and Redemption* (Penguin Books, 2007), 126.
5. Moyers, *Broken*, 126.
6. Moyers, *Broken*, 127.
7. Moyers, *Broken*, 339.
8. Moyers, *Broken*, 339 (italics in the original).
9. Moyers, *Broken*, 339–40.
10. Moyers, *Broken*, 203.

most. The person she had let into her heart had broken her heart in two," and as a result "she was suffering physically and mentally . . . experiencing memory lapses, disorientation, fears for her safety, anxiety attacks, and depression."[11] Mary is clearly a victim; what is unclear is to what degree she is a victim of Moyers and to what degree she is a victim of his addiction. There is not a clear line demarking when Moyers is rightly considered an agent and when he is enslaved by a compulsion.

How we define addiction determines where we place it along these parallel scales, which in turn has a tremendous effect on how we treat addiction. As Sonia Waters succinctly puts it, "definition drives care."[12] If addiction is a disease affecting the brain, a medical response is appropriate. If, on the other hand, addiction is a moral failure, it makes more sense to send those with addiction to the justice system. Similarly, if addiction is a coping mechanism that people use to cope with their circumstances, a more socially oriented response would be appropriate. How we define and think about addiction has deep implications for how we treat those with addiction. In this chapter I lay out a few of the more prominent theories of addiction, which will lay the groundwork for the next chapter, in which we delve into how we might think about addiction theologically. In what follows, I begin with models on the "freedom" end of the spectrum and move from one end to the other, ending with the brain disease model of addiction, which falls more on the "compulsion" end of the spectrum.

The Moral Model of Addiction

The assumption behind the moral model of addiction is that people have the capacity, freedom, and agency to not use drugs, even once they have been using for quite some time. It assumes that people could, to quote Nancy Reagan, "just say no," and that their decision to use is indicative of a moral flaw.[13] To be clear, very few people would say that they hold to a moral model of addiction. While this model is not the predominant way we *say* we think about addiction in the United States, the fact that people are still regularly incarcerated for possession of drugs indicates that many still view addiction as an issue of morality best dealt with in the justice system, as opposed to an issue of health. Of course, as has been well documented by the likes of Michelle Alexander, financial incentives, political gain, and most importantly, racist ideologies were the predominant drivers of mass incarceration in the war on drugs.[14] The political rhetoric that was used to obscure these racist motives, however, was largely based in morality,

---

11. Moyers, *Broken*, 203.
12. Sonia Waters, *Addiction and Pastoral Care* (Eerdmans, 2019), 33.
13. "Just Say No," The Ronald Reagan Presidential Foundation and Institute, accessed March 19, 2025, https://www.reaganfoundation.org/ronald-reagan/nancy-reagan/her-causes.
14. Michelle Alexander, *The New Jim Crow: Mass Incarceration in the Age of Colorblindness*, 10th Anniversary ed. (The New Press, 2020).

and the fact that this rhetoric was widely accepted demonstrates that the moral model of addiction still plays a significant role in our thinking about addiction even if we do not outwardly name it as such.

Hanna Pickard, who does not adhere to this model, explains that it relies on two premises. The first is "that drug use is a choice even for those who are addicted."[15] Incarcerating people for possession of drugs or for using in a public space only makes sense if we assume the person has the capacity to choose otherwise. The second premise Pickard names is more difficult to prove. She argues that society tends to condemn those who are addicted because we assume that "addicts are people of bad character who embrace a life of hedonism."[16] At times, even our best efforts to help prevent addiction through education can have these overtones. As Henderson and Dressler argue, "through attempting to teach students not to use drugs, these programs are teaching students to stigmatize people with substance use disorder," because the underlying message is that drug use is a "deviant and self-destructive behavior that goes against moral norms."[17] The U.S. Department of Education, for instance, advises that schools can "help to prevent youth and young adult substance misuse" by teaching students "the dangers of illicit drug use" and "support[ing] [students] in developing skills to resist the pressure to experiment with and misuse drugs and build healthy lifestyle choices."[18] Although much of the education is grounded in the neuroscience of addiction, framing addiction as something one must resist through healthy choices has inadvertent moral overtones.

While the moral model is no longer openly espoused by most people, it is still present in the way many respond to those with addiction. Moyers's friend's incredulity over what he did to his wife, Mary, is indicative of the moral model of addiction.[19] Moyers says that people responded "as different as night and day" to his addiction and to his cancer diagnosis in that "no one ever suggested" in relation to cancer that he "gave [him]self the illness or that it was in any way [his] fault. . . ."[20] Moyers explains, "It was a completely different story with my addiction," in that "from the beginning, we all thought the disease was partly if not wholly my fault."[21] Similarly, *Alcoholics Anonymous: The Big Book* points to this difference when it says, "if a person has cancer all are sorry for him and no one is angry or hurt." Alcoholism, on the other hand, tends to

---

15. Hanna Pickard, "What We're Not Talking about When We Talk about Addiction," *Hastings Center Report* 50, no. 4 (2020): 37, https://doi.org/10.1002/hast.1172.

16. Pickard, "What We're Not Talking About," 37.

17. Nicole L. Henderson and William W. Dressler, "Medical Disease or Moral Defect? Stigma Attribution and Cultural Models of Addiction Causality in a University Population," *Culture, Medicine, and Psychiatry* 41 (2017): 493, https//doi.org/10.1007/s11013-017-9531-1.

18. "Preventing and Reducing Youth and Young Adult Substance Misuse: Schools, Students, Families," U.S. Department of Education, last reviewed March 11, 2025, https://www.ed.gov/opioids/.

19. Moyers, *Broken*, 339.

20. Moyers, *Broken*, 337.

21. Moyers, *Broken*, 339.

produce "disgusted friends and employees" and "fierce resentment."[22] When a person relapses on their addiction, no one shows up with casseroles and well-wishes. Those around the person relapsing tend to be angry and often blame the person for relapsing. I sometimes catch myself inadvertently harboring some of these feelings about my fellow travelers in recovery who relapse (even though I relapsed many times myself, especially at the beginning!). These feelings are undoubtedly grounded in the shame and self-blame I felt when I relapsed. These common responses belie many of our claims that we do not see addiction as a moral problem.

The Choice Model

The choice model of addiction has similarities to the moral model in that it recognizes a tremendous amount of agency and freedom in the person with addiction. This can be very empowering for a person trying to get well. However, the choice model is very different from the moral model in that it does not view addiction as an issue of morality. Proponents of the choice model also do not see addiction as a simple choice between using or not using. This model of addiction is used most often by those who do research in behavioral economics, which, neuroscientist Marc Lewis explains, "blends social psychology with economic thinking." This is a field in which researchers attempt to make sense of "why people make the choices they make, including the choice to take addictive substances."[23] This model of addiction asserts that addiction is, in some ways, a rational choice.

Gene Heyman, a psychologist, researcher, and senior lecturer at Boston College, is a proponent of this model. He argues in *Addiction: A Disorder of Choice* that there are two ways of framing options. He calls one "local choice" and the other "global choice."[24] Someone who is addicted to alcohol has a choice between two options each day. The one option is to drink; the other is not to drink. Were the person with addiction to make this choice from a local (i.e., daily) perspective, the choice to drink is always the more rational option. On any single day, the pain of withdrawal far outweighs the pain of drinking. While drinking certainly loses its appeal over time due to the negative consequences of continuous drinking (e.g., daily hangovers, loss of jobs, friends, etc.), the value of not drinking is still lower. On any given day, not drinking would involve dealing with the hangover, job loss, and angry friends while undergoing withdrawal, and without the numbing effects of alcohol. Hence, from a local perspective, continuing to drink is entirely rational. Kent Berridge and Terry Robinson, who are not proponents of this model, explain the choice model as follows: "drugs are taken first because they are pleasant and then after repeated drug use, drugs are then taken also to avoid the unpleasant

---

22. *Alcoholics Anonymous: The Big Book*, 18.
23. Marc Lewis, *The Biology of Desire: Why Addiction Is Not a Disease* (PublicAffairs, 2016), 2.
24. Gene M. Heyman, *Addiction: A Disorder of Choice* (Harvard University Press, 2010), 119.

withdrawal symptoms that would ensue upon the cessations of use."[25] As long as the person with addiction continues to view her drinking from a local perspective, it makes sense that she chooses to continue to drink.

Heyman argues that another way to approach this choice between drinking and not drinking is from a global perspective. He says, "In the global choice, the options . . . reflect the dynamic relationships between choice and changes in value" over time.[26] In this perspective a person with addiction would have to think of her alcohol use over the next ninety days, for instance. The global perspective asks, If I were to drink over the next ninety days, would my life be better or worse at the end of those ninety days than if I chose not to drink? If the person with addiction chooses to continue to drink for ninety days, the value of her pleasure in daily life will likely be lower than it was ninety days before. If she chooses to stop drinking, the value of her pleasure in daily life will likely diminish in the first few days or even weeks. However, over time, she is likely to begin to feel better because she no longer has to deal with daily hangovers, loss of friends, etc. Over time, her friends may learn to trust her again, and she will begin to feel physically better. From a global perspective (i.e., over the long run) it is more rational to stop drinking than to continue. Heyman believes people make rational decisions, and hence the trick is to somehow help those with addiction see this global perspective.

The choice model falls closer to the "freedom" end of the spectrum by explaining that even the choice to use when life is falling apart all around the person using is, in some sense, rational in that the benefits of using outweigh the detriments of not using on any given day. At the same time, this model recognizes that using is not a value-neutral choice. That is, it is not the case that the pull to use and not use are of equal measure and that a moral flaw or a reckless hedonism in the person leads them to choose to use. Rather, from a local perspective the scales are weighted toward choosing to use. Thus, this model does not fall quite as clearly on the freedom side of the spectrum as the moral model does. One of the benefits of this model is that it helps explain why self-help groups, such as Alcoholics Anonymous, are so effective at helping people recover from addiction. Many people with addiction recover through participation in Twelve-Step groups, which rely, at least in part, on the ability of the person with addiction to make different choices (even if merely the choice of doing what a sponsor suggests).[27] Other interventions that have proven helpful include offering people small rewards for amounts of time in sobriety. These small rewards help tip the scales from a local to a global choice perspective and

---

25. Kent C. Berridge and Terry E. Robinson, "Drug Addiction as Incentive Sensitization," in *Addiction and Responsibility*, ed. Jeffrey Poland and George Graham (MIT Press, 2011), 24.
26. Heyman, *Addiction*, 119.
27. Note that this is my read of AA. Proponents of the Twelve Steps argue that the addicted person is powerless and is able to recover by turning her will over to a Higher Power. However, even the act of turning the will over demonstrates a capacity to make choices.

help people make incremental steps toward long-term sobriety.[28] The choice model offers hope in that it empowers those with addiction to create healthier lives through the practice of making different choices. At the same time, the choice model may attribute too much agency to the person suffering.[29]

The Self-Medication Model

The self-medication model encompasses a range of theories on addiction that all center around the notion that people use in order to cope. Some of these focus on societal factors that create environments in which it makes sense for people to use, while others focus more on psychological factors. Addiction specialists who focus primarily on psychological factors note that people who have had traumatic experiences, such as engaging in warfare, a major car accident, the death of a loved one, or (ongoing) childhood or adult sexual, physical, or psychological abuse, often attempt to reduce the stress of unresolved traumas by using drugs or alcohol. Marc Lewis notes that "substance abuse among those with PTSD is as high as 60–80 percent." However, over time the addiction to alcohol and drugs "itself becomes a source of stress—often *the* major source of stress."[30] People with addiction often suffer terrible consequences as a result of their use of drugs and alcohol. They may lose contact with loved ones, lose jobs, or harm others in ways that cause shame. Hence, where those suffering initially used drugs and alcohol to deal with the stress of childhood (or adult) trauma, they continue to use to deal with the stress of the addiction itself.

Edward Khantzian proposes that people use because "drugs of abuse relieve psychological suffering" and "a person's preference for a particular drug involves some degree of psychopharmacological specificity." What he means by this is that people tend to gravitate toward specific drug classes to counteract specific symptoms of psychological suffering. Thus, a person suffering from high states of "isolation and emptiness and related tense/anxious states" tends to prefer fast-acting depressants, such as alcohol; those who suffer from "the internally fragmenting and disorganizing effects of rage" alongside the "disruptive aspects of such affects to interpersonal relations" tend to prefer opiates; those who suffer

---

28. See, e.g., Heyman, *Addiction*, 105–8; Nancy M. Petry, Jessica M. Pierce, and Maxine L. Stitzer, "Effect of Prize-Based Incentives on Outcomes in Stimulant Abusers in Outpatient Psychosocial Treatment Programs," *Archives of General Psychiatry* 62, no. 10 (October 2005): 1148–56, https://doi.org/10.1001/archpsyc.62.10.1148; Maxine L. Stitzer, Nancy M. Petry, and Jessica Pierce, "Motivational Incentives Research in the National Drug Abuse Treatment Clinical Trials Network," *Journal of Substance Abuse Treatment* 38, supplement 1 (June 2010): S61–S69, https//doi.org/10.1016/j.jsat.2009.12.010; Hanna Pickard, "What We're Not Talking about When We Talk about Addiction," 40.

29. For other examples of the choice model (to various degrees) see, Gene Heyman, "Addiction: A Latent Property of the Dynamics of Choice," in *What Is Addiction?* ed. Don Ross, Harold Kineaid, David Spurrett, and Peter Collins (MIT Press, 2010), 159–91; Hanna Pickard, "Addiction and the Self," *Noûs* 55, no. 4 (December 2021): 735–61, https://doi.org/10.1111/nous.12328; Sally Satel and Scott O. Lilienfeld, "Addiction and the Brain-Disease Fallacy," *Frontiers in Psychiatry* 4 (March 2, 2014): article 141, 1–11, https://doi.org/10.3389/fpsyt.2013.00141.

30. Lewis, *Biology of Desire,* 3 (italics in the original).

from "deenergized" and depressive states tend toward stimulants. Interestingly, stimulants are also often effective at calming "hyperactivity" and "emotional lability." Importantly, Khantzian does not argue that psychological distress is the *only* reason people use. The basic theory is that substances reduce psychological distress and help those who are unable to express and regulate high emotions.[31]

Memoirs of addiction regularly talk about using in order to deal with psychological distress. In her memoir, *Stash: My Life in Hiding*, Laura Cathcart Robbins talks about Ambien as a kind of anesthetic for psychological pain: "These pills lull me into a state that has allowed me to accept the unacceptable."[32] Similarly, Sarah Hepola says in her memoir, *Blackout*, "I needed alcohol to drink away the things that plagued me. Not just my doubts about sex. My self-consciousness, my loneliness, my insecurities, my fears."[33] Drugs and alcohol can be powerful analgesics to life's difficulties—for a while at least.[34]

Others propose links between attachment styles and addiction. As Sonia Waters explains in *Addiction and Pastoral Care*, a caregiver's capacity to attune to the needs of infants and young children has tremendous effect on that child's development. Humans develop attachment styles based on childhood relational experiences, especially with caregivers. Children who are securely attached are able to manage "affect and stress regulation," develop "emotional intelligence," and gain a sense of who they are within a larger social whole.[35] Those with insecure attachment styles lack some of the above-named capacities and struggle to regulate emotions. In general, this version of the self-medication model suggests that "positive attachment experiences and secure patterns strengthen reward from social contact and decrease the risk for addictive behaviors," while "negative attachment experiences and insecurity . . . lead to insufficient reward from social contact and to a heightened risk to replace it with addictive behavior." Specifically, insecure attachment, which occurs in people "who do not experience a sufficiently secure base" in childhood, is often linked to substance use disorders among other mental health issues.[36] Further, in agreement with Khantzian's work, some argue that certain substances are linked more closely with certain attachment styles.[37] Importantly, insecure attachments, while sometimes the result of abusive childhood experiences, are not necessarily caused by parents.

---

31. E. Khantzian, "The Self-Medication Hypothesis of Substance Use Disorders: A Reconsideration and Recent Applications," *Harvard Review of Psychology* 4, no. 5 (1997): 232–34, https://doi.org/10.3109/10673229709030550.

32. Laura Cathcart Robbins, *Stash: My Life in Hiding* (Atria Paperback, 2024), 7.

33. Sarah Hepola, *Blackout: Remembering the Things I Drank to Forget* (Grand Central Publishing, 2016), 23.

34. The same is true for many other addictive behaviors, such as gambling, sex, gaming, etc.

35. Waters, *Addiction and Pastoral Care*, 63.

36. Andreas Schindler, "Attachment and Substance Use Disorders—Theoretical Models, Empirical Evidence, and Implications for Treatment," *Frontier in Psychiatry* 10 (October 14, 2019), article 727, 4, 2, https://doi.org/10.3389/fpsyt.2019.00727.

37. Schindler, "Attachment and Substance Use Disorders," 4.

Further, parents are, of course, themselves also shaped by their own upbringing and life circumstances, much of which are beyond their control.[38]

Psychological distress of the varieties described above are not the only factors at play in the self-medication model of addiction. Other proponents of this model, such as Bruce Alexander, focus more on societal factors. Bruce Alexander and several of his colleagues attempted to demonstrate this self-medication model in action through an experiment that came to be known as the "Rat Park" experiment. In this experiment, rats were divided into two camps. In one camp the rats lived in complete isolation. In the other the rats enjoyed life in a rat-friendly environment with lots of stimulation, comfort, and interaction with other rats. This environment came to be known as Rat Park. Each group of rats was offered both regular sweetened water and an opiate drug solution. Researchers found that the rats in isolation consumed a far greater amount of the opiate solution than those in Rat Park. Alexander and his colleagues published their findings in 1980 in an article titled, "Effects of Early and Later Colony Housing on Oral Ingestion of Morphine in Rats."[39] Where it was previously argued that opiates were addictive by nature and that any presence of opiates would result in drug addiction, Alexander demonstrated that the environment of a person was a greater predictor of opiate addiction than the availability of drugs.

In his more recent research, Alexander shifted his focus to patterns of drug and alcohol use among Indigenous peoples in Western Canada. He notes that when "the English colonial empire overran hundreds" of Indigenous communities, they often took over the land, moved the communities onto much smaller reservations, destroyed the "economic basis of their cultures," forced their children to go to "'residential school' to be taught the white man's culture," and forbade them to speak their native tongue, resulting in a sense of isolation and estrangement upon returning home.[40] Alexander discovered that while these Indigenous communities originally faced many of the same problems as their English colonizers, one problem they did not seem to have was addiction. He says, "There was so little addiction that it is very difficult to prove from written and oral histories that it existed at all." Once colonized, however, "alcoholism became close to universal."[41] The English colonizers assumed alcoholism became rampant due to a genetic predisposition in Indigenous peoples and the availability of alcohol. However, neighboring Indigenous communities that were not destroyed by colonization also had access to alcohol, and in those communities, addiction was not nearly as universal as in the colonized groups. Further, the prohibition of alcohol in the colonized communities did not resolve the addiction issue. Relying on his previous research with the rats in Rat Park, Alexander argues instead

38. Waters, *Addiction and Pastoral Care*, 58.
39. Bruce K. Alexander et al., "Effect of Early and Later Colony Housing on Oral Ingestion of Morphine in Rats," *Pharmacology, Biochemistry, and Behavior* 15, no. 4 (October 1981): 571–76, https://doi.org/10.1016/0091-3057(81)90211-2
40. B. K. Alexander, "Addiction: The View from Rat Park," Bruce K. Alexander, 2010, http://www.brucekalexander.com/articles-speeches/rat-park/148-addiction-the-view-from-rat-park.
41. Alexander, "Addiction."

that the colonized Indigenous peoples of Western Canada became addicted to alcohol as a result of being in "an environment that produces social and cultural isolation." Alexander notes that Indigenous peoples "have described the anguish of being deprived of their traditional cultures and social networks . . . and have explained how drunkenness relieved their misery temporarily, even as it ultimately led to self-destruction," and he argues that alcohol only became "*irresistible when the opportunity for normal social existence [was] destroyed.*"[42]

While not a pure version of the self-medication model, Isaac Horwedel offers an interesting take on addiction in "Free Compelled, Compulsively Free: A Critical Pastoral Approach to Addiction" that relies on some of the logic of the self-medication model. Horwedel argues that the entire capitalist enterprise within which the United States (and many other societies) operate sets people up for addiction such that "addiction is not an *aberration* within a social life under capitalism that is otherwise free," but is rather "a symptomatic expression of, and response to, necessary crises internal to forms of social life under capitalism that are mediated and circumscribed by the competitive compulsions of private production geared toward limitless accumulation."[43] Addiction is, in other words, a natural outcome of living in a capitalist society. If the human version of Rat Park is the ideal environment for the formation of healthy people, Horwedel would argue that capitalist societies create ideal conditions for the formation of addicted people.

In summary, the self-medication model sees addiction as a type of self-medication that an individual uses to deal with difficult psychological or environmental states. Similar to the choice model, it recognizes that people have good reason to use. However, unlike the choice model, proponents of this model suggest that some of these underlying reasons must be dealt with for a person to have the capacity to choose otherwise. That is, people cannot simply shift perspective from local to global in order to stop. The circumstances (psychological or environmental) that led to using must be dealt with first. One of the benefits of this way of thinking about addiction is that it takes into account the many studies that show a correlation between childhood and adult trauma and substance abuse.[44] This model also helps to account for the fact that psychotherapy is often an effective means of treating addiction.

---

42. Alexander, "Addiction" (italics in the original).

43. Isaac Horwedel, "Freely Compelled, Compulsively Free: A Critical Pastoral Approach to Addiction" *Pastoral Psychology* 71 (July 17, 2021): 69, https://doi.org/10.1007/s11089-021-00965-2 (italics in the original).

44. E.g., Lamya Khoury et al., "Substance Use, Childhood Traumatic Experience, and Posttraumatic Stress Disorder in an Urban Civilian Population," *Depression and Anxiety* 27, no. 12 (December 2010): 1077–86, https://doi.org/10.1002/da.20751; Amar Mandavia et al., "Exposure to Childhood Abuse and Later Substance Use: Indirect Effects of Emotion Dysregulation and Exposure to Trauma," *Journal of Traumatic Stress* 29, no. 5 (October 2016): 422–29, https://doi.org/10.1002/jts.22131; Philip L. Reed, et al. "Incidence of Drug Problems in Young Adults Exposed to Trauma and Posttraumatic Stress Disorder: Do Early Life Experiences and Predispositions Matter?," *Archives of General Psychiatry* 64, no. 12 (December 2007): 1435–42, https://doi.org/10.1001/archpsyc.64.12.1435; E. Y. Deykin and S. L. Buka, "Prevalence and Risk Factors for Posttraumatic Stress Disorder among Chemically Dependent Adolescents," *The American Journal of Psychiatry* 154, no. 6 (1997): 752–57, https://doi.org/10.1176/ajp.154.6.752.

Others, however, point out that the over-focus on the underlying reasons for using (e.g., unresolved trauma or environmental factors) can be detrimental to those with addiction, especially when it is assumed that dealing with the underlying factors will automatically solve the problem of addiction. Lembke, among others, indicate that this is a faulty assumption and can prohibit people with addiction from getting the help they need for their addiction.[45] Further, it is often difficult to parse out comorbidities in addiction. That is, it is hard to tell if a person is using in order to alleviate depression, for instance, or if depression is a symptom of addiction.[46] Thus, it is important to deal with both issues simultaneously. Additionally, Khantzian's notion that certain traumas and affect states correlate with specific drugs is unlikely to be the case as many drug users use varieties of drugs (both stimulants and depressants).[47]

The various forms of the self-medication model of addiction account for both the difficulty in changing addictive patterns and the possibility of recovery. In this sense it moves further away from the "freedom" end of the spectrum toward the "compulsion" end. While there is some freedom of choice, these choices are severely limited by people's circumstances. Alexander would argue that responsibility lies more with the way governments structure society than with the individual.[48]

Each of the models thus far (moral, choice, and self-medication) have progressively moved along the spectrum from freedom toward compulsion and simultaneously from responsibility in the form of blame to blamelessness. The next model moves closest to the compulsion end of the spectrum.

---

45. A. Lembke "Time to Abandon the Self-Medication Hypothesis in Patients with Psychiatric Disorders," *The American Journal of Drug and Alcohol Abuse* 38, no. 6 (August 28, 2012): 526–27, https://doi.org/10.3109/00952990.2012.694532; Robert L. DuPont and Mark S. Gold, "Comorbidity and 'Self-Medication," *Journal of Addictive Diseases* 26, sup. 1 (2007): 13–23, https://doi.org/10.1300/J069v26S01_03.

46. Lembke, "Time to Abandon the Self-Medication Hypothesis," 526.

47. Shane Darke, "Pathways to Heroin Dependence: Time to Re-Appraise Self-Medication," *Addiction* 108, no. 4 (April 2013): 663, https://doi.org/10.1111/j.1360-0443.2012.04001.x; Lembke, "Time to Abandon the Self-Medication Hypothesis," 526.

48. For other examples of the self-medication model of addiction as well as some critiques, see Adam C. Alexander and Kenneth D. Ward, "Understanding Postdisaster Substance Use and Psychological Distress Using Concepts from the Self-Medication Hypothesis and Social Cognitive Theory," *Journal of Psychoactive Drugs* 50, no. 2 (April 2018): 177–86, https://doi.org/10.1080/02791072.2017.1397304; R. Castaneda, et al., "Empirical Assessment of the Self-Medication Hypothesis among Dually Diagnosed Inpatients" *Comprehensive Psychiatry* 35, no. 3 (May–June 1994): 180–84, https://doi.org/10.1016/0010-440X(94)90189-9; Verena Ertl, et al., "Drinking to Ease the Burden: A Cross-sectional Study on Trauma, Alcohol Abuse and Psychopathology in a Post-Conflict Context," *BMC Psychiatry* 16 (June 24, 2016): 1–13, https://doi.org/10.1186/s12888-016-0905-7; Johann Hari, *Chasing the Scream: The First and Last Days of the War on Drugs* (Bloomsbury Publishing, 2016); E. Khantzian, "The Self-Medication Hypothesis of Addictive Disorders: Focus on Heroin and Cocaine Dependence," *American Journal of Psychiatry* 142, no. 11 (November 1985): 1259–64, https://doi.org/10.1176/ajp.142.11.1259; Khantzian, "Addiction as Self-Regulation Disorder and the Role of Self-Medication," *Addiction* 108, no. 4 (2013): 668–69, https://doi.org/10.1111/add.12004; Gabor Maté, *In the Realm of Hungry Ghosts*, illustrated edition (North Atlantic Books, 2008).

Neuroscience and Addiction

The brain disease model of addiction (BDMA) is currently the most widely accepted model of addiction in the United States, not least because it has a robust body of research and is supported by government institutions, such as the National Institute on Drug Addiction (NIDA). The BDMA is also one of the most contested models of addiction, because it relies on a particular interpretation of the neuroscientific data on addiction. Most addiction researchers agree on the neuroscientific data. What they do not agree on is what that data means about addiction. Thus, before discussing the BDMA, I offer a rudimentary sketch of what happens in the brain in addiction and then discuss how this data is interpreted by those who hold to the BDMA and by those who do not.

NIDA explains in one of its publications, "Drugs, Brains, and Behavior: The Science of Addiction," that drugs alter the brain's communication system by "interfering with the way neurons normally send, receive, and process signals via neurotransmitters."[49] The brain passes information from one part of the brain to another via a communication system made up of neural pathways. These pathways consist of a string of neurons connected to each other. Neurons carry messages from one part of the brain to the other. In order for these messages to be transmitted they must cross gaps between one neuron and another. At these gaps, called "synaptic clefts," neurons fire neurotransmitters from one neuron to the other. These neurotransmitters come in the form of a variety of chemicals, such as dopamine, serotonin, endorphins, and more.

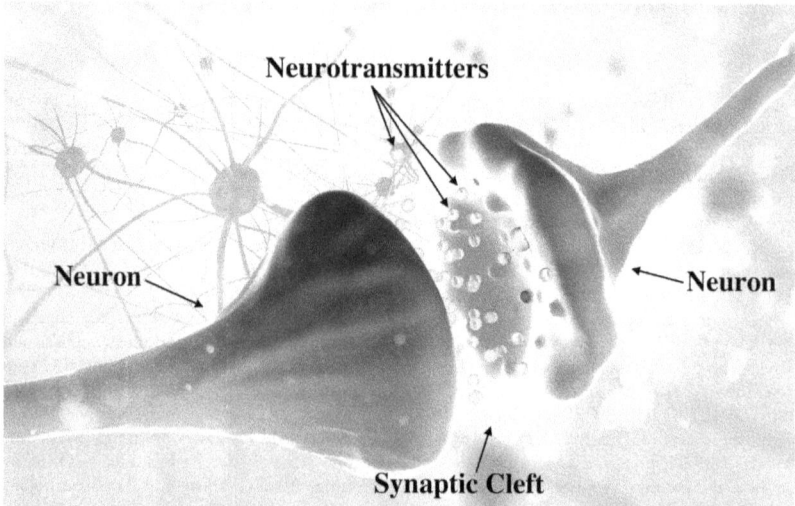

Fig. 1.3 Synapse and Neuron Cells Sending Electrical Chemical Signals by solvod, October 07, 2016, iStock, https://www.istockphoto.com/photo/synapse-and-neuron-cells-sending-electrical-chemical-signals-gm605755864-103852273 (labels and arrows are my additions).

---

49. National Institute on Drug Abuse, "Drugs and the Brain," last modified July 6, 2020, https://nida.nih.gov/publications/drugs-brains-behavior-science-addiction/drugs-brain.

What makes the process of crossing these synaptic gaps even more complex is that each type of neurotransmitter attaches to a specific receptor on the receiving neuron, much like a puzzle piece. They cannot be accepted by just any receptor. If that receptor is blocked, the neurotransmitter is not taken up by the receiving neuron and stays in the synaptic gap. Once neurotransmitters attach, a process begins by which they are either passed on, destroyed, or passed back to the sending neuron (a process called reuptake). In this way messages are sent from one part of the brain to the other, causing alterations in mood, new learning or behaviors, the formation of memories, and more.[50]

Substances that are commonly abused wreak havoc on this system of communication. Some substances mimic neurotransmitters, activating neurons. Others attach to the receptors or prevent the neurotransmitters from being taken up again, causing an overflow of a certain neurotransmitter in the synaptic gap. These effects all translate into a variety of experiences for the user.[51]

Almost all drugs that are commonly abused involve the neurotransmitter dopamine. These drugs cause a momentary flood of dopamine in the system, which creates the powerful good feeling that keeps people coming back for more. Different drugs target the system in different ways. Cocaine, for instance, blocks the reuptake of the neurotransmitter dopamine, which leaves an excess in the system. Amphetamines cause a surge of the production of dopamine, which also causes an excess. The excess of dopamine is one reason drugs of abuse are initially so pleasurable. Dopamine is not the only neurotransmitter involved. Opiates, for instance, mimic endorphins, the excess of which creates a feeling of relaxation.[52] However, I will focus primarily on dopamine, since it plays a major role in the addiction cycle of almost all drugs.[53]

Dopamine is a neurotransmitter (the chemical that gets passed across the synaptic cleft from one neuron to the other) that is responsible for rewarding survival salient behaviors (i.e., behaviors that help us survive, such as eating, hydration, sexual activity, etc.). In other words, when we engage in something that helps us (individually and as a species) survive, such as sex, the brain naturally produces dopamine, which makes us feel good, and in turn encourages us to engage in more of these behaviors. This is one way the brain ensures we survive. Using drugs disorders this survival mechanism by flooding the system with dopamine.[54]

So far, this doesn't sound like bad news. Who doesn't want a continual excess of dopamine in the brain? The problem is not the excess of dopamine but what the brain does to compensate for this excess. As Judith Grisel explains in *Never Enough*, the brain is always looking for equilibrium. Thus, "any stimulus that

---

50. Carlton K. Erickson, *The Science of Addiction: From Neurobiology to Treatment* (W. W. Norton, 2007), 32–49.
51. NIDA, "Drugs and the Brain."
52. Judith Grisel, *Never Enough: The Neuroscience and Experience of Addiction* (Vintage, 2020), 67–68.
53. Dopamine also plays a significant role in process addictions (e.g., addictions to gambling, pornography, gaming, shopping, etc.).
54. NIDA, "Drugs and the Brain."

alters brain functioning to affect the way we feel will elicit a response by the brain that is exactly the opposite to the effect of the stimulus."[55] In response to an excess of dopamine caused by methamphetamines, for instance, the brain radically lowers its own natural production of dopamine. Once the surplus of dopamine and its accompanying high wears off, a person using methamphetamines goes into a state of crushing anhedonia, unable to enjoy pleasurable activities they used to enjoy. The person is not just experiencing the dissipation of the excessive amount of dopamine that methamphetamines produce; the brain also lowers its natural production of dopamine in response to the initial excess such that a person feels even more depressed.

The more a person uses, the more the brain attempts to compensate by lowering the natural production of dopamine or "by reducing the number of receptors that can receive signals."[56] Since the brain is now operating at a severe deficit of dopamine in its normal state (to make up for the excess that methamphetamines provide), more and more of the drug is needed to create a high. Eventually a high becomes more and more elusive, and a person needs to use just to feel normal.[57] This is called drug tolerance and is one of the hallmarks of addiction.[58] Tolerance, by itself, is not necessarily indicative of addiction. We develop tolerance to drugs all the time. A person using oxycodone after surgery, for instance, will develop tolerance to the drug but is not necessarily addicted. Most people are able to get off the drug by slowly tapering the use of medications.

It is important to note that while dopamine is often associated with pleasure, it is actually a chemical that fuels desire rather than pleasure.[59] The enjoyment of eating or sex is not as important for survival as our desire for it, because desire helps us to keep seeking out these substances and behaviors and thus helps us to survive. Using drugs *disorders* this survival mechanism by flooding the system with dopamine, giving the brain the cue that this behavior is important for survival, thus reinforcing the use and desire for drugs.[60] Specifically, addiction tends to affect the striatum, a part of the brain that, when fueled by dopamine,

---

55. Grisel, *Never Enough*, 36.
56. NIDA, "Drugs and the Brain."
57. The brain's search for balance is not just confined to dopamine. It happens in response to any surge or deficit of neurotransmitters caused by a drug's capacity to mimic a neurotransmitter or by a drug's ability to target the receptors of the neurotransmitter. This is simply how the brain functions. As Grisel explains, lots of medications rely on the brain's drive for balance. Many anti-depressants work because they block the reuptake of the neurotransmitter serotonin, leaving an excess in the system, which helps a person's mood. This is similar to the way cocaine works in that cocaine creates a high by blocking the reuptake of dopamine, which leaves a surplus of dopamine in the system. (Grisel, *Never Enough*, 41).
58. NIDA, "Drugs and the Brain," *Diagnostic and Statistical Manual of Mental Disorders*, 546.
59. Kent C. Berridge and Terry E. Robinson, "Liking, Wanting, and the Incentive-Sensitization Theory of Addiction," *American Psychologist* 71, no. 8 (2016): 670–79, http://dx.doi.org/10.1037/amp0000059; Anne Lembke, *Dopamine Nation* (Dutton, 2023), 48–49; Lewis, *Biology of Desire*, 56.
60. NIDA, "Drugs and the Brain"; Lewis, *Biology of Desire*, 58. It is important to note that while Marc Lewis agrees with the neuroscience of addiction, he does not hold to the BDMA.

"translates past pleasures into present desires."[61] This produces what is known as craving in addiction.

Craving is an incredibly intense experience in which the boundaries between a strong desire and a survival need become blurred. Using the wisdom of neuroscience, Moyers describes his experience of using in his memoir as one of the brain being hijacked. However, he goes on to say that while this "explains the biochemical process, it doesn't get close to describing the desperate hunger, the consuming thirst, the unbearable craving, the furious yearning, the excruciating need that grabs you and shakes you and won't let you go." He says it is "a howling internal torment that overrides the need for food, for water, for sleep, for love."[62] In some ways Moyers is describing a survival type need, similar to that for food and water, and at times stronger than even those needs. However, "furious yearning" implies that this is not truly a survival need. He talks about it as both a need and a strong desire. Jowita Bydlowska also describes craving in her memoir, *Drunk Mom*. She says, "This is no ordinary wanting. This is the wanting that has no end. It's an obscene appetite; it's uncontrollable with mouth wide open, insisting. It's a baby—a wet, hungry baby that no one is picking up to soothe." Throughout her memoir, Bydlowska walks the line between desire and need. She says of alcohol that "it is not necessary. Yet it is a need." Still later she describes her drive to drink not as an "urge," but rather "a calling. An order from the sky or from the ground below me, or from the air around me, who knows."[63] A calling is not quite a need, yet it is much more than a strong desire. Both Bydlowska and Moyers demonstrate what the brain changes in addiction look like on the ground. The experience of the system flooded with dopamine, over time, produces an insatiable yearning that is almost indistinguishable from a survival need.

These experiences of craving are important to take in because people often confuse craving with wanting. This happens in part because we use the word craving to describe a range of experiences in everyday speech. We talk about craving ice cream or chocolate, for instance, as well as craving meth—yet these are profoundly different experiences. A craving for chocolate has more affinity with a strong desire, while a craving for meth (for someone who is addicted) would feel more like a survival need. What makes it confusing is that meth is not a survival need. While some drugs, when taken regularly and in high amounts, require medical intervention to prevent severe withdrawal that could be lethal (e.g., severe alcohol use), most people are able to stop using without the dangers of severe withdrawal. In that sense the drug is not literally a survival need yet feels the same to the person experiencing it. A common experience that comes closer to the experience of craving is that of sexual arousal. When one is aroused, it isn't necessary (until pushed to the edge) to have an orgasm, yet the closer one

---

61. Lewis, *Biology of Desire*, 56 (italics in the original).
62. Moyers, *Broken*, 278.
63. Jowita Bydlowska, *Drunk Mom: A Memoir* (Penguin Books, 2014), 4, 44, 119.

gets to having an orgasm, the harder it becomes to tell the difference between a strong desire and a need. Eventually, everything in the body and mind pushes for an orgasm. It is in some sense simply a strong desire, yet it feels like a need. Since craving is a unique marker of addiction, it is important to differentiate it from everyday desires so that we don't trivialize the experience of addiction.[64]

The more drug use is linked to specific feelings and thoughts, the more a kind of neural highway is created, whereby using becomes more and more automatic when these feelings and thoughts (or even behaviors) arise. This is especially pronounced with activities involving dopamine release.[65] Thus, if a person drinks every time they feel stressed, stress and drinking become linked, such that stress can, over time, almost automatically result in drinking. Similarly, a person might come to associate certain objects, such as a syringe, spoon, or belt, with drug use, such that the sight of a syringe almost automatically results in a craving for heroin. People recovering from intravenous drug use, therefore, often find it extremely triggering to get a blood draw.

This happens in part because "dopamine is released in the brain . . . well before the reward itself is ingested."[66] Robbins describes this experience in her memoir, *Stash*: "Sometimes . . . it was just the idea—the knowledge that I was about to get loaded that sent me into that euphoric stratosphere."[67] Problematically, this pre-ingestion rush doesn't immediately disappear when people stop using. At the beginning of her stay in rehab, Robbins was given smaller doses of the drug she was addicted to (Ambien) to slowly wean her off the drug altogether. Eventually, she is able to stop using Ambien altogether yet finds that when she stands in line to receive her other medications, just as she used to stand in line to receive Ambien, she feels intense cravings for Ambien: "Apparently my body doesn't know that I won't be getting the good drugs anymore, because waiting in this line is still like ringing the dinner bell for my addiction."[68] The same happens for a person in recovery who administered drugs intravenously in their addiction when they see a needle in a doctor's office.

These neural highways can be likened to the tracks created for cross-country skiers. When I lived in Trondheim, Norway, for a short time, I was regularly invited to go cross-country skiing. While I had some downhill skiing experience, I had never done any cross-country skiing but figured, "how hard can this be?" While moving forward was awkward at first, the parallel deep grooves prepared for skiers in the snow (i.e., the tracks—see fig. 1.4) helped me stay on the course, and eventually I could use them to propel myself forward.

---

64. Over the years, people have asked me if the difference between desire and craving is one of degree or kind, and I must admit that I don't know. Having experienced both, I can say that even if the difference between desire and craving is just a difference in degree (i.e., craving is simply a very strong desire), that difference in degree is so pronounced that it feels like a difference in kind.
65. Lewis, *Biology of Desire*, 59.
66. Lembke, *Dopamine Nation*, 59.
67. Robbins, *Stash*, 145.
68. Robbins, *Stash*, 145.

Fig. 1.4 Ski Track for Cross Country by Maksym Ponomarenko, February 25, 2020, iStock, https://www.istockphoto.com/photo/ski-track-for-cross-country-gm1207956835-348977109.

While I certainly didn't look like I had been doing this my whole life, I didn't make a fool of myself either—at least not initially. That only happened when I encountered my first downhill slope. My experience with downhill skiing had taught me that creating a downward facing "V" shape with my skis would help me to control my speed. The tricky thing about cross-country skiing, however, is that you first need to lift one of your skis out of its track and then use that ski to break by pushing it out to the side next to the track, creating the "V." The theory seemed straightforward enough, and those who went before me made it look easy. What I was not prepared for is just how difficult it is to pull your ski out of the track that was designed for it. I could not figure out how to keep my balance on my left ski while going downhill, so that I could pull my right ski out of the track in order to control my speed. It was as if my mind could not comprehend the idea of stepping outside of the well-worn track created for these skis. I tried again and again to lift my right leg while whizzing down the hill to no avail. Every single hill undid me. I would ski the first half and fall the rest of the way down to the great delight of everyone on the track. I think of neural highways as the cross-country ski tracks of the brain. While it isn't impossible to step out of the well-worn track, it is exceedingly difficult.

Some people love the thrill and challenge of skiing off track. These people go and explore hiking paths covered in snow that haven't been groomed for cross-country skiing. While skiing off-track is certainly possible, it can be very challenging. Similarly, if someone drinks every time she is stressed, the path between stress and drinking is akin to that of the ski tracks. It is the path of least resistance. However, it is not impossible for her to act otherwise. Just as a skier can ski off-track, a person with addiction can choose not to drink when stressed. If this were not the case, no one would ever recover. It is, however, very difficult *not* to follow the dopamine-driven well-worn track from stress to alcohol use. Resisting takes tremendous energy and practice and is hard to sustain over time.

In his memoir, *Tweak*, Nic Sheff describes a relapse after a period of sobriety: "One night, I said I was going to a meeting, but drove to hook up crystal instead. The car just seemed to drive itself across the bridge to Oakland."[69] Sheff takes the neural highway toward scoring meth because it is the way of least resistance and has over time become a habit. At the same time, resistance isn't impossible. Sheff does eventually stop using, but it takes extraordinary effort to step out of those well-worn tracks of addiction.

Over time, exposure to drugs can lead to longer lasting changes in the brain.[70] Brain images have demonstrated that one of the areas of the brain that suffers longer-lasting effects from drug use is the prefrontal cortex (PFC). The PFC is the part of the brain that is responsible for executive functioning and decision making. It is responsible for our capacity to regulate and reflect.[71] Neuroscientist Marc Lewis explains that addiction becomes automatic in much the same way other habits do. The more the cue to use a substance leads to almost automatic use of the substance, the less communication there is in the brain between the PFC and the midbrain. The part of the brain responsible for "critical reasoning, remembering, planning, and self-control" (the dorsolateral PFC) becomes more and more cut off from the process of using as habits form, such that over time "the communication between the prefrontal control and striatal compulsion isn't only constricted; it's fragmented or inaccessible."[72]

Long-term drug use eventually reduces gray mass volume in the PFC.[73] This reduction and the lack of communication between the midbrain and the PFC is likely one of the reasons people suffering from addiction keep using drugs despite severe negative consequences. Since the PFC is also responsible for our capacity to reflect on our own behavior, a reduction in gray matter volume in the PFC can also help explain why people suffering from addiction often suffer from a sense of denial by which they seem incapable of seeing their predicament clearly.[74]

---

69. Nic Sheff, *Tweak: Growing Up on Methamphetamines* (Atheneum Books for Young Readers, 2009), 18.

70. This is not always detrimental. As Grisel says, for "antidepressants, this is actually the therapeutic point" (*Never Enough*, 41). For drugs like methamphetamine or alcohol, however, this can be incredibly detrimental and can make it much more difficult to stop using.

71. Lewis, *Biology of Desire*, 45.

72. Lewis, *Biology of Desire*, 131.

73. Ahmet O. Ceceli, et al., "The Neurobiology of Drug Addiction: Cross-Species Insights into the Dysfunction and Recovery of the Prefrontal Cortex," *Neuropsychopharmacology* 47, no. 1 (January 2022): 284, https://doi.org/10.1038/s41386-021-01153-9; Rita Z. Goldstein and Nora D. Volkow, "Dysfunction of the Prefrontal Cortex in Addiction: Neuroimaging Findings and Clinical Implications," *Nature Reviews Neuroscience* 12, no. 11 (November 2011): 657, https://doi.org/10.1038/nrn3119; Lewis, *Biology of Desire*, 131.

74. Goldstein and Volkow, "Dysfunction of the Prefrontal Cortex in Addiction," 664.

Thus, on the one hand, the flood of dopamine causes the person with addiction to value the drug of "choice" as necessary for survival, which drives the person to use more and more.[75] At the same time, the brain's search for balance causes a depletion in dopamine, which means more and more of the drug is necessary to just feel normal. The accompanying anhedonia caused by dopamine depletion when a person isn't using causes a person to disregard other important and survival-salient activities (e.g., eating). Further, over time, the connection to the prefrontal cortex as well as the volume of gray matter in the prefrontal cortex are diminished, making it more and more difficult for a person to critically reflect and make rational choices in their best interest. In other words, there is a dual process at play here: the "reward value of drugs" is increased, while the "ability of the agent to resist" is decreased.[76]

These structural changes in the brain help answer some of the more baffling questions about addiction. Why do seemingly intelligent people continue to use despite clear negative consequences? Why do people in active addiction and early recovery often make such poor choices (e.g., the choice to use again after a period of abstinence)? The neuroscience of addiction helps to demonstrate that when people with addiction say that they don't know why they used again, or how they ended up making such poor choices, they are describing a neurological reality. That is, it is not true that a person with addiction simply lacks the moral fiber to behave differently.

The Brain Disease Model of Addiction (BDMA)

Where the neuroscience of addiction describes what happens in the brain in addiction, the BDMA offers an interpretation of that description. Those who adhere to the BDMA argue that the neuroscience of addiction (described above) demonstrates that addiction is a disease. They argue that neuroscience demonstrates that significant changes occur in the brain with repeated drug use and that these changes are indicative of disease. The National Institute of Drug Abuse (NIDA) defines addiction as "a chronic, relapsing disorder characterized by compulsive drug seeking and use despite adverse consequences." NIDA sees it as "a brain disorder, because it involves functional changes to brain circuits involved in reward, stress, and self-control. Those changes may last a long time after a person has stopped taking drugs." These changes in the brain are characteristic of disease in the same way that changes in heart functioning are indicative of heart disease: "both disrupt the normal, healthy functioning of an organ in the body, both have serious harmful effects, and both are, in many cases, preventable and treatable. If left untreated, they can last a lifetime and may lead to death."[77]

---

75. While "drug of choice" is a common way to refer to the primary drug a person used in addiction, I put "choice" in quotation marks to indicate that (as the neuroscience of addiction demonstrates) choice is not exactly the right word as it implies more agency than a person with addiction likely has.
76. Neil Levy, "Addiction, Responsibility and Ego Depletion," in *Addiction and Responsibility*, ed. Jeffrey Poland and George Graham (MIT Press, 2011), 91.
77. NIDA, "Drug Misuse and Addiction."

Similarly, Carlton Erickson argues in *The Science of Addiction* that diseases entail a "disruption of normal cell activity."[78] In the case of addiction, this disruption occurs in nerve cells (neurons), which causes dysregulation in neural pathways. As explained above, this "neurotransmitter dysregulation" shows up in the form of the over (or under) production of certain neurotransmitters, such as dopamine, or by blocking the reception of these neurotransmitters. Erickson notes that it is difficult to pinpoint an exact cause of the disease. It may be that the "neurotransmitter dysregulation" is already "present before the person takes a drug," or that it is caused by a "psychosocial stressor, such as trauma" or by repeated drug use. The fact that some people get addicted while others don't is indicative of the possibility that some dysregulation or genetic propensity is present in some people, pointing to the notion that addiction is a disease.[79]

The brain disease model of addiction has the benefit of explaining the changes that occur in the brain as a result of addiction.[80] Further, this model provides opportunities for government funding which allows scientists to do more research in the area of addiction etiology and treatment. Research on the neuroscience of addiction has, for instance, led to the production of naltrexone, a medication that can help curb the "euphoric and sedative effects of opioids, such as heroin, morphine, and codeine."[81] This model also has the benefit of moving addiction out of the sphere of the justice system (e.g., the war on drugs) and into the realm of the health department, allowing people with addiction to get help. This model also has the greatest potential of removing the stigma of moral failure or lack of willpower from addiction. If changes in the brain make it legitimately difficult for a person to behave otherwise, the problem is not one of willpower. A reduction in stigma is important because it may ultimately motivate more people with addiction to talk about it and seek out help.

78. Erickson, *Science of Addiction*, 50.
79. Erickson, 50, 51–52.
80. For more on the brain disease model of addiction, see David T. Courtwright "The NIDA Brain Disease Paradigm: History, Resistance and Spinoffs," *BioSocieties 5*, no. 1 (March 2010): 137–47, https://doi.org/10.1057/biosoc.2009.3; Norman Doidge, *The Brain That Changes Itself: Stories of Personal Triumph from the Frontiers of Brain Science* (Penguin Books, 2007); Katie Givens Kime, "Interpretive Phenomenological Analysis of the Spiritual Characteristics of Recovery Experiences in the Context of the Brain Disease Model of Addiction," *Pastoral Psychology* 67, no. 4 (August 1, 2018): 357–72, https://doi.org/10.1007/s11089-018-0816-2; George F. Koob, Michael A. Arends, and Michel Le Moal, *Drugs, Addiction, and the Brain* (Academic Press, 2014); Michael Kuhar, *The Addicted Brain: Why We Abuse Drugs, Alcohol, and Nicotine* (FT Press, 2015); Leshner, "Addiction Is a Brain Disease, and It Matters," *Science* 278, no. 5335 (October 1997): 45–47; Nora Volkow, "Drug Addiction," *Vital Speeches of the Day* (June 2006). Please note that the above resources reference and explain the brain disease model of addiction but do not all necessarily endorse the brain disease model of addiction.
81. Substance Abuse and Mental Health Services Administration (SAMHSA), "Naltrexone," last updated March 29, 2024, https://www.samhsa.gov/medications-substance-use-disorders/medications-counseling-related-conditions/naltrexone.

Other Interpretations of the Neuroscience of Addiction

Besides being the most popular model in the United States, the BDMA is also the most contested model. Almost everyone involved in addiction research agrees that the changes described above occur in the brain when a person repeatedly uses certain drugs. Researchers diverge, however, on how they interpret this data. Those who hold to the BDMA see the neuroscientific data as a sign of disease. Others interpret the data differently and argue that what happens in the brain as a result of repeated drug use is not a sign of disease but rather a sign of the brain doing precisely what it is meant to do under those conditions.

Some researchers, such as Marc Lewis and Maia Szalavitz, propose that addiction should rather be seen as a type of learning disorder that is the result of neuroplasticity (i.e., the capacity of the brain to change).[82] According to Lewis, "the kind of brain changes seen in addiction also show up when people become absorbed in a sport, join a political movement, or become obsessed with their sweetheart or their kids."[83] While it is true that the outcome of the changes in the brain brought on by repeated drug use are more severe and deeply painful, for Lewis the fact that these changes occur is not indicative of a brain disease. Erickson would likely counter that one of the things that is difficult to explain within the learning model paradigm is why some people get addicted, and others seem to be able to use without issue.[84]

Hanna Pickard points out that the explanation that addiction is a compulsion by which people have no choice but to use is a fallacy because evidence shows that those suffering respond to incentives, which would not be possible if it were a compulsion. When people with addiction are offered incentives, such as money, prizes, or jobs, for clean urine tests, many are able to abstain.[85] The BDMA is not able to account for the success of these programs. Contingency management (e.g., offering incentives for clean urine tests) aligns well with the choice model of addiction and the self-medication model in that both allow for the possibility that given better alternatives, people with addiction have the capacity to choose not to use. Strict versions of the BDMA do not allow for this possibility.

---

82. See, for instance, David Belin et al., "Parallel and Interactive Learning Processes within the Basal Ganglia: Relevance for Understanding of Addiction," *Behavioral Brain Research* 199 (April 12, 2009): 89–102, https://doi.org/10.1016/j.bbr.2008.09.027; B. J. Everitt, A. Dickinson, and T. W. Robbins, "The Neuropsychological Basis of Addictive Behaviour," *Brain Research Reviews* 36, no. 2–3 (October 2001): 129–38, https://doi.org/10.1016/S0165-0173(01)00088-1; Lewis, *Biology of Desire*; Marc Lewis, "Brain Change in Addiction as Learning, Not Disease," *The New England Journal of Medicine* 379, no. 16 (October 12, 2018): 1551–60, https://doi.org/10.1056/NEJMra1602872; Maia Szalavitz, *Unbroken Brain: A Revolutionary New Way of Understanding Addiction* (St. Martin's Press, 2016). Please note that the above resources rely to varying degrees on a learning model of addiction.

83. Lewis, *Biology of Desire*, 26.

84. Erickson, *Science of Addiction*, 51–52.

85. Pickard remains "agnostic" about whether addiction is a disease because there is not yet enough information to make a claim one way or the other. She is clear, however, about the fact that she does not think it is a compulsion. Pickard, "What We're Not Talking about When We Talk about Addiction," 40–41.

Part of the controversy about whether addiction is a brain disease has to do with how one interprets the facts about what happens in the brain. The other part, however, has to do with other factors, including the consequences of viewing it as a brain disease or something else. Some researchers take issue with NIDA's contention that addiction is chronic, stating that many people simply outgrow addiction and recover without any intervention.[86] Sally Satel and Scott Lilienfeld argue that one of the downsides of viewing addiction as a brain disease is the implication that medical intervention alone can help. They note that "recovery is a project of the heart and mind" and that those in recovery often need a variety of interventions, including the creation of a new social network and drug-free environment.[87]

Further, viewing addiction as a disease has the potential of robbing those with addiction of agency and creating the assumption that the person is doomed to engage in addictive behaviors forever. In that sense, the BDMA can seem somewhat fatalistic. Lewis notes that "personal motivation, a sense of empowerment, and belief in one's own agency are the most important psychological resources for overcoming addiction."[88]

Additionally, those who oppose the BDMA also point out that stigma is not necessarily reduced through a claim that addiction is a disease.[89] Proponents of the BDMA often see the reduction of stigma as a primary advantage of the disease model of addiction. However, as Pickard points out, "many diseases (such as leprosy and HIV/AIDS) are highly stigmatizing" and "stigmatization may be associated with a disease label rather than countered by it."[90]

Finally, the BDMA doesn't account for the way that people tend to recover from addiction. That is, for most, a medical intervention (e.g., medication) is not the primary way they recover from addiction. As theologian Kent Dunnington points out in *Addiction and Virtue*, "the paradox of alcoholism is that alcoholics" on the one hand, "acknowledge the futility of their own willpower to resist alcohol," yet on the other appear to "find access to a power sufficient to reinvigorate the once-impotent will . . . in a nonmedicalized program of recovery."[91]

Importantly, none of those who oppose the BDMA would contend that it is easy to stop using, or that addiction is not painful. What they object to is the idea that it is a disease located in the brain and that people cannot help but use because of this disease. Satel and Lilienfeld helpfully note that what is in question is not whether addiction is a disorder or not but rather whether it is a disease of the brain. They remark that "disorder" is more commonly used in psychiatry than "disease," "because the etiologies of mental illness are not yet well understood."[92]

---

86. Lewis, *Biology of Desire*, 21.
87. Satel and Lilienfeld, "Addiction and the Brain Disease Fallacy," 5.
88. Lewis, "Brain Change in Addiction," 1553.
89. Pickard, "What We're Not Talking About," 38; Lewis, "Brain Change in Addiction," 1552.
90. Pickard, "What We're Not Talking About," 38.
91. Kent Dunnington, *Addiction and Virtue: Beyond the Models of Disease and Choice* (IVP Academic, 2011), 32.
92. Satel and Lilienfeld, "Addiction and the Brain-Disease Fallacy," 2.

Most researchers recognize that prolonged drug use does not produce effective and healthy behavior, and in that sense, it can be characterized as a disorder. What is in question is whether the cause of addiction is a disease located in the brain, akin to Alzheimer's.[93]

WHICH MODEL IS CORRECT?

Researchers on addiction clearly do not agree on what addiction is or how it comes to be. The general public also views addiction through a range of lenses, varying from moral to disease. Interestingly, people often hold multiple and conflicting models of addiction at the same time.[94] *The Big Book*, for instance, describes addiction as an "allergy" that "sicken[s]" the body, on the one hand, and a problem that is "of our own making" rooted in "selfishness," on the other.[95]

Pickard argues that addiction is likely "a unified construct at a superficial level only." That is, people who use display a range of similar behaviors yet engage in these behaviors for a variety of reasons ranging from traumatic experiences, difficult life circumstances, simultaneous other mental health challenges (e.g., depression, bipolar, etc.), or even an unconscious formation of a sense of identity with addiction.[96] Others suggest that addiction is better characterized as a syndrome—that is, "a cluster of symptoms and signs related to an abnormal underlying condition."[97] Seeing addiction as "a cluster of symptoms and signs" allows for viewing both substance (e.g., cocaine, alcohol, etc.) and behavioral (e.g., sex, gambling, etc.) addictions under the same umbrella and highlights the ways in which different expressions of addiction share common features. The syndrome model also allows for a range of causes that include neural changes to the brain, genetic predisposition, psychological vulnerabilities (e.g., difficulty self-regulating), environmental vulnerabilities, trauma, etc. While NIDA is known for characterizing addiction as a brain disease, it also recognizes many of the vulnerabilities and risk factors (e.g., genetic predisposition, trauma, environment, comorbidity with other mental health disorders, etc.) that other models highlight.

My sense of the meaning of addiction is informed by the likes of Shaffer and Heilig et al., who recognize the importance of the BDMA yet advocate for viewing addiction from an interdisciplinary perspective relying on a range of models.[98] That is, addiction is best viewed as a mixture of many of the models

---

93. Satel and Lilienfeld, "Addiction and the Brain-Disease Fallacy," 2.
94. See Kime, "Interpretive Phenomenological Analysis," 361.
95. *Alcoholics Anonymous: The Big Book*, xxvi, 62.
96. Pickard, "What We're Not Talking About," 42.
97. Howard Shaffer et al., "Toward a Syndrome Model of Addiction: Multiple Expressions, Common Etiology," *Harvard Review of Psychiatry* 12, no. 6 (December 11, 2004): 367, https://doi.org/10.1080/10673220490905705.
98. Markus Heilig et al., "Addiction as a Brain Disease Revisited; Why It Still Matters, and the Need for Consilience," *Neuropsychopharmacology* 46 (2021): 1715–23, https://doi.org/10.1038/s41386-020-00950-y.

described above with the exception of the moral model and a strict version of the brain disease model of addiction. While neural changes are significant in addiction, there are additional factors at play that a strict version of the BDMA cannot account for. Most of the remaining models (e.g., choice, self-medication, a looser version of the brain disease model, and the syndrome model) are not mutually exclusive, and each seems to highlight a different aspect and cause of addiction, all of which can be at play in a person suffering. While I would not characterize addiction as a disease in the way that, for instance, lung cancer is seen as a disease, I do see it as a disorder akin to depression and other mental health issues. That is, something significant happens in the brain that goes beyond the norm. At this point the neuroscience of addiction is so well documented that any responsible model of addiction must take it into account. Thus, I would place addiction closer to the compulsion side of the spectrum than the freedom side. At the same time, I also see great value in the insights of the other models, particularly the self-medication model. In the next chapter, I propose a theological model for thinking about addiction that is consonant with the neuroscience of addiction yet leaves room for some of the causes highlighted by the other models.

Chapter 2

Addiction

Sin or Disease? A Theological Account of Addiction

"Is addiction a sin or a disease?" This is the question I am asked more than any other when I tell people I write about addiction and theology. When I dig a little deeper, I usually discover that what is behind this question is a deep sense of pain. Some ask because they have an addiction, and no matter how much they want to believe otherwise, they secretly wonder if it's their fault. Others ask because they have a friend or family member with an addiction. Some feel a sense of helplessness and sadness as they watch their loved one suffer. They want so much for their loved one to get well but don't know what to do or where to turn. They want to understand what addiction is so they can figure out if their loved one needs medication, prayer, therapy, connection, rehab, a recovery group, church, or maybe just a good kick in the pants. Or perhaps they feel exasperated with their loved one for using, yet again, and secretly wonder if their loved one could do better if they just tried a little harder. Parents of children who suffer from addiction sometimes wonder if perhaps it's their fault that their child is using. Whether asked by those suffering from addiction or those who love them, what is almost always behind the question is desperation and pain.

The other element behind this question is a specific (and faulty) theology of sin. What people are often asking when they ask if addiction is sin or disease is whether the person using is free to act otherwise or compelled to use. They are asking where addiction falls on the freedom-compulsion and blame-blamelessness scales I discussed in chapter 1. In other words, when people ask if addiction is a sin, they are often asking whether addiction is a moral failing.

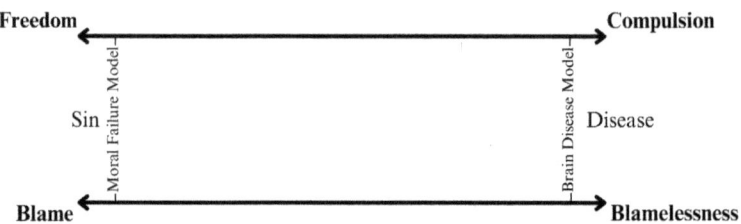

Fig. 2.1. Sin–Disease Spectrum

Theologian Alistair McFadyen points out that for many contemporary Christians sin presupposes "views of the human which take the individual and her autonomy as primary."[1] While McFadyen disagrees and offers a far more compelling view of sin in his book *Bound to Sin*, he explains that contemporary Christians often see something as sinful when someone can rightly be blamed for the act. He explains that for someone to bear the blame for something, she must be the *cause* of the act, have been able to *will* otherwise, and been *free to act* otherwise. For instance, a person caught stealing from a supermarket is prosecuted on the assumption that she caused the event (i.e., she stole an item and was not held under duress—e.g., at gunpoint—to do so). Further, it is assumed that she is morally capable of choosing. That is, if she had a brain injury that affected her capacity for moral reasoning, she would likely not be held responsible for this event. Finally, she must be shown to be free. If she were prescribed medication by a doctor and suffered the unfortunate side effect of sleepwalking, during which time she stole from the supermarket, she would unlikely be held responsible for stealing. These three elements of blame—causation, will, and freedom—are used to determine whether a person can rightly be blamed for an action. In much of contemporary popular theology, something is considered sin when it meets the abovementioned criteria. Hence, sin is often subsumed under the category of morality and only includes those acts for which we can rightly blame someone.[2]

Thus, when people ask if addiction is sin or disease, they are asking whether someone with addiction ought to be held morally responsible for their addiction. As I pointed out in chapter 1, this dichotomy between a moral model of sin and a disease concept is not merely limited to Christian notions of addiction. Hanna

---

1. Alistair McFadyen, *Bound to Sin: Abuse, Holocaust and the Christian Doctrine of Sin* (Cambridge University Press, 2000), 22.
2. McFadyen, *Bound to Sin*, 19–22, 25–26.

Pickard points out that people often see the disease concept of addiction and the moral failure model of addiction as the only two possible ways of viewing addiction.[3] Addiction is either a disease, and hence outside the scope of the person's responsibility, or a moral failure for which we can hold the person responsible. The person with addiction is either free to choose or compelled to engage in the addiction.

To further complicate matters, people with addiction do not resolve the conflict, as they tend to describe their experiences as a hellish mixture of compulsion *and* volition. Thus, Jowita Bydlowska says of alcohol, "It is not necessary. Yet it is a need."[4] Much of a sufferer's struggle seems to occur right on the knife's edge of wanting and needing, and willing and being compelled, such that a person with addiction does not even know where one ends and the other begins. Laura Cathcart Robbins describes moments when she stops using Ambien for (short) periods of time. In those moments she thinks, "*Perhaps I won't pick up my refill at the pharmacy next week after all and just get this . . . out of my system for good.*"[5] She has moments where she wills herself to stop using. At the same time, she also describes "being an addict is like being strapped into a roller coaster." She says, "You can try and pry the bar up on your own, you can scream at the top of your lungs, but you're locked in, and you can't get off until the ride is over."[6] On the one hand, the compulsion to continue to drink or use drugs is so strong that it is, for all intents and purposes, a survival need; on the other hand, this compulsion feels very much like an act of the will. The condition of addiction, therefore, does not seem to map neatly onto the categories of disease and moral sin.

In this chapter, I propose a different way of thinking about addiction that breaks free of the binaries of the disease/moral sin models of talking about addiction by retrieving the ancient theological concept of the bondage of the will.[7] I propose that addiction is best described as a manifestation of the bondage of the will because it incorporates the wisdom of the addiction models described in chapter 1, resonates with people's experiences of addiction, and allows for a way of talking about addiction from a faith-based perspective without attaching undue blame and shame to those suffering. I rely on Augustine and John Calvin to retrieve a theology of the bondage of the will yet detach it from the concept of original guilt to talk about addiction as a condition that affects the sufferer's relationship with God without attaching blame to the person suffering. I begin with a description of the concept of the bondage of the will.

---

3. Hanna Pickard, "What We're Not Talking about When We Talk about Addiction," *The Hastings Report* 50, no. 4 (July–August 2020): 38, https://doi.org/10.1002/hast.1172.

4. Jowita Bydlowska, *Drunk Mom: A Memoir* (Penguin Books, 2014), 44.

5. Laura Cathcart Robbins, *Stash: My Life in Hiding* (Atria Paperback, 2024), 9.

6. Robbins, *Stash,* 95.

7. I am not the first to consider addiction in light of the concept of original sin (though I do not, in the end, see addiction as original sin). While I focus primarily on Augustine and Calvin in this chapter, I engage other theologians who have asked similar questions in the next chapter.

THE CONCEPT OF THE BONDAGE OF THE WILL

To understand the concept of the bondage of the will, it is helpful to go back to Augustine's conception of the will more generally. Augustine is often credited with developing a more complex understanding of the will than was present in philosophy and theology before him and spends considerable time talking about the will in his corpus.

Augustine's early writings on the will are often targeted at the Manichean philosophy with which he was enamored in his younger years. Augustine writes about the freedom of the will in these texts to resolve a question about the existence of evil. Manicheans held a dualistic view of the cosmos whereby light and darkness, good and evil, and the spiritual and material realms were at war with each other. The existence of evil is thus easily explained since evil is simply one of the two powers at play in the cosmos. Matter (e.g., the earth, human bodies, etc.) is inherently evil, while the spiritual realm is inherently good. After Augustine converts to Christianity (and rejects Manicheism), however, he struggles to explain the existence of evil in light of God's creation. He sums up the question as follows: "If sins originate with souls which God has created, and which therefore have their origin from God, how are sins not to be charged against God at least immediately?"[8] That is, if we say that God created everything, aren't we also obligated to say that God created evil? Where else could evil come from, after all?

This is the question Augustine discusses with his counterpart Evodius in *On Free Will*. He tells Evodius there are "two classes of things, the eternal and the temporal."[9] However, unlike the Manicheans, Augustine does not see the temporal as inherently evil. The temporal is, after all, created by God, and all that God creates is good. The temporal is, rather, simply a lesser good, and it is in the desire for these lesser goods that Augustine sees the possibility for the existence of evil. The potential for evil resides in the human capacity to choose this lesser good *over* the ultimate good.

Augustine argues in *On Free Will* that "doing evil is . . . to neglect eternal things which the mind itself perceives and enjoys and loves and cannot lose, and to pursue, as if they were great and wonderful, temporal things which are perceived by the body, the lowest part of human nature, and can never be possessed with certainty."[10] It is in the act of desiring the temporal and pursuing it as if it were eternal that sin enters the world. Thus, he says, "We charge the soul with sin when we show that it has abandoned the higher things and prefers to enjoy lower things."[11] Desiring something finite and giving it the weight of the transcendent is something we all do, in big and small ways, all the time. There are moments in my life, for instance, when I unwittingly attach my sense of identity

---

8. Augustine, *On Free Will*, in *Augustine: Earlier Writings*, ed. John Baillie, John T. McNeill, and Henry P. Van Dusen, trans. John H. S. Burleigh (Westminster, 1953), II.ii.4.
9. Augustine, *On Free Will*, I.xvi.34.
10. Augustine, *On Free Will*, I, xvi, 34.
11. Augustine, *On Free Will*, III.i.2.

to my job. How I feel about myself in those moments is entirely dependent on how well I do my job. There is nothing inherently wrong with caring about my work. However, if my sense of worth becomes attached to how well I do my job, I end up basing my worth in the temporal and the fickle ups and downs of my work as opposed to basing it in God's view of me as worthy (no matter what I do or do not do). Some people give a particular sport a divine place in their lives, some allow another person to take this spot, and yet others pursue wealth as if it were a god. Addiction is an extreme example of our attempt to ask a finite good to meet infinite needs. For Augustine, evil resides in these choices for the temporal over the ultimate. None of these things (a job, a particular sport, another person, or money) are inherently evil, but pursuing them as if they are God is. This is, of course, idolatry.

In his later writings, Augustine sums up his position when he explains that sin entered the world through "the misdirected love whereby the will fell away from the immutable to the mutable good."[12] It is important to note that the faculty of the will is good and that that which is desired is in itself also good. That is, all that God created is good. But evil entered the world through an inordinate desire for lesser goods.[13]

Evil is thus a privation. That is, it doesn't really exist as a created entity among other created entities. Rather, evil is found in the human capacity to choose something or someone other than God over God. Augustine argues that humans are responsible for this free choice to pursue the temporal because God's punishment of human sin would be "unjust unless the will was free not only to live aright but also to sin."[14] In other words, it only makes sense for God to hold us accountable for sin if we were able to choose not to sin. It is not clear whether Augustine, at this point in his career, imagines humans to have free will only prior to the fall or also after the fall.[15]

This question of whether the will is free to choose the good after the fall becomes the center of his argument with Pelagius later in Augustine's life. Fourth-century theologian Pelagius believed that pre- and postlapsarian humans (i.e., humans before and after the fall respectively) have the capacity to freely choose. He argued that the will is, in essence, neutral and entirely self-motivated.

---

12. Augustine, *The City of God*, trans. Marcus Dods (Hendrickson, 2016), book 12.8.
13. Augustine, *City of God*, book 12.8.
14. Augustine, *On Free Will*, II.i.3.
15. Augustine's position on the extent to which humans have free will to do good is notoriously difficult to pin down. This is due, at least in part, to the fact that Augustine is often writing in opposition to a particular theology or person. He may, therefore, state his theology more starkly than he might were he writing a work on free will that had no opposing view in mind. Some Augustine scholars argue that he changes his mind (from a position in which he espouses greater free will to one in which he espouses almost no free will) over the course of his career, while others argue for a more consistent view (i.e., severely limited free will). A full exploration of Augustine's view of the will is beyond the scope of this book. Further, there are many scholars who do precisely this work, such as Han-Luen Kantzer Komline, *Augustine on the Will: A Theological Account* (Oxford University Press, 2019); James Wetzel, *Augustine: The Limits of Virtue* (Cambridge University Press, 1992); Eleanore Stump, "Augustine on Free Will," in *The Cambridge Companion to Augustine,* ed. David Vincent Meconi and Eleanore Stump (Cambridge University Press, 2014).

That is, it is not compelled in one direction or another.[16] In his letter to Demetrias, for instance, Pelagius says,

> It was because God wished to bestow on the rational creature the gift of doing good of his own free will and the capacity to exercise free choice, by implanting in man the possibility of choosing either alternative, that he made it his peculiar right to be what he wanted to be, so that with his capacity for good and evil he could do either quite naturally and then bend his will in the other direction too.[17]

Thus, Pelagius argues, humans have the capacity to choose both good and evil. In this letter Pelagius wants to encourage Demetrias in her decision for consecration and in her capacities to do the good and thus demonstrates to her that humans have the capacity to do the good.

Where Pelagius writes about the freedom of the will as a source of encouragement for Demetrias, part of what is also at stake for him, especially in his arguments with Augustine, is human culpability. To make his point, Pelagius uses Augustine's own words against him and quotes Augustine's *On Free Will* and says that Augustine was right in saying that if humans are sinners "*because [they] could not have been otherwise,*" then they are "*free from blame.*"[18] It only makes sense for God to hold humans accountable for sin if humans were able to act otherwise. However, Augustine seems to hold a more complex position on the will even in this earlier work (*On Free Will*) when he says,

> all that a man does wrongfully in ignorance and all that he cannot do rightly though he wishes, are called sins because they have their origin in the first sin of the will when it was free. These are its deserved consequences. . . . So we apply the word "sin" not only to that which is properly called sin, that is, what is committed knowingly and with free will, but also to all that follows as the necessary punishment of that first sin.[19]

Thus, the necessity of committing sins is a consequence of the fall. Humans inherit this consequence, and thus cannot do otherwise, yet are responsible for it. A consequence of the fall is that our desire is now directed at lesser goods, and we are unable of our own volition to fully desire the ultimate good (God). This misdirected desire co-opts the will so that it is now bent toward lesser goods.

---

16. See McFadyen, *Bound to Sin,* 168–72 for a helpful explanation of Pelagius's position on the will.

17. Pelagius, "To Demetrias," trans. B. R. Rees Ferrante, in B. R. Rees, *Pelagius: Life and Letters* (Boydell, 1998), 3.2.

18. Augustine is here quoting a piece from Pelagius's writings in which Pelagius quotes Augustine to show that even Augustine used to hold to Pelagius' notion of free will. Augustine, *On Nature and Grace,* in *Saint Augustine: Four Anti-Pelagian Writings,* ed. Thomas P. Halton et al., trans. John Mourant and William J. Collinge (Catholic University Press, 1992), section 9 (italics in the original).

19. Augustine, *On Free Will,* III.xix.54.

On the one hand Augustine is pushing against the fatalism of the Manicheans who see evil as intrinsic to the material realm (as opposed to the spiritual realm) while on the other hand pushing against the Pelagian notion of full freedom (after the fall).

Fig. 2.2. Pelagian–Manichean Spectrum

The questions about human freedom and compulsion that I've been wrestling with in relation to addiction are clearly not new. Had the category of addiction existed in the fourth century, a Pelagian might thus have seen addiction as a choice, while a Manichean would likely see it as more of a compulsion inherent to the material realm. Augustine attempts to walk the line between these two by holding to the concept of the bondage of the will. While Augustine leans more toward compulsion than freedom, it is unclear where exactly he would place himself as he seems to argue for both sides, depending on who he is arguing against. As such, interpreters of Augustine have varying views on his position on the will, some arguing for a limited sense of free will, with others arguing for no free will.

John Calvin interprets and relies on Augustine's concept of the bondage of the will to argue that postlapsarian humans do not have freedom, at least not in the way that we think of the concept. Given Calvin's influence on Reformed thinking about human willing, I briefly explore Calvin's position, before arguing for a more moderate position based on Eleanore Stump's interpretation of Augustine.

The concept of the bondage of the will is deeply embedded in the broader concept of original sin. Calvin defines original sin as "a hereditary depravity and corruption of our nature, diffused into all parts of the soul, which first makes us liable to God's wrath, then also brings forth in us those works which Scripture calls 'works of the flesh' [Gal. 5:19]."[20] In other words, original sin is (1) a hereditary condition (the bondage of the will), (2) for which we are held responsible and liable (hereditary guilt), which (3) brings forth immoral acts (sins). These three elements constitute original sin. What is particularly important about this definition for Calvin is that not only is Adam's sin passed on but also his guilt, by which all persons are then held liable to God. Hence, everyone inherits guilt. Further, Calvin notes that humankind is "overwhelmed—as by a deluge—from

---

20. John Calvin, *Institutes of the Christian Religion*, ed. John T. McNeill, trans. Ford Lewis Battles (Westminster, 1960), 2.1.8.

head to foot, so that no part is immune from sin and all that proceeds from him is to be imputed to sin."[21] As a result of sin, humankind's nature is so transformed and corrupted that it does not simply become sinful when a sin is committed but is now sinful in and of itself. In other words, we are born into the condition of already being sinful (i.e., the bondage of the will).

It is difficult to understand what it means to be born into this external condition because we have never known life without it. It is similar to trying to describe what water is to a fish. Several years ago, I had an experience that gave me a glimpse into what it is like to step into an external condition, which proved useful for helping me to understand the effect such a condition can have on a person.

I took a trip with a friend to "the most magical place on earth" (or perhaps more realistically, the most magical place in Florida). From the moment we entered the parking lot we were immersed in Disney's world. Music piped from hidden speakers all over the car park, indicating that we were, indeed, in a "magical place." Friendly parking lot attendants directed us to the shuttle that took us into the park. Once on the shuttle, a friendly and slightly goofy host gave us his spiel to get us in the mood for Disney, joking around with the passengers and thankfully reminding us to take note of our parking area and space. The parking areas were named after heroes and villains of Disney stories, reminding us that we were in "a whole new world." Music was piped throughout the park, no matter where we went. Even the restrooms offered no respite from Disney joy as "It's a Small World" echoed in the stalls. The staff, from parade actors to ride operators to street sweepers, all presented as slightly goofy, ready with a corny joke at a moment's notice. With its attention to the very minute details, Disney transported us from our daily lives and, for a moment, drew us into a world of their making.

The magic and joy of Disney was a condition or situation that we stepped into. It was a condition imposed from without through music, props, staff, and so on. Disney created for us a totalizing experience, such that it was hard to step outside of the world they created. Every detail evoked this magical world of goofy joy and reverie. The condition that Disney crafted through its music, props, characters, and more was clearly outside of us. Some of this imposed reverie, however, infiltrated from without to within. For instance, I found myself, days later, absentmindedly whistling Disney tunes to the great annoyance of those around me.

Disney World gives us a taste of what it is to enter into a situation not of our own making. It gives us a glimpse of the totalizing effect an imposed condition can have on us. This trivial illustration may help to shed light on what John Calvin means by original sin in the *Institutes*. For Calvin, sin is not just a collection of immoral acts. Similarly, Disney World is not simply a collection of Disney characters, though it is that too. Rather, Disney is a world that we step

---

21. Calvin, *Institutes*, 2.1.9.

into and Calvin describes sin as a totalizing situation (the bondage of the will) that we are born into.

Of course, original sin is not the magical and fun totalizing condition of Disney. Rather, it is a complex world we are born into. Serene Jones gives a more sobering reflection in *Call It Grace* of what this looks like. She describes going on a fun fishing outing with her grandfather and Mr. Porter, "the first African American elected to state senate," delighting in their presence.[22] And yet when she comes home and has dinner with her extended family the next day, she sees more clearly for the first time how complex her grandfather really is. On the one hand, he is in a close friendship with Mr. Porter, and yet on the other hand, he regularly spews racist jokes over dinner. Further, he purposefully "brushes up against" her as she sets the table, "his loins . . . pressing against [her] back." During that particular dinner he tells a drawn-out misogynistic joke, and as he finishes his story, Jones feels a menstrual cramp; she writes, "The violence of the story kept sinking into me, descending further and further into my belly, deep into my bones, into my blood, and burying itself between my legs," and "that small place, down there inside of me, the place from where my blood came, mocked me with the hard truth: I wasn't now and never would be a fisher 'man' the likes of Dick and Melvin. I would always be more like the 'woman' in their jokes than they would ever be." Later she realizes that her grandfather was both enacting his own rage and living into a larger system of which he was a part. She says, "Dick Jones's inheritance of original sin was twofold, its wellspring in his personal history and his gender's assumed right of sexual dominance." Dick Jones stepped into systems of racism and sexism that conditioned him and yet also acted from within those systems himself.

Serene Jones, recognizing at fifteen that she will always be the butt of her grandfather's jokes, finds herself co-opted by the same systems that co-opted her grandfather:

> I leaned back in my chair, arms hanging loose on the sides, trying on the pose of a comfortable man.
>
> I tried on the words to go with the pose. Manlike words that would make my cramps disappear like a bad dream. And earn me a proud seat back in the boat, not a shameful place, victimized on the shoreline.
>
> I tried to speak with bravado "Tell another, Grandpa." I said. "Tell us about Mrs. Colliers, the one with the big jugs."
>
> After I said it, I couldn't believe what had come out of my mouth; it was as if some evil spirit were inside my brain. . . . I was torn between my pride and my desire to belong, on the one side, and my own bleeding body and my fear of his virulent, abusive relation to women, on the other.

Jones finds herself conditioned by the very systems of violence she hates. She says, "I didn't realize it as completely then, but I was experiencing the full force of what Calvin called *original sin*, that persistent and all-too-human pull toward

---

22. Serene Jones, *Call It Grace: Finding Meaning in a Fractured World* (Penguin Books, 2020), 37.

our own destruction."[23] Jones names the reality that Calvin describes of being both born into a system, and having it condition us from without, and yet also being infected by it from within.

Calvin notes that the change effected by Adam's sin not only affects the external world we are born into but also transforms us from within. Where I was able to step out of the world Disney crafted at any moment by simply leaving the park, the condition of sin that we are born into is such that we cannot step outside of it to see what life without it would be like. Hence, an important difference (besides the obvious) between the situation Disney crafts and original sin is that while Disney does its very best to draw us into a different world, it cannot and does not fully infiltrate us from within. Serene Jones's narrative demonstrates what it is to be fully drawn in and co-opted by a system of violence. Calvin argues that the condition of original sin is not just a situation we are born into. That is, it is not just that we are born into a world that is already sinful (an outward circumstance), but rather that this condition has already infiltrated us from within. There is no part of us that is not infected by this condition. Hence, Calvin describes original sin as a "corruption of our nature, diffused into all parts of the soul."[24]

This all-encompassing effect of original sin is very similar to the totalizing effect addiction has. People with addiction often experience their lives as being overwhelmed by the drive for the addictive substance, and as a result their lives become diminished. Much as someone in active addiction may try to compartmentalize their addiction, the addiction invariably infects every relationship and every part of their being. In her memoir, *Parched*, Heather King says, "My world was getting smaller by the minute."[25] Similarly, Mary Karr notes in her memoir *Lit* that addiction is a kind of "ambition-deficit disorder" that "ensures . . . life gets lived in miniature." She says, "Liquor . . . shrinks me to a plodding zombie state in which one day smudges into every other—it blurs time." Where it used to allow her to feel "taller, faster, funnier," it now simply diminishes her existence into a kind of daily nothingness.[26]

Addiction absorbs so much of a person's life and personality that they are overcome, as Calvin so aptly describes, "as by a deluge—from head to foot—so that no part is immune" from the addiction.[27] Where a social drinker, for instance, can enjoy a few beers with friends without having it alter her personality, a person suffering from a substance use disorder becomes so consumed with alcohol that she makes choices that seem to be in direct conflict with her values. William Moyers, for instance, tells the story of leaving his wife and children, whom he loves deeply, to live in a crack house in his memoir *Broken*.[28] Moyers's values

---

23. Jones, *Call It Grace*, 43, 45, 48, 46 (italics in the original).
24. Calvin, *Institutes*, 2.1.8.
25. Heather King, *Parched: A Memoir* (New American Library, 2006), 212.
26. Mary Karr, *Lit* (Harper Perennial, 2009), 47, 171.
27. Calvin, *Institutes*, 2.1.9.
28. William Cope Moyers, *Broken: My Story of Addiction and Redemption* (Penguin Books, 2007), 2.

and life goals alter drastically as he is overtaken by his addiction, and no part of his life, not even his children, is immune from his addiction.

A college student on a binge may find her personality altered while drunk at a bar, such that she laughs or feels ashamed the next day at what she did while intoxicated. This is very different, however, from the experience of a person with addiction, whose very drives and desires are so caught up in the addictive substance that there is no moment of real reprieve in which she can look back in embarrassment at last night's activities. She may wake up to a dreaded memory of last night, but her very being is so caught up in pursuing the addictive substance that this memory simply propels her toward another binge. Calvin's description of the bondage of the will as an overwhelming condition that alters a person from top to bottom is very much in line with the way people experience their addictions.

While Calvin demonstrates that we do not have free will in the ways that we understand the term, he does hold to a sense of the human capacity to will. Calvin makes a complicated distinction between the will and free will in order to argue that we have a will, and yet the will is not actually free. Calvin argues that "man was created with free choice," but that "our choice is now held captive under the bondage of sin," because of "Adam's misuse of free choice when he had it."[29] After the fall, Calvin argues, we no longer have free choice. Calvin does not always seem consistent on this point. At times he claims we have limited free will and at others he claims we do not. Calvin explains this apparent inconsistency by saying, "if freedom is opposed to coercion, I both acknowledge and consistently maintain that choice is free."[30] He is careful to maintain that humans are not coerced by an outside force to choose evil. In that sense, we are free. Hence, "Man . . . sinned willingly, not unwillingly or by compulsion; by the most eager inclination of his heart, not by forced compulsion; by the prompting of his own lust, not by compulsion from without."[31] Calvin argues that we are not compelled to act but rather prompted by our own desire. What's at stake for Calvin here is human liability for sin. Yet, this desire is not within our control in the way we might think. We cannot, on our own steam, override it or choose to desire differently. In that sense, we are not free. Calvin seems to recognize that we experience ourselves as making choices, while at the same time recognizing that we do not have control over our choices. Thus, Calvin makes the complicated argument that we sin out of necessity (an inner drive) rather than compulsion (an outside force) and can therefore be held responsible.

Heather King attempts to name this paradox of having a will and yet feeling, in a sense, compelled to do the very thing she does not want to do:

---

29. Calvin, *The Bondage and Liberation of the Will: A Defense of the Orthodox Doctrine of Human Choice against Pighius*, ed. A. N. S. Lane, trans. G. I. Davies (Baker Books, 1996), II.263.
30. Calvin, *Bondage and Liberation*, II.279.
31. Calvin, *Institutes*, 2.3.5.

> It was as if the part of my brain that governed experience had been lobotomized, and this sense of being so deeply separated from my truest, sanest self—the fact that on the one hand, I felt *compelled* to engage in behavior that basically consisted of doing the same thing over and over again and expecting different results, and that on the other hand I was somehow *willing* it—created a moral/psychic conflict of such ghastly proportions and satanic complexity I simply tuned it out.[32]

Much of an addicted person's struggle seems to occur right on the boundary of wanting and needing, and willing and being compelled, such that a person with addiction does not even know where one ends and the other begins. This is the experience of craving I described in the last chapter. On the one hand, the compulsion to continue to drink or use drugs is so strong it is, for all intents and purposes, a survival need. The person with addiction is compelled (a word Calvin would not want to use)—enslaved to the addiction. King names it as such when she calls the drive to drink a "slavering need."[33] On the other hand, King also experiences herself as having a functioning will. People with addiction are able to choose in their own best interest at times. If this weren't the case, people with addiction would never recover.

Carl Fisher describes the paradox of addiction well in his book, *The Urge: Our History of Addiction*: "The thing that is terrifying" to those with addiction "is that they watch themselves making a choice while feeling there is something wrong with the choosing." He says, "It is, in other words, an issue of *disordered choice*. . . ."[34] This paradox of both feeling compelled and yet having some sense of agency is, in some ways, the essence of the problem of addiction. It is this element of addiction that many theories of addiction try to explain. Thus, Calvin's description of the will as being bound and yet functional (e.g., willing to sin "by the most eager inclination of [the] heart") deeply resonates with the experiences of people with addiction.[35]

However, Calvin takes this paradox and tries to resolve it and in so doing creates a deeply troubling theology. Calvin first says that humans do not really have free will in the way that we think of the term. He rightly recognizes that people often assume that applying the word "free" to the "will" means "that it [the will] therefore has good and evil within its power, so that it can by its own strength choose either of them."[36] Calvin expressly denies the will this kind of freedom. He therefore says in both the *Institutes* and in *The Bondage and Liberation of the Will* that he would prefer it if "free will" were banned from common usage.[37] For all intents and purposes, Calvin does not believe humans

---

32. King, *Parched*, 148 (italics in the original).
33. King, *Parched*, 51.
34. Carl Erik Fisher, *The Urge: Our History of Addiction* (Penguin Books, 2023), 7–8 (italics in the original).
35. Calvin, *Institutes*, 2.3.5.
36. Calvin, *Bondage and Liberation*, II.279.
37. Calvin, *Bondage and Liberation*, II.279; Calvin, *Institutes*, 2.2.8.

(apart from God's grace) have free will as we understand the term. Our desires are so warped that we cannot choose the good without God's intervention.

What is at stake for Calvin is the necessity of God's grace (something that is important to Augustine as well) and God's sovereignty. For Calvin, humans can do nothing outside the will of God as God is Lord over all that is. This is so important to Calvin that he takes the concept of God's sovereignty to its logical and unpleasant conclusion and says that "God not only foresaw the fall of the first man, and in him the ruin of his descendants, but also meted it out in accordance with his own decision."[38] In other words, he says that "God willed, not only permitted, Adam's fall and the rejection of the reprobate."[39] The argument Calvin makes here is clearly deeply troubling, and theologians in Calvin's own time and many since have strongly refuted it.[40]

What is at stake for Calvin in all of this is actually a pastoral concern. He says, "All this [teaching] has no other purpose but to make the believer rest, free from anxiety, in the omnipotence of God." He finally argues that "this entire teaching trains a person only to be humble, to fear God, to place his trust in God, and to ascribe glory to God, which are the chief components of true religion. . . . "[41] Calvin's concern is for the believer to be free of anxiety and full of gratitude. The logic he uses to meet this pastoral concern, however, is deeply troubling. Calvin resolves the paradox of feeling both compelled and yet having a will by taking the illogical position that humans are both fully responsible for sin and the fall (i.e., having free will) and yet unable to act otherwise (i.e., being compelled). On the freedom/compulsion and blame/blamelessness continuum we've been exploring, this would look as follows (recognizing that Calvin would want to use the word "necessity" over "compulsion"):[42]

---

38. Calvin, *Institutes*, 3.23.7.
39. Calvin, *Institutes*, 3.23.8.
40. In "The Eternal Predestination of God," for instance, Calvin expressly writes against his contemporary critics, Albertus Pighius and Georgius of Sicily (John Calvin, "The Eternal Predestination of God," in *Calvin's Calvinism: The Eternal Predestination of God and the Secret Providence of God*, trans. Henry Cole [Wipf & Stock, 2019]). Likewise, Calvin's *The Bondage and Liberation of the Will: A Defense of the Orthodox Doctrine of Human Choice against Pighius* is a response to his critic, Albertus Pighius. In the twentieth century, Karl Barth doesn't directly refute the doctrine of double predestination but does famously revise it (see Karl Barth, *Church Dogmatics: Doctrine of God, Vol. II.2*, ed. Geoffrey William Bromiley and Thomas Forsyth Torrance [T&T Clark, 1957], II.2.vii.32–35) and thereby undoes some of Calvin's more problematic ideas. Barth is often "accused" of promoting universal salvation as a result.
41. Calvin, *Bondage and Liberation*, II.258.
42. Calvin would not approve of the word "compelled" in this and later sentences. He would likely want me to use the language of necessity instead of compulsion, because necessity does not imply coercion by an outside force. Calvin argues that we sin of necessity in the same way that God does good of necessity. We would never say that God is compelled by an outside force to do the good, nor would we say that God does not have free will. Similarly, Calvin argues we have free will insofar as we can choose between varieties of evil, and we are not compelled by an outside force to choose evil. We do so with our will intact (Calvin, *Institutes*, 2.3.5). Again, what is at stake for Calvin is our liability for sin. I deliberately choose the language of compulsion, however, because we frequently use the language of compulsion when talking about addiction, precisely because it names the fact that a force outside of the person struggling (the addiction) drives a person to keep seeking out the addictive substance despite clear negative consequences. At the same time, however, the person also *feels* as if they are making choices. Further, the distinction Calvin attempts to make between

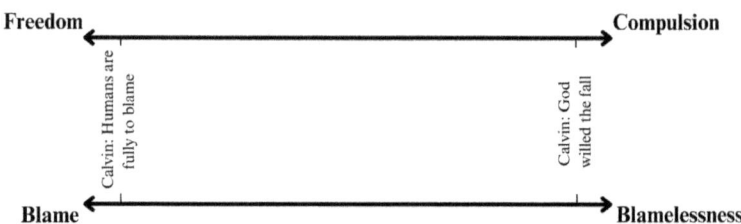

Figure 2.3. Calvin on Freedom–Compulsion Spectrum

Thus, while Calvin's descriptions of the totalizing effect of sin are helpful in naming the experience of addiction, the extremes he goes to in an attempt to hold to God's sovereignty is ultimately both illogical and unhelpful. Augustine offers a useful, though inconsistent, middle ground that allows for an apt description of the effects of sin, while also holding to minimal free will. Augustine says that while postlapsarian humans do not have the freedom to do or even will the good, they do have the freedom to ask for God's help. Thus, according to Augustine, "You are not held guilty because you are ignorant in spite of yourself, but because you neglect to seek the knowledge you do not possess. You are not held guilty because you do not use your wounded members but because you despise him who is willing to heal them."[43] It seems, then, that while we are not fully free, we are free to "seek the knowledge [we] do not possess." This is, at any rate, Augustine's stance at the time of writing *On Free Will*.

In "Augustine on Free Will," Eleanore Stump describes Augustine's position on the will (in *On Free Will*) by making a distinction between first- and second-order volition. For Augustine, the will is bent toward evil because the will follows desire, and human desire is directed at lesser goods. Humans cannot change this first order desire. However, humans can desire to desire differently (second-order volition), and that is where human freedom (and responsibility) reside for Augustine in *On Free Will*.[44] Without some agency (even if just the agency to ask for help), a person could not be held liable for sin. As noted earlier (see footnote 15), some scholars think Augustine changes his mind over the course of his life and that while he held to some degree of free will in his earlier writings (e.g., *On Free Will*), he lets go of this notion in his later writings.

Stump, however, demonstrates that Augustine holds to his initial position (that we have the freedom to ask for help) even in his later works. She notes that when Pelagius uses Augustine's own words from *On Free Will* against him to demonstrate that Augustine holds to the concept of human free will, Augustine says that he always believed (even in *On Free Will*) that humans are not free to

---

necessity and compulsion falls apart when you take his theology of predestination into account. If the fall was predestined by God, and the result of the Fall is that we now will evil of necessity, we are, for all intents and purposes, compelled (by God, in Calvin's theology) to will evil.

43. Augustine, *On Free Will*, III.xix.53.
44. Eleanore Stump, "Augustine on Free Will," 166–71.

do the good on their own but are free to ask for God's assistance in resisting temptation and guarding against sin.[45] If this were not so, the Lord's Prayer (i.e., "Lead us not into temptation," Matt. 6:13) would seem unnecessary.[46] Similarly, Stump points to Augustine's *On Grace and Free Choice* (a later work, written in 426–427 CE) where Augustine argues, "Now God has revealed to us through His own Scripture that human beings have free choice of the will." He goes on to say, "the divine precepts would themselves be pointless for human beings unless we had free choice of the will, by which we might reach the promised rewards through carrying them out."[47]

Beyond the ability to ask for help, Augustine also sees postlapsarian humans as having the freedom of will to accept the grace that God gives.[48] Thus, Augustine says in *On the Spirit and the Letter*, "For the soul cannot receive and possess the gifts there spoken of [i.e., grace], but by consenting. What it is to possess, what it is to receive, pertains to God: the receiving and the possessing necessarily to him who receives and possesses."[49] Stump notes that Augustine, in this passage and others, is wrestling with the idea that God must be responsible for our desires to will the good as humans rely fully on God's grace for the good, and willing the good is a kind of good. However, if God is responsible for this second-order desire, then why wouldn't God give that desire to everyone? Stump helpfully argues that in the passage quoted above, Augustine attempts to show that God does give it to everyone, and it is up to humans to decide whether to receive it or not.[50]

Stump notes that Augustine, in the end, attempts to solve a problem he cannot solve. He wants to both hold humans responsible for sin and thus attribute some sense of free will, while also holding to the notion that humans can only do the good through God's grace.[51] Where Calvin solves it by coming to the conclusion that God must have willed the fall *and* that humans are yet fully to blame for the fall, Augustine stays in the paradox and at times in both early and later works claims that it is possible to have a second-order volition to will the good

---

45. Augustine, "On Nature and Grace" in *Saint Augustine: Four Anti-Pelagian Writings*, ed. Thomas P. Halton et al., trans. John Mourant and William J. Collinge (Catholic University Press, 1992), section 9.

46. Augustine, "On Nature and Grace," section 9; see Stump's argument in "Augustine on Free Will" on pp. 171–73.

47. Stump, "Augustine on Free Will," 171–73; Augustine, *On Grace and Free Choice*, in *On the Free Choice of the Will, On Grace and Free Choice, and Other Writings*, trans. and ed. Peter King (Cambridge University Press, 2010), 2.2.

48. Stump, "Augustine on Free Will," 174.

49. Augustine, *On the Spirit and the Letter*, in *Augustine: Later Works*, ed. John Baillie, John T. McNeill, and Henry P. Van Dusen, trans. John Burnaby (Westminster, 1955), section 60.

50. Stump, "Augustine on Free Will," 174. Interestingly, even receiving grace can be problematic for Augustine as it could be seen as a human capacity to do the good outside of God's grace (i.e., the good of receiving grace). Stump offers an interesting solution to the problem Augustine faces by suggesting that perhaps there is a middle way between receiving and rejecting grace. She suggests that perhaps Augustine's problem would be solved if he accepted the notion that humans have the capacity to stop rejecting grace. That is, humans do not have the capacity to accept grace, and in their normal state are prone to reject grace. Yet, humans do have the capacity to stop rejecting grace and thereby open the door to receiving it (Stump, 178–81).

51. Stump, "Augustine on Free Will," 177–78.

(something Calvin expressly denies) and receive the good given to us, and at others claims even this is a gift of God.[52]

Protestant, and particularly Reformed, understandings of the bondage of the will tend to be based on Calvin's interpretation of Augustine and thus leave no room for humans to do the good on their own. A total lack of free will to choose the good does not align with our experience of reality, however. That is, while I certainly frequently experience the frustration of doing what I do not, in fact, want to do, I also have experiences of making healthy choices toward the good. It seems disanalogous to my experience to call all of these choices toward the good as God's work in me, and all of the choices toward evil as my work. I experience both as within the workings of my own will.

Therefore, I follow Stump's interpretation of Augustine and hold to a concept of the bondage of the will that allows for a limited capacity to do the good. Theologian Christopher Cook offers an analysis of addiction in which he relies closely on Stump's interpretation of Augustine. He notes in *Alcohol, Addiction, and Christian Ethics* that while we cannot actively seek to desire the good, we can cease to reject grace, and in so doing an addicted person "becomes open to a second-order volition for abstinence, conferred (using the language of AA) by a Power greater than the Self." Cook thus describes addiction as an experience of the divided will. Relying on McFadyen, Cook also recognizes the pervasiveness of sin and the pernicious power of sin to co-opt victims to become participants in their own destruction. Thus, he says, "[S]in is experienced as a power which adversely influences human choice and decision-making, and which engages people in the very processes which bring about their own enslavement."[53] Cupcake Brown offers a tragic example of this kind of co-opting in her memoir *A Piece of Cake*. Brown describes her childhood in foster care, among abusive foster parents and predatory men. In order to escape foster care, she needs money, and the only way she knows how to make money as a young adolescent is through "tricks." She says, "The lessons were clear: men want you only for sex; sex makes you money; money bought necessities like food, shelter, booze and drugs; drugs and booze make life—and sex—not so bad."[54] In some sense, she has the ability to make choices, yet her choices are severely limited. There is no world in which she has the freedom to walk away from the foster care system and into the arms of a loving family. She can run away from the evils of her foster home but has limited skills in surviving on the streets as a child. The only way she knows how to survive is by having sex with men she does not want to have sex with, and the only way she knows how to survive that is to use drugs and alcohol, which is yet one more step in the process of bringing about her own destruction. She is caught in a system not of her own making, within which she is forced to make choices

---

52. On Calvin's denial of second-order volition to will the good, see Calvin, *Bondage and Liberation*, II.257.

53. Christopher Cook, *Alcohol, Addiction, and Christian Ethics* (Cambridge University Press, 2006), 160, 165, 167.

54. Cupcake Brown, *A Piece of Cake: A Memoir* (Broadway Books, 2006), 52.

that cause her harm. Cook rightly recognizes that the will is co-opted and bent toward evil. While I deeply appreciate Cook's analysis of addiction, and especially his reliance on McFadyen and Stump, I ultimately diverge in that I am hesitant to attach the category of "sin," no matter how nuanced, to addiction, because of the tremendous potential for harm this category can do to those with addiction. I explore this further in the next chapter when I engage with other theologians who write about addiction.

Instead, I see addiction as a manifestation of the bondage of the will. Augustine's concept of the bondage of the will allows for a way of talking about addiction that aligns with the experiences of those suffering from addiction, while being consonant with scientific understandings of addiction. It also allows for more pastoral responses to those with addiction, which I will explore in the next chapter.[55]

THE BONDAGE OF THE WILL AND EXPERIENCES OF ADDICTION

The metaphor of bondage is an apt one, because it names the deep frustration of both having a will and yet not being able to direct it as freely as one would like.[56] Augustine's description of the corruption of the will is similar to the way those suffering from addiction describe the complex interplay between compulsion and volition in addiction. On the one hand, those suffering from addiction recognize that they are using their will and at the same time feel almost forced to engage in their addiction. It seems as if they are choosing, and yet they continue engaging in the very behaviors they do not want to engage in.

Jowita Bydlowska shows this co-opting of the will when she says, "When I walk into a liquor store—against my will, not because I want to, I promise, I swear—I know that I own my two feet but I don't, really; they're no longer mine. And as soon as I'm inside the store . . . I know that no power in this world can make me leave before I've gotten something."[57] Similarly, Nic Sheff says in his memoir *Tweak*, "It's like I'm being held captive by some insatiable

---

55. I am indebted to Ellen Ott Marshall for the many conversations we had about this chapter, and for helping me to find a structure for the argument for the bondage of the will that focuses on these three elements (i.e., resonance with experiences of addiction, consonance with scientific understanding of addiction, and pastoral implications).

56. As is true for most of our theological concepts, the bondage of the will is a metaphor. That is, the will is not literally bound. Because we are not always aware of the fact that these concepts are metaphors, I intentionally emphasize them as such. Seeing our theological concepts as metaphors reminds us that none of these are true in an ultimate sense. In this case, they point toward a truth about the human situation. Recognizing these concepts as metaphors gives us the space to experiment with these concepts and to test them for their capacity to clarify our realities. I delve more deeply into the concept of metaphors in chapter 4.

57. Bydlowska, *Drunk Mom*, 16–17.

monster that will not let me stop."⁵⁸ Both Bydlowska and Sheff describe an almost out-of-body experience, in which a drive within them simply takes them toward the addictive substance. In AA this phenomenon is described as "powerlessness." "Alcohol," Bill W. writes, "bleeds us of all self-sufficiency and all will to resist its demands." He goes on to explain that alcoholics are "the victims of a mental obsession so subtly powerful that no amount of human willpower could break it."⁵⁹ Of course, this is both true and not true. Were it true that alcoholics were entirely powerless, there would be no point in having Twelve Step meetings, or any part of the AA program at all.

The metaphor of the bondage of the will resonates with the experiences of those with addiction as described in the memoirs. In this way, it offers validation of the experience and, in a sense, normalizes it. The beauty of this metaphor is that it elucidates the tension between compulsion and volition that those suffering from addiction are so familiar with. Further, the metaphor of bondage aptly represents the deep sense of disturbance this tension brings about.

As quoted in the last chapter, Elizabeth Vargas describes this experience painfully well in her memoir, *Between Breaths*, when she comes home from her third stay in rehab and relapses within four days. She asks herself, "Why on earth would I do this? Why would I risk everything, undoing all I had accomplished?"⁶⁰ She experiences a deep sense of self-loathing and shame. She wants to stop yet seems unable. She experiences herself as having a will and yet being unable to fully control it to gain sobriety.

Of course, this exasperating experience of having a sense of having free will and yet often doing precisely what we do not want to do is not limited to those with addiction. The experience of addiction merely highlights this intense struggle that is part of the human condition. Paul talks about this universal experience in Romans, where he says, with what appears to be a significant amount of frustration, "I do not understand my own actions. For I do not do what I want, but I do the very thing I hate" (Rom. 7:15). The metaphor of the bondage of the will names both the tension we feel within ourselves between compulsion and volition and the deep frustration this tension creates in us. Addiction is an especially painful manifestation of this tension. The concept of the bondage of the will clearly resonates with the experiences of those who suffer from addiction. However, experience is not the only litmus test of this theology of addiction. As I indicated in chapter 1, theologies of addiction must also take into account the scientific theories and models of addiction.

---

58. Nic Sheff, *Tweak: Growing Up on Methamphetamines* (Atheneum Books for Young Readers, 2008), 6.

59. *Twelve Steps and Twelve Traditions* (Alcoholics Anonymous World Services, 1953), 21, 22. Bill W. is not the only author of the *Big Book* and the *Twelve Steps and Twelve Traditions*, though he wrote the bulk of the material.

60. Elizabeth Vargas, *Between Breaths: A Memoir of Panic and Addiction* (Grand Central, 2016), 197.

THE BONDAGE OF THE WILL
AND THE MODELS OF ADDICTION

In the last chapter, I indicated that a mixture of several models of addiction likely comes closest to explaining what addiction is. In particular, I highlighted the importance of recognizing aspects of the self-medication model, which points to the ways our environments (recall the rats in Rat Park vs. the rats in isolated cages), traumas, and pasts affect our propensity for addiction. I also noted that whether you hold to a pure version of the brain disease model of addiction or not, responsible researchers must take into account the neuroscience of addiction since these processes in the brain are so well documented. In this section, I demonstrate that the concept of the bondage of the will captures important elements of these two models of addiction.

As I explained in the last chapter, neuroscientists demonstrate that addiction is fueled in the brain by dopamine, a neurotransmitter associated with desire. The drug-fueled flood of dopamine in the brain gives the brain the faulty impression that taking the drug is an activity necessary for survival. The drug then becomes just as important, if not more, than other activities necessary for survival, such as eating. Thus, a person suffering from addiction will often prioritize the procurement of drugs and alcohol over all other activities, including activities necessary for survival, such as eating and sleeping. In other words, the desire for those things that are necessary for survival is misdirected at a good that does not, in fact, help humans survive.

Further, the vicious cycle of addiction leads the person suffering to make more and more "choices" in the direction of the addiction, which in turn further impairs the person's ability to make choices toward recovery. The drug becomes the solution to every problem so that the person with addiction ends up trying to make the drug meet infinite needs. Dunnington notes that the drug of "choice" becomes the meaning-making principle of the addicted person's life, so that everything revolves around this singular purpose of getting and using the drug.[61]

While fourth-century theologian Augustine clearly didn't know anything about dopamine or the neuroscience of addiction, the process he describes in the bondage of the will, whereby desire is misdirected at finite goods, and these are given the prominence of the infinite good (i.e., God), is remarkably similar. This misdirection of desire ensnares the will such that while it still functions, it keeps making choices in the direction of lesser goods. The problem, of course, is that finite goods do not, ultimately, deliver. In this sense, the concept of the bondage of the will describes in theological terms what the neuroscience of addiction describes in biological terms. The benefit of the bondage of the will is that it is able to identify and explain an experience (i.e., the malfunctioning of the will) that feels central to addiction in a way that neuroscience alone cannot. While

---

61. Kent Dunnington, *Addiction and Virtue: Beyond the Models of Disease and Choice* (IVP Academic, 2011), 150–52.

the neuroscience of addiction is able to explain *how* (in terms of physiology or chemistry) the will is co-opted, the bondage of the will does a better job of naming what it feels like to have a will that is co-opted by misdirected desire.

Similar to the neuroscience of addiction, the metaphor of the bondage of the will also recognizes the ways in which repetition and habit play into our condition of being bound. The neuroscience of addiction demonstrates that the brain changes as more and more "choices" are made in the direction of using so that it becomes legitimately difficult to make "choices" in one's own best interest. Heather King describes this narrowing of choices in her memoir: "I didn't know that by taking that first drink I had surrendered my free will: the thing that distinguishes a human being from an animal."[62] In many ways, King's description of freely taking the first drink only to then surrender her free will is very similar to Augustine's description of his struggle with lust. In the *Confessions*, Augustine writes,

> I was bound not with the iron of another's chains, but by my own iron will. The enemy held my will; and of it he made a chain and bound me. Because my will was perverse it changed to lust, and lust yielded to become habit, and habit not resisted became necessity. These were the links hanging one on another . . . and their hard bondage held me bound hand and foot. . . . Habit had grown stronger against me by my own act, since I had come willingly where I did not now will to be.[63]

Augustine is not offering a systematic theology of the will in the *Confessions*, so it is hard to draw conclusions about what exactly Augustine means by the will here. What is interesting about this particular description of the will is the way he describes the limiting of the will over time. His description resonates with the description of what happens in the brain in addiction. The landscape of choices becomes smaller and smaller over time, such that it seems those suffering from addiction lack free will almost entirely.

Further, the concept of the bondage of the will describes both an external and internal condition. That is, postlapsarian humans (i.e., all of us) are born into a world that is already infected. This is not just an abstract theological reality but something we live every day. We encounter this systemic infection in the justice system that still incarcerates Black people at almost five times the rate of their white counterparts.[64] We experience it in the gender wage gap that still exists in most countries in the world. We witness it at schools in the State of Georgia, for instance, where, on average, 20 percent of children experience food insecurity.[65] Further, many children are born into homes with abusive and neglectful parents.

---

62. King, *Parched*, 67.
63. Augustine, *Confessions*, ed. Michael P. Foley, trans. F. J. Sheed, 2nd ed. (Hackett, 2006), 8.v.10–11.
64. "U.S. Criminal Justice Data," The Sentencing Project, accessed April 7, 2025, https://sentencingproject.org/research/us-criminal-justice-data/.
65. "Map the Meal Gap," Feeding America, accessed April 7, 2025, https://www.feedingamerica.org/sites/default/files/2019-05/2017-map-the-meal-gap-child-food-insecurity_0.pdf.

We are all born into systems that are already broken, and some experience the brunt of these systems more than others.

As Serene Jones demonstrates in *Call It Grace*, these external systems we are born into have a deep impact on our internal conditions as well. When Jones tells the story of her asking her grandfather to tell the story "'about Mrs. Colliers, the one with the big jugs,'" she demonstrates the power these external systems of sexism and racism can have on one's internal compass, and how, in turn, the internal has an effect on the external.[66] By mimicking her grandfather's sexism, she inadvertently contributes to and perpetuates the sexism in her family and society. The concept of the bondage of the will describes the ways in which external and internal influence each other to create perpetuating systems of brokenness.

In the last chapter, I described the self-medication model of addiction, which accounts for the ways external conditions (e.g., social location, traumatic experiences, family of origin, etc.) can affect a person's propensity toward addiction. The concept of the bondage of the will provides a rich description of addiction that recognizes the power that external conditions can have on us. This interplay between the external and internal is often missing from stricter models of addiction (apart from the syndrome model) that attempt to encompass the condition of addiction by relying primarily either on internal factors (e.g., the strict version of the brain disease model of addiction, or the moral model) or external factors (e.g., Bruce Alexander's Rat Park).[67] The metaphor of the bondage of the will offers depth to the conversation on addiction in that it is able to recognize the power of both internal and external factors.

Beyond the ability to include the wisdom of both the self-medication model and the neuroscience of addiction, the concept of the bondage of the will also allows conversations around addiction to break free from the disease/sin and blamelessness/blame binaries that currently govern a lot of conversations about addiction in churches and beyond. Augustine's recognition that humans are held in bondage in both external and internal systems that co-opt the will helpfully breaks free of moral models of sin that see sin as a moral failing perpetrated by people operating from a neutral stance with the full range of choices at their disposal to do good or evil. Augustine demonstrates that our choices are far more limited. At the same time, an interpretation of Augustine that allows for limited free will to do the good allows for a sense of agency and responsibility that people often don't attribute to the concept of disease, especially when pitted against sin in conversations about addiction.

Admittedly, I push Augustine's concept of the bondage of the will further (toward freedom) than he would allow for. Specifically, while recognizing the severe limitations of human freedom, I allow for more agency and freedom than Augustine. More importantly, I don't hold to Augustine's concept of inherited guilt.

66. Jones, *Call It Grace*, 46.
67. See chapter 1 for a description of these models of addiction.

While Augustine's concept of the bondage of the will is helpful, his concept of original sin includes more than just the bondage of the will. As I discussed earlier, the concept of original sin holds within it three elements: namely, the bondage of the will, sinful acts, and hereditary guilt. Augustine (and Calvin after him) thus couples the hereditary condition of the bondage of the will with inherited guilt. For Augustine, we do not simply inherit the postlapsarian condition of having a co-opted will but also the guilt for that condition. For Augustine, this is, at least in part, a theodical move in that he wants to account for the existence of suffering. As Ian McFarland explains in his work *In Adam's Fall*, Augustine uses the concept of original sin "to explain apparently unmerited suffering." McFarland goes on to say that "Augustine argued that the range and intensity of misery experienced by infants could only be squared with God's goodness if they are born guilty of sin."[68] While I see great value in the concept of the bondage of the will and recognize that we hold at least some responsibility for the acts we engage in within this condition, I do not hold to the concept of inherited guilt, which blames humans for the existence of the condition that we are born into after the fall. Thus, I stretch the concept of the bondage of the will further than either Calvin or Augustine would allow and explicitly separate it out from the condition of original sin, which includes inherited guilt.

I propose a reconstruction of the metaphor of the bondage of the will that truly holds the tension between compulsion and volition. The metaphor of bondage is helpful to understand this tension. Bondage, on the one hand, recognizes that the will is held and directed by a force outside the control of the person in bondage. On the other hand, the metaphor of bondage also allows us to appreciate that the will has some freedom, however limited that may be. Those who are bound are robbed of many freedoms yet are not completely bereft of agency and freedom. A person whose hands are bound, for instance, is severely limited in what they are able to do. They cannot stretch out their arms to hug another person, or depending on how tightly their hands are bound, clap their hands. If their hands are bound in front of their body, they can, however, use their hands to eat an apple, for instance. Bondage implies severe limitations but not complete incapacity. The word connotes captivity, which is an appropriate way to look at the compulsion of addiction. Yet even within captivity, people have some sense of agency, however limited that may be. The metaphor of bondage both illuminates the tension between compulsion and volition and allows for what Ellen Ott Marshall would call "moral agency under constraint," which she describes as "moral action in contexts of limited freedom and choice."[69] Were there no freedom at all, as Calvin suggests, there would be no room for human actions toward health and happiness. Augustine allows for limited freedom and agency, which includes the freedom to ask for help and receive it. I push that limited

---

68. Ian A. McFarland, *In Adam's Fall: A Meditation on the Christian Doctrine of Original Sin* (Wiley-Blackwell, 2010), 32.
69. Ellen Ott Marshall, "Moral Agency under Constraint," Moral Agency under Constraint, accessed April 7, 2025, https://scholarblogs.emory.edu/moralagency2019/.

freedom a little further because a more expansive, though still limited, sense of freedom rings true to the human condition, at least as I experience it.

CONCLUSION

In this chapter I've offered a theological model for thinking about addiction that both resonates with experiences of addiction and is consonant with significant scientific models of addiction. In the next chapter, I focus on why it matters to see addiction as a version of the bondage of the will by exploring the implications of this model for offering pastoral responses to those suffering from addiction. Theological models are, after all, only effective insofar as they are able to promote human flourishing (and the flourishing of all creation).

Chapter 3

The Bondage of the Will and Pastoral Responses to Addiction

Thus far, I have made an argument for understanding addiction as a version of the bondage of the will. I demonstrated that this both resonates with experiences of addiction and is consonant with significant scientific models of addiction. Importantly, the concept of the bondage of the will captures the wisdom of both the self-medication model and the neuroscience of addiction, recognizing that those with addiction are co-opted both by forces outside of themselves (e.g., social location, past trauma, etc.) and forces within themselves (e.g., what happens in the brain in addiction). Further, this metaphor allows the conversation around addiction to break free from the disease / moral sin binary that people are often stuck in. In this chapter, I move beyond these benefits to look at the pastoral implications of seeing addiction as a version of the bondage of the will. The main point I make in this chapter is that seeing addiction as a version of the bondage of the will has the pastoral value of reducing the shame and stigma that those suffering from addiction often experience. I begin with an overview of how shame functions in the lives of those with addiction and then demonstrate how the concept of the bondage of the will helps alleviate this shame.

THE PROBLEM OF SHAME IN ADDICTION

Even though substance use disorder is a common problem, affecting 17 percent of the US population (age twelve or older) in 2023, it nevertheless elicits an enormous amount of shame.[1] Over the course of my fifteen-year recovery journey in Twelve-Step and SMART recovery groups, I have heard thousands upon thousands of stories which, though differing in context and detail, almost all include an abiding sense of shame. This is not surprising given the fact that "for many addicts, shame is the central organizing principle of their identity and the primary cause of the addiction."[2] Others who research the link between shame and addiction make similar observations.[3] Substance use disorders frequently function as a response to or defense against shame that is often, though not always, the result of traumatic experiences in childhood: the link between childhood trauma and addiction is common enough to warrant recognizing it as one of the primary contributing factors in the establishment of addiction.[4] The addictive behavior becomes a

---

1. "Key Substance Use and Mental Health Indicators in the United States: Result from the 2023 National Survey on Drug Use and Health," Substance Abuse and Mental Health Services Administration (SAMHSA), July 2024, https://www.samhsa.gov/data/sites/default/files/reports/rpt47095/National%20Report/National%20Report/2023-nsduh-annual-national.pdf, p. 26, fig. 28. In 2015 this percentage was 7.8 percent compared to 17.1 percent in 2023 ("Key Substance Use and Mental Health Indicators in the United States: Results from the 2015 National Survey on Drug Use and Health," SAMHSA, September 2016, https://www.samhsa.gov/data/sites/default/files/NSDUH-FFR1-2015Rev1/NSDUH-FFR1-2015Rev1/NSDUH-FFR1-2015Rev1/NSDUH-National%20Findings-REVISED-2015.pdf, p. 21, fig. 27). This percentage held fairly steady until 2020 when the percentage nearly doubled to 14.5 percent ("Key Substance Use and Mental Health Indicators in the United States: Results from the 2020 National Survey on Drug Use and Health," SAMHSA, October 2021, https://www.samhsa.gov/data/sites/default/files/reports/rpt35325/NSDUHFFRPDFWHTMLFiles2020/2020NSDUHFFR1PDFW102121.pdf, p. 29, fig. 27) and then continued to climb. The 2020 report highlights indicate that the COVID-19 pandemic likely had a negative impact on these numbers ("Highlights for the 2020 National Survey on Drug Use and Health," SAMHSA, accessed April 9, 2025, https://www.samhsa.gov/data/sites/default/files/2021-10/2020_NSDUH_Highlights.pdf, p. 3). At the time of this writing, the 2023 report was the most recent available report.
2. Christiane Sanderson, *Counselling Skills for Working with Shame* (Jessica Kingsley, 2015), 146.
3. E.g., Ronald Potter-Efron, "Therapy with Shame-Prone Alcoholic and Drug-Dependent Clients" in *Shame in the Therapy Hour*, ed. R. L. Dearing and J. Tangney (American Psychological Association, 2011), 219–35; and Shelly A. Wiechelt, "The Specter of Shame in Substance Misuse," *Substance Use & Misuse* 42, no. 2–3 (2007): 399–409, https://doi.org/10.1080/10826080601142196.
4. See, A. L. Giordano et al., "Addressing Trauma in Substance Abuse Treatment," *Journal of Alcohol and Drug Education* 60, no. 2 (August, 2016): 55–71; Lamya Khoury et al., "Substance Use, Childhood Traumatic Experience, and Posttraumatic Stress Disorder in an Urban Civilian Population," *Depression and Anxiety* 27, no. 12 (November 2010): 1077–86, https://doi.org/10.1002/da.20751; A. Mandavia et al., "Exposure to Childhood Abuse and Later Substance Use: Indirect Effects of Emotion Dysregulation and Exposure to Trauma, *Journal of Traumatic Stress* 29, no. 5 (September 13, 2016): 422–29, https://doi.org/10.1002/jts.22131; and P. L. Reed, J. C. Anthony, and N. Breslau, "Incidence of Drug Problems in Young Adults Exposed to Trauma and Posttraumatic Stress Disorder: Do Early Life Experiences and Predispositions Matter?," *Archives of General Psychiatry* 64, no. 12 (December 2007): 1435–42, https://doi.org/10.1001/archpsyc.64.12.1435.

coping mechanism that allows the person momentarily to escape or blunt the feelings of shame.[5]

Mary Karr's memoir *Lit* offers one example of this link between childhood trauma, shame, and addiction. She describes her alcoholic mother and says, "her lack of maternal posture always unconsciously felt like some failure of mine on the child front."[6] She does what children often do when they are harmed by parents. She assumes that she is at fault. She recalls a particularly harrowing incident when her mother took Karr and Karr's sister's toys and "doused . . . every toy with gas and tossed on a match." She says, "Much of the night's a blur but for her standing over us with a carving knife." When her therapist asks her whose fault that night was, Karr says, "Probably mine, like I said, I was a pain in the ass. My sister's to blame maybe a little, but she was older and way less trouble."[7] The idea that either of them were to blame is, of course, preposterous, and yet children often take on the shame of their caregivers in order to survive the trauma of abuse.

Tragically, Karr finds herself perpetuating the cycle of shame and addiction by becoming an absent mother who "hides in [her] study drinking" as her husband and son play in the next room.[8] She stops breastfeeding her son early so that she can continue drinking. Karr feels the crushing shame of not being a "good" mother and tells herself, "You're the bad mom in the afterschool special, the example other moms—little parentheses drawn down around their glossy mouths—go to the principal about."[9] As often happens in addiction, she feels shame that she is not present to her son because she drinks, and yet the only way she knows how to deal with this shame is to continue drinking.

While many people use addictive substances to cope with shame, somewhat ironically shame is also often a result of the addictive behavior itself. For example, in *Drunk Mom*, Jowita Bydlowska recalls going on a binge and leaving her baby "in his wicker basket . . . screaming, possibly trying to outdo the bombastic sounds coming out of the speakers . . . soaked in piss and milk." She frequently takes her baby on liquor runs and drinks large amounts while supposedly caring for her baby. She says, "I know what this looks like. This is exactly what it looks like, although, naturally, I'm pretending otherwise. But if you need to know the truth: Yes, I am ashamed to be here with a stroller."[10] Once these feelings of shame arise as a result of using, it becomes incredibly tempting to drink or use again in order to mute the feelings of shame, generating an addiction spiral driven by shame.[11]

---

5. Large portions of this section were previously published in Jennifer Carlier, "Penal Substitutionary Atonement and the Problem of Shame in Addiction," *Pastoral Psychology* 72, no. 5 (July 17, 2023): 659–73, https://doi.org/10.1007/s11089-023-01089-5.

6. Mary Karr, *Lit* (Harper Perennial, 2009), 105.

7. Karr, *Lit*, 62.

8. Karr, *Lit*, 181.

9. Karr, *Lit*, 9.

10. Jowita Bydlowska, *Drunk Mom: A Memoir* (Penguin Books, 2014), 29–30, 98.

11. Ronda L. Dearing, Jeffery Stuewig, June Price Tangney, "On the Importance of Distinguishing Shame from Guilt: Relations to Problematic Alcohol and Drug Use," *Addictive Behaviors* 30,

Shelly Wiechelt names this cycle the "shame-addiction spiral" and argues that shame is thus a central factor in the initiation *and* continuation of addiction.[12]

Caroline Knapp describes this cycle poignantly in her memoir, *Drinking: A Love Story*, when she relays her friend Janet's story. Janet suffered from, among other things, alcoholism and bulimia.[13] She would be tempted to binge, and then "she'd try to talk herself out of another binge, and then she'd talk herself back in ('Just this one time, just one more time and then I'll stop') and then she'd go out and just *eat*, the same way you go out and just get drunk."[14] Then Knapp writes,

> Later, when she finished eating and throwing up, or when she woke up in the morning bloated and hung over, she'd hate herself, loathe herself, and the stage would be set for a repetition of the cycle: any sense of herself as competent or worthy would have been drowned away by the liquor, or flushed away down the toilet; any conviction that she could find a better way to manage her fears or her feelings would be undermined by another degree or two; not believing in her soul that she was a capable or valuable human being, a woman who deserved to be fed in a nurturing way, she'd simply, inevitably, repeat the cycle again.[15]

Her binge and purge would reinforce the belief that she couldn't possibly stop the cycle, much less be worthy of trying, which in turn would lead to shame and self-loathing, which in turn would lead to another binge and purge cycle. The emotion of shame, in other words, would drive both her bulimic and alcoholic behavior forward.

To complicate matters further, people suffering from addiction not only experience shame as a result of each instance of using but also often feel profoundly ashamed simply for being addicted.[16] William Cope Moyers describes feeling "humiliated and helpless" and says he saw himself as a "'bad man,'" and a "weak-willed pathetic thirty-year-old man who couldn't control his own behavior."[17] Early in his memoir he notes that "shame and my drug use ran along parallel lines until they eventually merged and became one." Moyers says, "I drank because I was ashamed, and I was ashamed because I drank."[18]

---

no. 7 (August 2005): 1392–1404, https://doi.org/10.1016/j.addbeh.2005.02.002; Potter-Efron, "Therapy," 221–22; Sanderson, *Counseling Skills*, 144–48; Wiechelt, "The Specter of Shame," 403.

12. Wiechelt, "The Specter of Shame," 403.

13. Knapp's friend suffered from a combination of addiction (in the form of alcoholism) and bulimia. She uses her friend's experience of both as a way of describing the cycle of shame that occurs in addiction. While the shame cycles of addiction and bulimia are quite similar, bulimia is not technically classified as addiction, and I am not here suggesting that it is. While there are many overlapping patterns, eating disorders have their own etiology, symptoms, and interventions.

14. Caroline Knapp, *Drinking: A Love Story* (Dial Press Trade Paperback, 1996), 136.

15. Knapp, *Drinking*, 137.

16. Potter-Efron, "Therapy," 221; Sanderson, *Counseling Skills*, 145; Wiechelt, "The Specter of Shame," 403.

17. William Cope Moyers, *Broken: My Story of Addiction and Redemption* (Penguin Books, 2007), 213, 232, 133.

18. Moyers, *Broken*, 74.

Part of that shame was generated by perpetually living in his father's shadow. Moyers initially pursued a career in journalism similar to his famous father, Bill Moyers. He says, "Dad's success was a bright flame that blinded me because it was all I could see. I was the moth that was about to get torched, but was it the fault of the flame or did the moth fly into it?"[19] Moyers is careful not to blame his father for his addiction. He says, "Over the years many people have asked me if I became an alcoholic and crack cocaine addict because of the pressures of being 'the son of.'" Moyers explains that he clearly had "issues with my father" and those issues certainly played into his addiction. He explains that "any unresolved issue . . . feeds the discomfort, the sense of not fitting in your own skin, the fear of meaninglessness, insignificance, the sense of shame, the hole in the soul that gives people who are vulnerable to addiction a really good excuse to get drunk or high." Shame is clearly a driver in Moyers's addiction that repeatedly leads him back to relapse. However, Moyers is also careful to note that shame is not the sole cause of his addiction. He says, "It isn't the issue that drives the addiction so much as the addiction that latches on to the issue for a free ride."[20]

Moyers illustrates the complexity of shame in addiction. He is clear about the fact that shame and addiction went hand in hand for him. He used out of shame, and his using also perpetuated his shame. That is, his unresolved issues with his father led to a tremendous amount of shame that contributed, at least in part, to his alcohol and drug use. While using, however, he is also aware of causing his first wife, his second wife, and his parents a great deal of pain, which leads to more shame, which in turn leads to more using. Moyers offers one example of the complex web of shame that is at play in the addiction cycle, created by the initial shame caused by outside factors, the shame caused by each instance of using, and the shame caused by the addiction itself and the loss of control associated with it. These three, however, are not the only factors at play.

Beyond the internal shame (described above) that those who have addiction experience, there is also external shame, which Christiane Sanderson describes as "the shame induced by the gaze and assessment of others."[21] Moreover, external shame seems to be due, at least in part, to a societal propensity to view addiction as a type of moral failure—this despite the growing popularity of the brain disease model of addiction in the United States.[22]

As I illustrated in chapter 1, Moyers describes this well when he notes that he and everyone around him assumed that his addiction was "partly if not wholly [his] fault." After receiving a cancer diagnosis, the distinction between how those around him viewed his illnesses of addiction and cancer clarified for him that societally, we have a tendency to blame those who suffer from substance use disorders for their addictions, while we have no such inclinations with other

---

19. Moyers, *Broken*, 90.
20. Moyers, *Broken*, 246–47.
21. Sanderson, *Counseling Skills,* 80.
22. For more information on the brain disease model of addiction, see chapter 1.

illnesses.[23] This external shame often exacerbates the internal shame that those struggling with addiction are already fraught with. Unfortunately, the *Big Book* at times plays into this external shame. While it frequently calls addiction an illness, it also at times seems to blame the addicted person for their addiction. It says, for instance, "Selfishness—self-centeredness! That, we think is the root of our troubles. . . . So our troubles, we think, are basically of our own making. They arise out of ourselves, and the alcoholic is an extreme example of self-will run riot, though he usually doesn't think so."[24] The underlying assumption is that the addicted person is to blame for their addiction and has the agency and freedom necessary to make different choices.[25]

The literature on shame suggests that external shame becomes particularly poisonous when the person is unable to adjust their behavior to meet societal standards. Sanderson gives a potent example of this when she talks about shame in sexuality. Not surprisingly, family and societal "messages about sex . . . wield a large impact on sexual feelings, thoughts and behaviours." However, when "sexual arousal is in opposition to cultural mores or expectations . . . the ensuing battle between sexual arousal and societal expectations becomes the crucible for unbearable shame," especially when the "sexual arousal cannot be controlled or managed." The resulting intensity of shame can "in severe cases" lead to sexually deviant behavior (e.g., compulsions or criminal behavior) or even "to suicidal ideation or suicide attempts."[26] What Sanderson so helpfully describes here is the intensity and danger of the internal shame that occurs when a person is blamed and shamed (external shame) for something they have minimal control over (in this case, sexual arousal). The memoirs demonstrate that the same occurs in addiction. The addicted person is often blamed and shamed for their addiction.

In the war on drugs, the mass incarceration of those with substance use disorders is a significant example of how society views addiction primarily as a moral failure. As Michelle Alexander argues in *The New Jim Crow*, Black men, in particular, are often the targets of mass incarceration as a result of racism.[27] The punishment of those with addiction only makes sense if drug addiction (at least in relation to some populations) is seen as a moral failure. The issue here, of course, is much more complex than one of shame alone, as the war on drugs is deeply embedded in racist ideologies.[28] The societal propensity to

---

23. Moyers, *Broken*, 339.
24. *Alcoholics Anonymous: The Big Book*, 62.
25. Paradoxically, Bill W. and AA more generally do not actually believe people have free will and agency to make different choices when it comes to alcohol. They describe an alcoholic as being powerless over addiction. Perhaps this inconsistency in characterizing addiction as both an "illness" and a kind of "selfishness" is indicative of Bill W.'s own wrestling with the notion of freedom and bondage in addiction.
26. Sanderson, *Counseling Skills*, 122.
27. Michelle Alexander, *The New Jim Crow: Mass Incarceration in the Age of Colorblindness*, 10th anniversary ed. (New Press, 2020); see also, Sonia Waters, "Punishing the Immoral Other: Penal Substitutionary Logic in the War on Drugs." *Pastoral Psychology* 68, no. 5 (October 2019): 533–48, https://doi.org/10.1007/s11089-018-0836-y.
28. See Alexander, *The New Jim Crow*.

blame and shame people with substance use disorders (particularly those in Black communities) exacerbates the internal shame burdening those dealing with these disorders and keeps them entangled in and weighed down by the addiction—often with lethal consequences, as we shall see.

Shame, therefore, plays such a key role in people suffering from addiction that Ronald T. Potter-Efron notes that shame can become "the characterological center of their psychological identities." Indeed, Potter-Efron observes that for some people with addiction, continued use is a way of offering "undeniable validation of their worthlessness." Addiction, for these sufferers, functions as "an advertisement of their shame."[29] The sense of shame propels the person to continue using.

Those suffering from addiction also describe the ways in which shame propels a person from one addiction to the other. Knapp describes this as "changing partners in a dance." She says, "A bout of compulsive overeating fills you with shame and sexual inferiority, which fills you with self-loathing and doubt, which leads you to a drink, which temporarily counters the self-hatred and fills you with chemical confidence, which leads you to sleep with a man you don't love, which leads you circling back to shame, and voilà: the dance can begin again." She describes in particular the ways in which shame in the form of self-hatred and loathing drive the cycle from one addiction to another: "The dance *will* begin again, for the music is always there in women's minds, laced with undertones of fear and anger, urging us on into the same sad circles of restraint and abandon, courtship and flight."[30] The music that always plays in the background is the music of shame. She describes the way in which emotions (shame, fear, anger), behaviors (drinking, overeating, etc.), and beliefs centered on shame (e.g., "I'm unworthy" or "I cannot stop even if I wanted to") each reinforce each other in a vicious cycle.

Beyond propelling the addiction cycle forward, shame also plays a key role in a person's ability to seek help. As Timothy McMahan King notes in *Addiction Nation*, shame drives those who have addiction to "remove [them]selves from others in the exact moments that [they] most need help and connection."[31] Shame isolates those who most need care, because a common strategy for dealing with shame is hiding.[32] The fact that shame and addiction propel each other forward, coupled with the fact that those who struggle with shame are least likely to ask for help, creates the dangerous and potentially lethal aforementioned cycle of destruction.

---

29. Potter-Efron, "Therapy," 221, 223.
30. Knapp, *Drinking*, 137 (italics in the original).
31. Timothy McMahan King, *Addiction Nation: What the Opioid Crisis Reveals about Us* (Herald, 2019), 46.
32. Jennifer M. Chilton, "Shame: A Multidisciplinary Concept Analysis," *Journal of Theory Construction & Testing* 16, no. 1 (Spring 2012): 4–8; King, *Addiction Nation,* 46; Potter-Efron, "Therapy," 225–26; Sanderson, *Counseling Skills,* 69.

Shame also plays a role on a societal level in that besides heart-wrenching grief, families often also experience shame when a family member dies from an addiction overdose or a suicide associated with addiction. As King says in *Addiction Nation*, this stigma creates a situation in which "the very people who would normally raise the alarm and demand action—those closest to the crisis" (e.g., parents of children who overdosed) "were keeping the true cause of their pain hidden."[33] Parents are often at the forefront of demanding action with regard to diseases on behalf of their children. However, addiction often creates a situation in which families hide the cause of death of their loved ones, where they would normally demand change. This stigma allows for the continuation of drug overdoses, the opioid crisis, and the crack epidemic.

Shame is, in short, not just an unpleasant feeling that those with addiction experience; it has potentially deadly consequences. Erin Khar writes about this reality in her memoir, *Strung Out*: "Shame is the gatekeeper that prevents people from getting help. Stigma is bred from that shame." She goes on to say, "That stigma has killed so many. That stigma almost killed me." She notes that Americans "are stuck in a spiral of shame, and that shame drives the vicious cycle of relapse that many drug users get caught in."[34] Since drug overdose deaths continue to occur at a staggering rate (e.g., 2021 saw a record high with over 107,000 deaths, a 15 percent increase over 2020 and a 51 percent increase over 2019), it is crucial to focus on the disruption of shame as one potential site of intervention.[35]

THE BONDAGE OF THE WILL AND THE DISRUPTION OF SHAME

The metaphor of the bondage of the will is helpful for disrupting shame in that it recognizes that those suffering from addiction are not as free as people often assume. Seeing addiction as a manifestation of the bondage of the will allows us to see that for a person suffering from addiction, the will is co-opted by

---

33. King, *Addiction Nation*, 43.
34. Erin Khar, *Strung Out: One Last Hit and Other Lies That Nearly Killed Me* (Park Row, 2020), 14, Kindle.
35. Mike Stobbe, "CDC says more than 107,000 Americans died of drug overdoses in 2021, setting 'staggering' record," *PBS NewsHour* (May 11, 2022), https://www.pbs.org/newshour/health/cdc-estimates-more-than-107000-americans-died-of-drug-overdoses-in-2021-setting-staggering-record. "Drug Overdose Death Rates," National Institute on Drug Abuse, accessed April 9, 2025, https://nida.nih.gov/research-topics/trends-statistics/overdose-death-rates. The most recent statistics thankfully show a decline for the first time in years of drug overdose deaths. While final numbers are not yet available, the CDC indicates a likely decline of 24 percent in the year from Oct. 2023–Sept. 2024. While incredibly promising news, the CDC also indicates in the same report that "overdose remains the leading cause of death for Americans aged 18–44" ("CDC Reports Nearly 24% Decline in U.S. Drug Overdose Deaths," CDC, February 25, 2025, https://www.cdc.gov/media/releases/2025/2025-cdc-reports-decline-in-us-drug-overdose-deaths.html#:~:text=New%20provisional%20data%20from%20CDC%27s,steep%20decline%20in%20overdose%20deaths).

the addiction, such that it is now bent toward seeking out the substance of "choice."[36] The person suffering is not simply making a series of faulty moral choices. There are mechanisms at play that are beyond the person's control which, when recognized, help alleviate the blame and shame that is often attached to addiction.

Brian Powers makes a similar claim about the capacity for the concept of original sin to reduce blame and shame in his work *Full Darkness*.[37] Powers, relying on McFadyen's *Bound to Sin*, retrieves Augustine's notion of original sin for the redemptive purpose of reducing the crushing sense of blame and guilt war veterans tend to experience. He notes that the Augustinian concept of original sin "frees individuals from absolutizing their own guilt . . . and opens up avenues for self-understanding that are not essentialized and can perhaps lead to experiences of healing."[38] In the war conditions that Powers references, this is, perhaps, easier to see. A soldier comes into a system (i.e., war) that is not of her own making and that is already indicative of "our collective broken and damaged nature."[39] Within that system, she has options, yet these options are severely limited, and what it means to do good within the system of war is complicated. Where killing another person would normally be morally reprehensible, within the system of war, killing an enemy is seen as permissible and even good. Her sense of morality is co-opted by the condition of war and bent toward that which benefits the war, which includes acts that would normally be immoral (i.e., killing another person).

A similar pattern is at play in addiction. However, where the co-opting force in war is a system (war) imposed from outside onto a soldier, the co-opting force in addiction is largely internal. This is part of what makes those with addiction so susceptible to external shame. Since no one can see the internal forces at work, it is easy to blame and shame a person with addiction for her condition. The concept of the bondage of the will has the potential to help "loosen the noose" around the necks of those with addiction by recognizing that those suffering from addiction are caught in a system not fully of their own making and are not fully to blame for the actions they partake in as a result of their addiction.[40]

Further, as Powers points out, "a critical point" in original sin "is that our willing is not individually self-contained, but is influenced by our collective

---

36. "Substance of choice" is a common way to name the substance a person is addicted to. As I did in previous chapters, I put "choice" in quotation marks because I question how much choice a person actually has.

37. While Powers' work has deeply influenced my own, I steer clear of the language of "original sin" but use it here and in the next few paragraphs because he relies on it.

38. Brian S. Powers, *Full Darkness: Original Sin, Moral Injury, and Wartime Violence* (Eerdmans, 2019), 145.

39. Powers, *Full Darkness*, 171.

40. I take the phrase "loosen the noose" from Tyler Boudreau's article, "The Morally Injured," *Massachusetts Review* 52, no. 3/4 (Autumn/Winter 2011): 753. He is arguing a different point, but I found the phrase particularly descriptive for what the concept of the bondage of the will has the potential to do for those with addiction.

broken and damaged nature."[41] Broadly, this means we are born into conditions not of our own making over which we have little control. As I talked about in chapter 2, people with substance use disorders are often born into conditions (e.g., socioeconomic conditions, trauma, abuse, etc.) that are fertile ground for the development of addiction.

Further, many of these fertile conditions for addiction are created by "our collective broken and damaged nature."[42] This is, again, easier to see in the case of war. The phrase "Thank you for your service," often spoken to military personnel, is one way of recognizing that people in the military are acting on our behalf. Whether we like it or not, we are collectively responsible for what happens in wars waged by the countries we are citizens of. And when we think these wars are unjust, we have a collective responsibility to do something about it, whether that is protesting, voting differently, going on strike, etc.

Similarly, the conditions our societies perpetuate that set people up for addiction are indicative of "our collective broken and damaged nature."[43] As I noted above, the links between childhood trauma and addiction have been well documented. Children suffering abuse often have other adults in their lives who know of or at the very least suspect the abuse yet fail to stop it. The movie *Spotlight* demonstrates the sometimes purposeful and sometimes unintentional ways in which people are complicit in systems of abuse. As one of the main characters, Mitchell Garabedian, says in one of the scenes, "If it takes a village to raise a child, it takes a village to abuse one."[44] Children are not usually abused in a vacuum.

Cupcake Brown describes this complicity in her memoir, *A Piece of Cake*. When she is in the foster system, she is regularly abused by her foster "mother," Diane (among others). Diane's abuse is cruel and relentless. Two times an adult notices marks on Brown's back from Diane's whip. Both times the adult in question (her aunt the first time, and the school nurse the second) notifies the police and foster system of the abuse, yet both times Brown is placed back in Diane's custody. The first time, the psychiatrist Brown talks to simply doesn't believe her. He tells the court "he doubt[s] any abuse occurred" and suggests the court place Brown back in Diane's custody. The second time, Cindy, a social worker from the foster care system, takes Brown back to Diane because she cannot find another home for her. Cindy takes Brown back even though Diane "had admitted to hitting" Brown.[45] Cindy assures Brown that they'll be watching Diane, but Brown never sees Cindy again, and the abuse continues. Communities turning a blind eye to abuse is one example of the ways we are complicit in systems that perpetuate addiction (among other things).

---

41. Powers, *Full Darkness*, 171.
42. Powers, *Full Darkness*, 171.
43. Powers, *Full Darkness*, 171.
44. *Spotlight*, directed by Thomas J. McCarthy (Participant Media, First Look Media, Anonymous Content, and Rocklin/Faust Productions, 2015), 0:57:39.
45. Cupcake Brown, *A Piece of Cake: A Memoir* (Broadway Books, 2006), 68, 73.

Likewise, many people are, to varying degrees, complicit in systems that allow for poverty, racism, and the mass incarceration of those in Black communities, for instance. These conditions, in turn, lead to higher rates of addiction. Thus, the problem of addiction is much larger than that of the individual, and society as a whole bears responsibility for these conditions.

For Powers, the concept of original sin relieves veterans of the burden of individual blame, allowing people to recognize that they are not solely responsible and are often parts of systems over which they have little control. I appreciate Powers's insight and recognize the same being true for addiction. However, while Powers recognizes and names these conditions as original sin, I explicitly separate out the bondage of the will from the concept of original sin, because the concept of sin, however well-defined and nuanced, tends to do more harm than good for those with addiction. This is also what sets my views apart from other theologians writing about addiction, such as Linda Mercadante, James Nelson, and Kent Dunnington, who all see addiction (to varying degrees) as a manifestation of original sin.

Nelson, for instance, calls alcoholism "the deepest experience of sin I have had." Relying on Augustine, he recognizes addiction as a kind of idolatry in which we give "ultimate significance to something that is not truly ultimate." Nelson names addiction as *both* disease *and* sin. Thus, he says, "Disease language . . . suggests the needs for treatment and therapy" and "sin language cries out for grace, forgiveness, and liberation."[46] While I resonate with much of what Nelson describes in this work, the word "sin" and its implication that those suffering from addiction need "forgiveness" generates and perpetuates shame. It would be theologically unsound and ethically problematic, for instance, to say that cancer or depression, a condition that is perhaps more similar to addiction, is something for which people need forgiveness. The language of liberation and freedom is appropriate for all those conditions. Forgiveness, however, implies that the person is somehow guilty of their condition. I explore these concepts further in the next chapter where I engage theologies of salvation in relation to addiction.

Mercadante makes a similar though more complex case to that of Nelson in her book *Victims and Sinners*. Relying on Reinhold Niebuhr's category of anxiety, Mercadante argues that addiction falls on a spectrum and is, in some cases, more a matter of a precondition to sin (in Niebuhr's terms, anxiety) and, in others, a manifestation of sin itself (in Niebuhr's terms, pride or sensuality). She says, "One cannot decide whether any particular addiction is . . . primarily original or actual sin."[47] While recognizing the difficulty of determining whether someone's particular addiction is a manifestation of original or actual sin, she still sees value in the concept of sin because it names the human condition in relation to God.

---

46. James B. Nelson, *Thirst: God and the Alcoholic Experience* (Westminster John Knox, 2004), 73 ,72, 77.

47. Linda A. Mercadante, *Victims & Sinners: Spiritual Roots of Addiction and Recovery* (Westminster John Knox, 1996), 43.

Yet she also recognizes that sin has been unhelpfully subsumed into the category of morality. She therefore attempts to parse out the condition of sin from individual sins in addiction and says, "It is helpful to realize that although there is equality of sin (sin is universal), there is inequality of guilt."[48] This is precisely the reason I name addiction as a manifestation of the bondage of the will as opposed to original sin. When we talk about addiction as a manifestation of original sin (the condition of sin) and try to differentiate expressions of addiction as either original or actual sins (even if we just do this about our own addiction and do not judge others), we find ourselves back inside the very moral game we were trying to step out of by naming addiction as original sin.

The bondage of the will separated from the concept of original sin (which includes both inherited guilt and actual sins) allows us to name the condition of addiction in relation to God and helps us to see it as a condition we need freedom from, but not forgiveness for. In this way, the metaphor of the bondage of the will helps to ameliorate the sense of crushing guilt (which often leads to shame), which people with addiction often feel as a result of their addiction, by taking at least some of the blame off of the person with addiction.

At the same time, while the metaphor helps illustrate the particularly restrictive experience of addiction, it does not doom the person suffering to a life of addiction in the way a strict version of the brain disease model of addiction does. As Dunnington rightly notes, while the BDMA alleviates the blame and shame attached to addiction, it makes "unintelligible the actual modes of recovery that addicted persons successfully undertake." That is, people recover outside the medical system. They recover by finding communities that walk alongside them. If addiction were purely a brain disease, the only solution would be a medical one, and yet people recover outside the medical system all the time. Like Mercadante and Nelson, Dunnington relies on the category of original sin which "mediates between an overly voluntarist Pelagianism on the one hand and an overly determinist Manichaeism on the other."[49] While I largely agree with Dunnington's assessment, I differ in that I steer clear of the language of original sin. As I have demonstrated, the category of the bondage of the will does the same work of mediating between "voluntarism" and "determinism" without including the moral categories inherent in the concept of original sin, with its inclusion of inherited guilt and actual sins.

Crucially, while the metaphor allows for the restrictive experience of addiction, it is not fatalistic. The will, even while bound, is still functional, and as such, those with addiction have the ability to make choices toward recovery. This allows for a limited sense of responsibility without blaming the person with addiction when they are not able to make those choices. Richard Garrett explains that recovery "is a matter of discovering the many things we *can* do to get our addictions under

---

48. Mercadante, *Victims and Sinners*, 41.
49. Kent Dunnington, *Addiction and Virtue: Beyond the Models of Disease and Choice* (IVP Academic, 2011), 134.

our rational control." He says, "*Right Effort* entails doing whatever we *can* do in order to do all of those good things [i.e., not use] that we rationally *would do* but irrationally *do not do*."[50] That is, we do what we can (e.g., go to meetings, get help from a therapist, pray, ask for help, etc.) to do what we cannot (i.e., stop using). This resonates with Augustine's notion that we have limited capacity to ask for help and to receive it yet cannot free ourselves without the grace of God. The metaphor of the bondage of the will helps both the person suffering from addiction and those around her to recognize that making choices toward health and recovery is tremendously difficult, especially at the beginning when the person is just coming out of active addiction. This recognition allows for both compassion for the struggle and hope that recovery is possible, even when setbacks occur again and again.

CONCLUSION

Thus, the metaphor of the bondage of the will allows for a robust theological understanding of addiction that alleviates shame and makes sense of the fact that recovery is often a deeply spiritual process. However, most people in the pews are only dimly aware of the concept of the bondage of the will. Churches regularly engage the concept of sin, on the one hand, and suffering on the other. We sing about our need for forgiveness of sins in hymns and songs and confess our individual and collective sins in prayers of confession. Though more infrequent now than fifty years ago, pastors also preach about sin and forgiveness. Similarly, we lift up those who are suffering in prayer, hear sermons, and sing about God's presence in the midst of pain. Painting with a very broad brush, we might say that we think about sinners as perpetrators and those experiencing suffering as victims (of other people, illnesses, circumstances, etc.). Yet, we rarely talk about the strange and far more common intermediate space between sin and suffering, where we find ourselves caught in systems, not of our making, that push us to do that which we do not want to do, and for which we are not to blame, yet are at least partially responsible.

Giving people language to name and understand that experience is to give them a pathway away from shame toward hope and freedom. Reviving the metaphor of the bondage of the will in Christian education, sermons, prayers, liturgies, and songs allows people to recognize the subtle space between volition and necessity. It helps us to step out of the victim/perpetrator binaries we so often find ourselves in and allows us to name the nuanced and messy realities of people's lives. Reintroducing the concept of the bondage of the will in churches would help people to recognize conditions like addiction for what they are. It would give pastoral counselors language to talk about the suffering of addiction

---

50. Richard Garrett, "Addiction, Paradox, and the Good I Would" in *Addiction and Responsibility,* ed. Jeffrey Poland and George Graham (MIT Press, 2011), 259 (italics in the original).

in relationship to God without attaching blame or shame to the person with addiction. At the same time, the concept of the bondage of the will also allows for ways of talking about responsibility without blame.[51] As Wendy Farley says in *Tragic Vision and Divine Compassion*, while "human action is located in an already corrupted environment . . . , corruption and fragility do not have the effect of destroying human responsibility."[52] The concept of the bondage of the will gives pastors and pastoral counselors room to talk about both the suffering of addiction and the sense in which we still carry responsibility without assigning blame. This is important because people with addiction tend to take on more self-blame and shame than is true to the situation and helpful in recovery.

While the language of the bondage of the will creates space and opportunities for the disruption of shame in those with addiction, it does not by itself free a person from that bondage. The bondage of the will allows us to accurately and compassionately discern the problem. The theological concept most suited to talk about the solution (i.e., freedom from bondage) is salvation (soteriology), which I will turn to in the next chapters.

---

51. For more information on the concept of responsibility without blame (from a non-theological perspective), see Hanna Pickard, "Responsibility Without Blame for Addiction," *Neuroethics* 10, no. 1 (January 7, 2017): 169–80, https://doi.org/10.1007/s12152-016-9295-2.

52. Wendy Farley, *Tragic Vision and Divine Compassion: A Contemporary Theology* (Westminster/ John Knox, 1990), 50.

Chapter 4

Penal-Substitutionary Atonement and the Problem of Shame in Addiction

In the last two chapters I've offered a theological understanding of what addiction is by relying on a modified version of Augustine's bondage of the will that holds the tension between compulsion and volition. This metaphor helps show the painful experience of both having a will and yet often doing precisely what we do not want to do.[1] It is this tension that creates the anguish of addiction and, I would argue, of the human condition in general. Where I've spent the last three chapters delving into the problem of addiction from both scientific and theological perspectives, in the next few chapters I ask what freedom from the bondage of addiction looks like from a theological perspective. Similar to my approach in the last chapters, I value theologies that resonate with the experiences of those in recovery from addiction, align with scientific understandings of how addiction and recovery work, and offer pastoral benefits to those with addiction by relieving them of the burden of shame.

The title along with large portions of the chapter were previously published in Jennifer Carlier, "Penal Substitutionary Atonement and the Problem of Shame in Addiction," *Pastoral Psychology* 72, no. 5 (July 17, 2023), 659–73, https://doi.org/10.1007/s11089-023-01089-5. Used with permission.

1. As I pointed out in chapter 2, Paul helpfully touches on this experience in Romans when he says, "I do not understand my own actions. For I do not do what I want, but I do the very thing I hate" (Rom. 7:15).

From a theological perspective, freedom from bondage is most often associated with the doctrine of salvation, which is a broad term that encompasses all of God's acts of deliverance and redemption. Like the concepts of sin and the bondage of the will, there are many ways people have thought about salvation over the centuries. I use this broad term because the term salvation is often collapsed into atonement and more particularly into a specific version of atonement. In this chapter and the next I explore this predominant way of thinking about salvation—namely penal-substitutionary atonement—in order to show how it can harm those with addiction on both a personal (this chapter) and societal level (chapter 5) in that it perpetuates the cycle of shame that those suffering from addiction are often caught in. I argue instead for the use of many metaphors to talk about salvation. In chapter 6, I turn to one such metaphor of salvation located in the story of the exodus and demonstrate why I see this model as particularly helpful for those suffering from addiction.

Each of the theologies of salvation I explore tells a particular story that is rooted in a metaphor. These metaphors, both in content (the stories they tell) and form (the fact that they are metaphors), powerfully influence how we think about the divine-human relationship. Before diving into the content of each of these metaphors, it is important to explore how metaphors function to create meaning and why they are so powerful.

METAPHORS AND THEOLOGY

In high school, I was taught that a metaphor is a literary device used primarily by poets. Similar to alliteration, simile, rhyme, or iambic pentameter, I was taught to think of metaphors as devices used by writers to artfully express what might have been expressed more literally yet tediously in wordy prose. Thus, when I say, "life is a rollercoaster," I am relying on the similarity of having ups and downs (among other things) that both life and rollercoasters have. I could also say, "Life can be unpredictable and full of ups and downs that can be both scary and exciting," but substituting this description with "life is a rollercoaster" is more efficient and evocative. In this understanding of metaphors, the metaphor relies on inherent similarities between the two things being compared (i.e., the ups and downs in the example above).[2]

A major shift in the theory of metaphor occurs in 1936 with the work of I. A. Richards in *The Philosophy of Rhetoric*. Richards argues that metaphor is not simply replacing one word or phrase with another to create an analogy but is the process by which meaning is created through the *interaction* of two thoughts.

---

2. This way of understanding metaphors (i.e., substitution theory) is based on Aristotle's theory of metaphor (Aristotle, *The Rhetoric and the Poetics of Aristotle*, trans. W. Rhys Roberts and Ingram Bywater [Modern Library, 1984]). The idea behind this theory is that metaphors are substitutes for literal descriptions and rely on inherent similarities between the two matters being compared.

That is, the meaning of the metaphor is not dependent on inherent similarities between the two elements but is rather created by the interaction between the two elements. Richards points out that the "mind is a connecting organ . . . and it can connect any two things in an indefinitely large number of different ways."[3] Thus, Richards would say that there is no obvious and inherent preexisting similarity between "rollercoasters" and "life" in my previous example (i.e., "life is a rollercoaster"). Rather, the mind works to connect "rollercoasters" and "life" in the metaphor, and it is in this interaction that meaning takes place. The mind determines that "rollercoasters" and "life" share the commonality of having ups and downs. It could just as easily have determined that "rollercoasters" and "life" are similar in being over before you know it.

Max Black takes up Richards's claim that metaphors force the reader to connect two ideas, which creates an interaction between them, and builds on it to argue that the two ideas do not simply interact but that the metaphorical word or phrase (e.g., the "rollercoaster" in the example above), in fact, frames the way we think about the target (e.g., "life"). When we say, "life is a rollercoaster," we conjure up a system of ideas related to the frame (i.e., the "rollercoaster"). For instance, we note that rollercoasters follow a winding path that has many ups and downs, that they are scary yet also exciting and fun, that they move fast, and that they require us to be strapped into cars. Everything we know about "rollercoasters" then becomes a window through which we view "life."

However, where the system of ideas related to "rollercoasters" is conjured up based on what one generally assumes a rollercoaster to be, the system of ideas related to "life" is not based on what one generally assumes "life" to be. The system of ideas surrounding "life" in this metaphor occurs only because thoughts about "life" are now framed by thoughts about "rollercoasters." Black explains that any characteristic of life "that can without undue strain be talked about in '[rollercoaster]-language' will be rendered prominent, and any that cannot will be pushed into the background." Our thoughts about "rollercoasters" organize and frame our thoughts about "life" in this metaphor. Black compares this to looking "at the night sky through a piece of heavily smoked glass on which certain lines have been left clear." Certain aspects of the target (i.e., "life" in this case) are obscured by the smoked glass, while others are highlighted by the clear lines left by the metaphorical world related to, in this case, "rollercoasters." Thus "the principal subject is 'seen through' the metaphorical expression."[4] In the example above, I might think about life as being fast, scary, exciting, fun, and having many ups and downs. Since being strapped into cars doesn't readily map onto life, that aspect of rollercoasters is ignored. The metaphor highlights aspects of life that are similar to rollercoasters (i.e., having ups and downs, being scary and exciting, etc.), and at the same time hides many other aspects of life (e.g.,

---

3. I. A. Richards, *The Philosophy of Rhetoric*, 1st ed. (Oxford University Press, 1965), 93–94, 125.

4. Max Black, *Models and Metaphors: Studies in Language and Philosophy* (Cornell University Press, 1962), 41.

that it involves aging, that it can be boring, tragic, and sad, etc.). Metaphors thus have the capacity to both highlight and obscure things about the target (i.e., "life" in this example).

George Lakoff and Mark Johnson take these ideas one step further in their seminal work, *Metaphors We Live By*, and argue that "metaphor is pervasive in everyday life, not just in language, but in thought and action."[5] For Lakoff and Johnson, and other proponents of the cognitive linguistic theory of metaphor, a metaphor is not simply a matter of substitution at the level of language, or even of interaction at the level of thought.[6] Rather "our ordinary conceptual system, in terms of which we both think and act, is fundamentally metaphorical in nature."[7] In short, we think in metaphors, and these influence not only the way we see the world but even how we live in it.[8]

Lakoff and Johnson's example of "ARGUMENT IS WAR" (emphasis in the original) demonstrates how this works. For Lakoff and Johnson, metaphorical language is a result of metaphorical thinking. Thus, when we say things like "your claims are *indefensible*," "he *attacked every weak point* in my argument" or "he *shot down* all my arguments," we are using what another cognitive linguistic theorist, Zoltán Kövecses, refers to as "metaphorical linguistic expressions."[9] These expressions are linguistic manifestations of the conceptual metaphor ARGUMENT IS WAR. Crucially, war is not simply the way we talk about arguments, but the notion of war influences how we conduct arguments. That is, "we can actually win or lose arguments."[10] We view those with whom we argue as opponents needing to be vanquished. This metaphor is so embedded that we find it hard to imagine a world in which this might not be the case, and in which arguments function more like a dance, for instance, in which the movements of the one require a response in kind from the other, and in which the whole is far more important than what each individual thinks and says.[11] The fact that metaphors can function to both *de*scribe and *pre*scribe reality means they are powerful influencers.[12]

---

5. George Lakoff and Mark Johnson, *Metaphors We Live By* (University of Chicago Press, 2003), 3.
6. Mark Johnson, "Introduction: Metaphor in the Philosophical Tradition," in ed. Mark Johnson, *Philosophical Perspectives on Metaphor* (University of Minnesota Press, 1981), 5–6. Other proponents of the cognitive linguistic theory of metaphor include Gilles Fauconnier and Mark Turner, *The Way We Think: Conceptual Blending and the Mind's Hidden Complexities* (Basic Books, 2003); Raymond W. Gibbs, *Metaphor Wars: Conceptual Metaphors in Human Life* (Cambridge University Press, 2017); Zoltán Kövecses, *Metaphor: A Practical Introduction* (Oxford University Press, 2010).
7. Lakoff and Johnson, *Metaphors*, 3.
8. Metaphors are far more complex than I have room (and expertise) to explore in this brief introduction. The conceptual theory of metaphor has expanded far beyond Lakoff and Johnson's initial idea. My point here is not to offer a full description of the intricacies of theories of metaphors but rather to point to a few broad implications of Lakoff and Johnson's and, to some extent, Richards and Black's notions of how metaphors function.
9. Lakoff and Johnson, *Metaphors*, 4 (italics in the original); Kövecses, *Metaphor*, 12.
10. Lakoff and Johnson, *Metaphors*, 4.
11. Lakoff and Johnson, *Metaphors*, 4–5.
12. As David Donaldson points out, there is, of course, an element of subjectivity in the way we interpret metaphors (see David Donaldson, "What Metaphors Mean," in *Philosophical Perspectives on Metaphor*, ed. Mark Johnson [University of Minnesota Press, 1981], 200–21) At the same time, there are generally accepted ways of interpreting metaphors in societies. That is, most people in the

This is especially true in theology. Feminist theologians, especially, have always been keenly aware of the ways in which language influences thought and action and have recognized the importance of metaphors for theology, particularly with regards to the way we talk about God.[13] Using metaphor is a strategy of necessity when talking about God because God is beyond human comprehension.

The language we use in theology is important because, as feminist theologian Sallie McFague notes in *Metaphorical Theology*, "whoever names the world owns the world."[14] Many feminist, queer, and womanist theologians note that the world of Western theology is drenched in patriarchal, heteronormative, ableist, and white supremacist language that excludes women, children, the elderly, those with disabilities, and BIPOC (Black, Indigenous, and People of Color) and LGBTQ+ communities. Problematically, the use of such language to talk about the Divine creates the illusion that, to give an example, "maleness is an essential character of the divine being." When male pronouns are used consistently to talk about God, it becomes easy to imagine that God is in God's essence male. Further, "whenever a segment of reality is used as a symbol for God, the realm of reality from which it is taken is elevated into the realm of the holy, becoming 'theonomous.'"[15] Thus, for example, when we consistently use the metaphor "father" to talk about God, fathers—and by extension men—become divinized. This is easy to see in the case of patriarchal language, but the deification of whatever we metaphorically attribute to God also comes into play in the metaphors we use to talk about salvation.

Delores Williams makes this argument in her seminal article, "Black Women's Surrogacy Experience and the Christian Notion of Redemption," and in her book *Sisters in the Wilderness*.[16] Williams contends that atonement theologies, such as penal-substitutionary atonement, divinize surrogacy in that Jesus is portrayed as the ultimate surrogate who stands in our place to take on our punishment. Since surrogacy is a prime location of Black women's suffering in both the antebellum and postbellum eras, the deification of surrogacy in penal-substitutionary atonement is highly problematic because it "supports and reinforces the exploitation

---

United States functionally think of arguments in terms of war, whether they are aware of it or not. Metaphors describe what is at play and prescribe how we live and think based on these broad, generally agreed-upon interpretations of metaphor, even while allowing room for subjective nuances. Further, it is possible to make an argument that all language is metaphorical in that it is symbolic. That is, words point to a reality but are not that reality. While that is an interesting philosophical argument, that is not what I am focusing on when I talk about metaphors.

13. E.g., see Elizabeth A. Johnson, *She Who Is: The Mystery of God in Feminist Theological Discourse* (Herder & Herder, 2017); Sallie McFague, *Speaking in Parables* (Augsburg Fortress, 2000); Sallie McFague, *Metaphorical Theology: Models of God in Religious Language* (Fortress, 1982); Sallie McFague, *Models of God: Theology for an Ecological, Nuclear Age* (Fortress, 1987).

14. McFague, *Metaphorical Theology*, 8–9.

15. Johnson, *She Who Is*, 33, 39.

16. Delores Williams, "Black Women's Surrogacy Experience and the Christian Notion of Redemption," in *Cross Examinations: Readings on the Meaning of the Cross Today*, ed. M. Trelstad (Augsburg, 2006), 19–33; Delores Williams, *Sisters in the Wilderness: The Challenge of Womanist God-Talk* (Orbis Books, 1993).

that has accompanied [Black women's] experience with surrogacy."¹⁷ Williams is concerned that accepting Jesus as ultimate surrogate leads to the passive acceptance of "the exploitation that surrogacy brings."¹⁸ Other theologians have critiqued penal-substitutionary atonement based on a similar logic, whereby our attribution of something to God (e.g., violence and abuse, or passivity and servanthood) gives it divine status.¹⁹

My own argument employs a similar logic in that I am concerned about the implications of the metaphors we use to talk about salvation. These metaphors deeply influence how we think about who God is, who we are in relation to God and each other, and what we can expect from a life lived in freedom. In the next section, I explore the logic of penal-substitutionary atonement and demonstrate how the metaphor that this theory relies on functions to keep those with addiction mired in a cycle of shame.

PENAL-SUBSTITUTIONARY ATONEMENT AND THE "LOGIC" OF PUNISHMENT

For many Christians, penal-substitutionary atonement functions as the primary and sometimes only theology of atonement.²⁰ Indeed, until I went to seminary in my young adulthood, I had no idea there were other ways of thinking about the cross and salvation (e.g., solidarity, moral influence, varieties of *Christus Victor*, including ransom theory, etc.). For many Christians, penal-substitutionary atonement is a comforting model for thinking about salvation in that it envisages a God who goes to great lengths to save us.

Broadly speaking, penal-substitutionary atonement is a metaphor for how God saves humanity. As metaphor, it attempts to give voice to the mystery of God and salvation and does so by placing atonement within a judicial system. Within this metaphor, God is a judge who deems humans to be criminals (due to their sinfulness) and requires punishment in the form of eternal damnation. Jesus, acting as an intermediary, takes upon himself our punishment and in so doing demonstrates God's tremendous love for us.

---

17. Williams, *Sisters,* 162.
18. Williams, *Sisters,* 162.
19. E.g., Rita Nakashima Brock, *Journeys by Heart: A Christology of Erotic Power* (Wipf & Stock, 2008); Rita Nakashima Brock and Rebecca A. Parker, *Proverbs and Ashes: Violence, Redemptive Suffering, and the Search for What Saves Us* (Beacon, 2001); Gregory A. Love, *Love, Violence, and the Cross: How the Nonviolent God Saves Us Through the Cross of Christ* (Cascade Books, 2010); J. Denny Weaver, *The Nonviolent Atonement* (Eerdmans, 2011).
20. Mark D. Baker and Joel B. Green, *Recovering the Scandal of the Cross: Atonement in New Testament and Contemporary Contexts* (IVP Academic, 2011), 161; Love, *Love, Violence,* 3; Leanne Van Dyk, *Believing in Jesus Christ* (Geneva, 2002), 87; Sonia Waters, "Punishing the Immoral Other: Penal Substitutionary Logic in the War on Drugs," *Pastoral Psychology* 68, no. 5 (Oct. 2019): 534, https://doi.org/10.1007/s11089-018-0836-y.

While Early Church Fathers alluded to versions of penal-substitutionary atonement, Martin Luther and John Calvin offered the first more systematic accounts of this theology of atonement. In this chapter, I rely primarily on John Calvin's account, even though the churches that taught me about penal-substitutionary atonement (without using that name) never mentioned John Calvin or Martin Luther in relation to this theology. Rather, it was taught to me as a matter of course. This simply was what salvation meant in the churches I grew up in. Nonetheless, a brief description of Calvin's version of penal-substitutionary atonement is helpful to get a more detailed sense of what this theology of salvation entails.

As I described in chapter 2, John Calvin sees human sin as a "corruption of our nature," which bends the will toward evil, for which we are held guilty (i.e., inherited guilt), and which results in sinful acts.[21] Because of our sinful nature, we are no longer in right relationship with God. Calvin says, "God's righteousness bars our access to him, and God in his capacity as judge is angry toward us."[22] At the same time, our sinful nature is so pervasive that that there is nothing we can do on our own steam to win back God's favor. "Hence," Calvin says, "an expiation must intervene in order that Christ as priest may obtain God's favor for us and appease his wrath. Thus, Christ to perform this office had to come forward with a sacrifice."[23]

Christ takes on the role of Mediator and offers himself as sacrifice to take on the punishment in our stead. It was necessary for the Mediator, as fully human, to live in full obedience and faithfulness to God and yet take on the punishment of death on our behalf. Only a true human could take such punishment on our behalf (since humans deserve the punishment for faithlessness). At the same time only God could live in full obedience to God's will and only God could overcome death. Thus, Calvin says, "In short, since neither as God alone could he feel death, nor as man alone could he overcome it, he coupled human nature with divine that to atone for sin he might submit the weakness of the one to death; and that, wrestling with death by the power of the other nature, he might win victory for us."[24]

For Calvin, who studied law, the manner of Jesus' death is important in that it attests to the point of his death: "If he had been murdered by thieves or slain in an insurrection by a raging mob, in such a death there would have been no evidence of satisfaction. But when he was arraigned before the judgment seat as a criminal, accused and pressed by testimony, and condemned by the mouth of the judge to die—we know by these proofs that he took the role of a guilty man and evildoer." Thus, Jesus dies not as an innocent man but as one carrying the sin of the world: "He suffered death not because of innocence but because of sin." Hence, he says, "Thus we shall behold the person of a sinner and evildoer

---

21. John Calvin, *Institutes of the Christian Religion*, ed. John T. McNeill, trans. Ford Lewis Battles (Westminster, 1960), 2.1.8.
22. Calvin, *Institutes*, 2.15.6.
23. Calvin, *Institutes*, 2.15.6.
24. Calvin, *Institutes*, 2.12.3.

represented in Christ, yet from his shining innocence it will at the same time be obvious that he was burdened with another's sin rather than his own."[25] Christ is crucified and cursed on our behalf. Calvin, relying on a judicial model, notes the importance of the manner of death because it demonstrates that Christ took a punishment in our stead. While the punishment is satisfied in Christ's death, the resurrection is what gives us new life.[26]

While it is helpful to get a clearer sense of Calvin's articulation of penal-substitutionary atonement, it is important to remember that when I talk about this theology of atonement, I am not confining this theology to Calvin alone. Indeed, Calvin's own theology of salvation includes more than penal-substitutionary atonement alone. Many theologians (e.g., Charles Hodge) after Calvin have shaped, refined, and solidified penal-substitutionary atonement as a prominent theology of salvation in churches. While theologians like Calvin, who adhere to penal-substitutionary atonement, are careful to point to God's love as primary in this model of atonement, I have found that this love often comes with a significant dose of condemnation, which can lead to a sense of shame.[27]

As discussed in chapter 3, shame can contribute to both the development and maintenance of addiction. The person uses to escape feelings of shame; the use, in turn, generates new feelings of shame, which reinforces the original sense of shame. Shame becomes the catalyst, result, and reinforcer of addiction, generating a dangerous and possibly lethal cycle. Those with addiction thus need an interruption to this cycle of shame in order to heal. Penal-substitutionary atonement does precisely the opposite: it adds divine sanction to shame by naming the human-divine relation as one of criminal and judge, which further entrenches the person and surrounding communities in a shame spiral that perpetuates the problem of addiction. By relying on the metaphor of humans as criminals, penal-substitutionary atonement reifies shame in the person with addiction. That is, instead of those who have addiction contending with *feeling* as if they are bad and in need of punishment (i.e., shame), penal-substitutionary atonement heightens the problem by saying they actually *are* bad and in need of punishment. Crucially, while Jesus Christ assumes the punishment for crime (i.e., sin), the identity of "criminal" is never fully erased. At best, humans are

---

25. Calvin, *Institutes*, 2.16.5.
26. Thus, Calvin says, "[W]e divide the substance of our salvation between Christ's death and resurrection as follows: through his death, sin was wiped out and death extinguished; through his resurrection, righteousness was restored and life raised up, so that—thanks to the resurrection—his death manifested its power and efficacy in us" (2.16.13). Christ's death absolves us of the punishment for sin, but it is only through the resurrection that we have full life.
27. Calvin wants to avoid pitting the Son's mercy against the Father's wrath, and thus points to God's mercy as the beginning of salvation. Calvin points us to Augustine to note that "the fact that we were reconciled through Christ's death must not be understood as if his Son reconciled us to him that he might now begin to love those whom he hated. Rather, we have already been reconciled to him who loves us, with whom we were enemies on account of sin" (2.16.4). He focuses on this because he does not want us to read him as if he pits the Father's wrath against the Son's love. The wrath and the love are both God's. Thus, Calvin says that in the atonement God "anticipates us by his mercy" and loves us first (2.16.2).

forgiven criminals in this metaphor for atonement. This status as (forgiven) criminal reifies the shame with which those with addiction already contend. Thus, penal-substitutionary atonement ontologizes shame and makes it part of the person's being, as opposed to being merely a difficult feeling with which they contend. Penal-substitutionary atonement heightens shame and names it as an identity with divine sanction. Thus, it is not merely that penal-substitutionary atonement does not offer the interruption to the shame cycle that those with addiction so desperately need, but rather that it further mires the person in the very addiction/shame cycle from which they seek redemption by adding divine sanction to the shame they already feel. While not specifically linked to penal-substitutionary atonement, divine-sanctioned shame is a persistent theme in addiction memoirs.

In her memoir, *Strung Out,* Erin Khar talks about the ways shame plays into her addiction. She recounts that childhood sexual abuse created a rage in her that she "turned into shame and guilt and self-loathing."[28] While there isn't a one-to-one relationship between the shame caused by the abuse and her addiction, the two are clearly related. When the memories of her abuse come crashing in, she changes her appearance in an effort to separate herself from "the one who had been carrying pain and shame and running from it in vain, faster and faster." Part of how she ran from the pain and shame was through her addiction to heroin. Yet with each hit, she also injected herself with more shame. At one point when she relapses, she says, "Shame is a gatekeeper. Shame takes old shame and turns it into a new shame."[29] The addiction cycle runs on shame. The old shame of childhood sexual abuse becomes the new shame of getting high, which becomes the old shame, which in turn becomes the new shame, and on and on it goes. Shame creates an endless cycle, pushing the addiction ever forward.

For Khar her shame took on God-sized proportions when she got an abortion. As she tried to sit up, she felt a "sharp stabbing cramp." Khar writes, "If I narrowed in on the pain, it took the shape and sensation of all the shame I'd ever felt in my body, of my body." She says, "I felt what I can only describe as God's judgment."[30] She doesn't actually believe in God, and yet shame brings to mind God's judgment. Of course, she took that old shame of getting an abortion and turned it into new shame. She says, "I did the only thing I thought would help: I got high." In Khar's story, there's a complex interplay between the shame she feels from childhood that she attempts to cover up through heroin use and the shame that is produced by her drug use itself. She says, "I couldn't recognize the blurred lines between the drugs and my depression and the trauma from sexual abuse. All those things melted together and became the filter through which I saw myself: the monster."[31] Shame becomes the frame through which she sees

---

28. Erin Khar, *Strung Out: One Last Hit and Other Lies That Nearly Killed Me* (Park Row, 2020), 71, Kindle.
29. Khar, *Strung Out,* 73, 149.
30. Khar, *Strung Out,* 150, 151.
31. Khar, *Strung Out,* 167.

herself, and all she sees is a monster. Importantly, shame is also the frame through which she assumes God sees her. Her sense of God in her state of self-loathing is that of a God of judgment and punishment.

Heather King similarly describes how shame becomes the engine that drives her addiction in her memoir, *Parched*. She describes herself as feeling as if she couldn't quite live up to her mother's high standards and says, "It wasn't that she made me feel second-rate for failing to meet her standards; it was that I already felt so second-rate myself I was afraid my myriad deficiencies would lead her to discount me altogether."[32] Drinking grants her a moment of reprieve from this constant sense of shame of being "second-rate." The first time she drinks, she "was transformed" and "suddenly felt pretty, competent, at ease . . . embraced and welcome."[33] Many people with addiction describe this sense of finally feeling at ease and okay once they drink. Drinking covers over the shame of being not enough, and yet, as King aptly notes, "the irony of instant gratification is that it leaves such lasting scars."[34] Over time, the drinking itself creates a sense of shame. At one point after years of drinking, she writes in her journal, "'Why must I be so utterly undisciplined, so moody, dreamy, lazy, despondent, eternally frustrated, unsatisfied and ultimately guilty with the knowledge that it is all MY FAULT?'" She wants so desperately to make her parents proud and yet sees herself instead as "sinking to the depths of slime and mire." She attempts to use alcohol to cover over her shame but discovers it leaves her a husk of a human being, robbed of "every emotion but self-loathing."[35]

Like Khar, King's God is also a God of judgment: "I did, of course, *believe* in God—judgement, eternal damnation: these were ideas that came easily to me. My idea of how He operated was pretty much based on New England weather: three months of paradise, nine of hell—I could do the math. Winter was obviously a *punishment* for summer, a reflection of the universal law that every moment of happiness had to be paid for with three of misery." King goes to Sunday School and hears the stories of redemption and healing yet finds them irrelevant: "The donuts in the foyer afterward were okay, but obviously lost sheep and prodigal sons and the man who lay paralyzed on his mat till Jesus came along had nothing to do with me."[36] While King grows up hearing stories of healing, reconciliation, and forgiveness, the God she feels most connected to in her drinking is the God of punishment. One day, while lying in the sun, hungover yet again, she thinks, "No sky should have been that blue, it seemed to me; no water that warm. There'd be a price to pay for such bounty, I kept thinking. There'd be a terrible, terrible price."[37] The idea that punishment is always just around the corner matches her theology of an angry God who makes humans pay for any

32. Heather King, *Parched: A Memoir* (New American Library, 2006), 24.
33. King, *Parched*, 65.
34. King, *Parched*, 119.
35. King, *Parched*, 198–99 (emphasis in the original), 210, 238.
36. King, *Parched*, 41, 42.
37. King, *Parched*, 97.

experience of bounty. The idea that she deserves punishment seems inextricably tied to her addiction and is, in some ways, a driver of it. Interestingly, both Khar's and King's shame drive them to imagine a God of punishment and anger. Their sense of God corroborates their sense of self-loathing and, in a sense, adds divine blessing to it.

This sense of God as One who affirms self-loathing and shame and demands punishment finds especially strong expression in penal-substitutionary atonement in that it names human beings as criminals in need of punishment. Problematically, the solution penal-substitutionary atonement offers is actually no solution at all but rather another instantiation of the problem. That is, the felt need for punishment is part of the problem of shame with which those with addiction contend, and offering a solution (i.e., someone else taking on the punishment) that adheres to the logic of shame and punishment symbolizes nothing other than the victory of shame. Paul Ricoeur talks about sin as the separation between humans and God that happens on the side of humans. That is, humans *feel* separated from God.[38] This resonates with the experience of shame with which many people with addiction struggle. As I mentioned in chapter 3, shame causes people to hide and separate themselves (both physically and emotionally) from the community.[39] The feeling of separation is, in some sense, the expression of their shame. The notion of punishment, however, says Ricoeur, is itself simply "another symbol of this same separation."[40] The idea that God would need to punish humans, far from being a solution to the problem of estrangement from God, is simply another symbol of the estrangement itself. The feeling of being bad (shame) causes a person to imagine that they require punishment. This need for punishment is then projected onto God and given divine sanction in penal-substitutionary atonement.[41]

What we need—what those suffering from addiction need—is to undo the logic of or connection between shame and punishment. Ricoeur helpfully unravels the logic of crime and punishment and demonstrates it to be absurd. The logic of retributive justice attempts to offer a punishment that is equal to the crime.[42] The more heinous the crime, the greater the punishment. This seems entirely logical. Ricoeur, however, demonstrates that the logic of equalization does not, in fact, make sense. Punishment attempts to equalize something that cannot be equalized. Punishment works on the logic of purification. Cleansing

---

38. Paul Ricoeur, "Interpretation of the Myth of Punishment," in *The Conflict of Interpretations: Essays in Hermeneutics,* ed. D. Ihde, trans. Robert Sweeney (Northwestern University Press, 1974), 354–77.

39. Jennifer M. Chilton, "Shame: A Multidisciplinary Concept Analysis," *Journal of Theory Construction & Testing* 16, no. 1 (Spring 2012): 5; Timothy McMahan King, *Addiction Nation: What the Opioid Crisis Reveals About Us* (Herald, 2019), 46; Ronald Potter-Efron, "Therapy with Shame-Prone Alcoholic and Drug-Dependent Clients," *in Shame in the Therapy Hour,* ed. R. L. Dearing and J. Tangney (American Psychological Association, 2011), 225–26; Christiane Sanderson, *Counseling Skills for Working with Shame* (Jessica Kingsley, 2015), 69.

40. Ricoeur, "Myth of Punishment," 371.

41. Ricoeur, "Myth of Punishment."

42. Ricoeur, "Myth of Punishment," 355; Waters, "Punishing the Immoral Other," 539; Weaver, *Nonviolent Atonement,* 2–3.

cancels out a stain, and the larger the stain, the more of a cleansing agent is needed. Punishment works on the same logic—only it isn't logical at all. The justice system assumes that the larger the crime, the more punishment is necessary. However, where stain and purification happen in the same subject, the effect of crime and the effect of punishment happen in different subjects. The one cannot cancel out the other. The effect of a crime on person A remains the same no matter what punishment person B receives for committing the crime. The two have nothing to do with each other, because they happen in different people. Punishment may have other benefits, such as perhaps a sense of validation of wrongdoing for the victim, or it can function as rehabilitative for the criminal, but it cannot cancel out a crime.[43]

This logic of seeking an equal measure of suffering for the perpetrator of a crime as that which she imparted to her victim is the logic of retributive justice: "What is most rational in punishment, namely, that it fit the crime, is at the same time most irrational, namely, that it erases it."[44] The idea, then, that God demands a punishment that is equal to the crime that humans commit is absurd. It is based on the logic of stain and cleansing with the problem that whereas cleansing can erase a stain, punishment cannot erase a crime.

While Ricoeur does not explicitly mention this, a similar fallacy of logic is at play when the idea of substitutionary atonement is moved from the realm of the marketplace, which is where Anselm originally placed it (see below), to the realm of the justice system. Anselm, who arguably gave the first clear and systematic description of the satisfaction model of atonement, situates atonement within the feudal system and the marketplace within which he lived and describes it as a process by which Jesus pays a debt that humans owe to God.[45] Anselm argues that since we owe full honor and obedience to God, once we sin, we cannot ever repay the debt, no matter how well we obey and honor God. Since, metaphorically, we already owe God everything we have, there is no possibility of giving God anything extra or sufficient to make up for past deficiencies. Anselm notes that only God could make up the difference, yet only humans owe the debt. Anselm sums up the situation as follows: "it is necessary that the heavenly city be made complete by human beings, and that cannot be the case unless this recompense is made—a recompense that only God can make and only human beings owe." The solution to the problem presented here according to Anselm is that "a God-man make this recompense."[46] Thus, only Jesus Christ, as both fully divine and fully human, is able to pay the debt on our behalf. Once paid,

---

43. Ricoeur, "Myth of Punishment," 354–58.
44. Ricoeur, "Myth of Punishment," 358.
45. While there are earlier accounts of versions of the satisfaction model of atonement, Anselm is understood to be the first to give a full and systematic description of this version of atonement (Gustav Aulén, *Christus Victor: An Historical Study of the Three Main Types of the Idea of Atonement*, trans. A. G. Herbert [Wipf & Stock, 2003], 84; Timothy Gorringe, *God's Just Vengeance: Crime, Violence and the Rhetoric of Salvation* [Cambridge University Press, 1996], 90.
46. Anselm, *Cur Deus Homo*, in ed. and trans. Thomas Williams, *Anselm: Basic Writings* (Hackett, 2007), II.6.

humans are no longer debtors, and God has been given what God is owed.[47] Change is affected in both the debtor, who is no longer a debtor once payment is made, and the creditor, who is paid what is owed.

Penal-substitutionary atonement becomes illogical precisely because it takes the substitution out of the realm of the marketplace and places it in the realm of the justice system. John Calvin, for instance, argues that our sin incites God's wrath and that God's justice demands punishment for sin. Jesus Christ as fully human is able to take on the punishment we owe and as fully divine is able to bear the punishment.[48] The problem, of course, is that Jesus taking on the punishment does not undo the crime committed and therefore effects no real change in God (against whom the crime was committed), nor in humans, who remain (forgiven) criminals. Just as the logic of stain and purification does not translate to crime and punishment, the logic of debt and payment does not translate either.

Ricoeur argues that what seems like an adoption of the logic of punishment (e.g., in the book of Romans) is, in fact, a description of the way the logic no longer functions. Thus, he says, "What would appear to us as a logic of identity" (i.e., the logic that the punishment must fit the crime) "becomes the lived contradiction which makes the economy of the law break apart." The absurdity of the logic of punishment implodes on itself and "by this absurd logic, the concept of law destroys itself and, with the concept of law, the whole cycle of notions which are governed by it: judgment, condemnation, punishment. This economy is now placed *en bloc* under the sign of death."[49] Ricoeur argues that what is offered instead is a gift of superabundance.

---

47. Anselm's argument is more complicated than I outline above. The logic he uses to demonstrate that Jesus's death is sufficient to pay the debt on our behalf is complicated and summarized below for those interested. He argues that Jesus is born free from original sin. Were this not so, he would have been unable to live free of sin. Further, Anselm notes that had Jesus lived a life free of sin, Jesus would have done nothing more than what God commands of every human being since full obedience is what God demands of everyone. Living a life in full obedience to God would have gained Jesus entry into paradise but could not have provided payment for anyone else. Thus, Jesus had to give a gift above and beyond what is asked of everyone (i.e., more than full obedience). Since the God-human (i.e., Jesus Christ) lives a sinless life, he is not subject to death in the way all other humans are. Because the God-human is not subject to death, giving his life on our behalf is the gift that he can give above and beyond full obedience to God. The fact that he offers his very life as payment for our sin and dies on our behalf is abundant payment for our sin. The payment is abundant because he is both fully human and fully divine, and as fully divine, his life is worth more than anyone could imagine. As a result of this gift, God now owed the God-human a reward, but "what reward will be given to one who lacks for nothing, one to whom nothing can be given and for whom no debt can be canceled?" (Anselm, *Cur Deus Homo*, II.19). Therefore, the God-human takes the reward that he is given, and instead of keeping it himself (since he does not need a reward), he gives it to humans and thereby pays the debt on humankind's behalf. It is as if God has a heavenly bank account, and the God-human causes an excess of funds. To maintain order, these funds must be disbursed, and the God-human chooses to give them to humanity to pay the debt they owe. (Anselm, *Cur Deus Homo*, II.11–19.)

48. Calvin, *Institutes*, 2.12.1–3.

49. Ricoeur, "Myth of Punishment," 373.

What I find helpful about Ricoeur's argument here is that he recognizes that what humans need liberation from is the *feeling* of judgment and the need for punishment, which I argue is rooted in shame. For those who have addiction, the feeling of being a bad person (shame) is one of the main things that needs healing. This is one of the reasons treatment centers tend to spend a significant amount of time talking about addiction as a disease. In addition to being true, it also allows the person with addiction to let go of the shame of feeling like a moral failure. Dealing with addiction is in part dealing with shame.

Sarah Hepola recognizes in *Blackout* that part of recovery is learning to stop the shame spiral. She says, "Self-destruction is a taste I've savored all my life. The scratch in my throat left by too much smoking, the jitteriness of a third cup of coffee, the perverse thrill of knowing a thing is bad and choosing it anyway—these are all familiar kinks, and one feeds the other. But was it possible to change my palate—to crave something good for me, to create an inspiration spiral instead of a shame spiral?"[50] Hepola has to learn to let go of the things that confirm shame and instead choose that which affirms life for her.

As I described in chapter 3, for those with addiction, the feelings of shame are often partly the result of the harms perpetrated against others within the addiction. However, they are also partly the result of harm done to the person suffering from addiction (e.g., childhood trauma) and of the harm addiction itself does to the person. Both the guilt of perpetrating harm under the influence of addiction and the shame of harm caused *to* the person suffering from addiction intermingle in complex ways, such that it becomes difficult, if not impossible, to untangle one from the other. Penal-substitutionary atonement, by naming humans criminals, harmfully "conflates the parts that hold guilt from commissions of sin and those that hold shame from experiencing the wounding of sin."[51] This is especially harmful for those who have experienced the trauma of abuse as children, because many people who experienced abuse as children take inappropriate responsibility for the abuse in order to cope and therefore imagine themselves to have been somehow deficient and deserving of this abuse.[52] Penal-substitutionary atonement plays into these unhealthy tendencies of taking inappropriate blame, especially for those with addiction, where the lines between being victim and perpetrator are blurry at best.

Ricoeur helpfully demonstrates that the need for punishment and the feeling of guilt and shame *is* sin, and it is precisely this need for punishment that needs to be vanquished. The feeling of being a bad person who needs punishment is the thing that requires healing. This is true in addiction as well. The person often feels as if they need punishment for being a "bad" person, but it is precisely *this shame* of feeling like a bad person that needs healing. Penal-substitutionary atonement cannot meet this need and, in fact, only heightens the problem. Within the metaphor, the best for which one can hope is to be a forgiven criminal.

50. Sarah Hepola, *Blackout: Remembering the Things I Drank to Forget* (Grand Central, 2015), 180.
51. Jennifer Baldwin, *Trauma-Sensitive Theology: Thinking Theologically in the Era of Trauma* (Cascade Books, 2018), 136.
52. Baldwin, *Trauma-Sensitive Theology*, 136.

More important, the judicial metaphor is, in a sense, a victory of shame itself. The idea that God looks upon humanity and deems it so bad that God demands eternal death as punishment signifies the victory of shame. The necessity of Jesus taking on this punishment in our stead is a confirmation of shame and the logic of punishment, thus further heightening the sense of shame that those who have addiction experience.[53]

PENAL-SUBSTITUTIONARY ATONEMENT: AN OVERUSED METAPHOR FOR SALVATION

If penal-substitutionary atonement was offered in churches as one metaphor for salvation among many others of equal value, the issues raised above would certainly still be problematic but not insurmountable. Problematically, however, penal-substitutionary atonement has become so common and dominant that it is difficult for people to remember that it is, indeed, a metaphor and not a literal description of what happens in salvation.[54]

Sallie McFague talks about the danger of metaphors becoming literalized in her work *Metaphorical Theology*. Metaphors contain both "similarity and difference."[55] That is, even while claiming similarity, metaphors "always contain the whisper, 'it is *and it is not*.'"[56] When we say that God is a rock, we recognize both similarities between a rock and God (e.g., steadfastness) and dissimilarities (e.g., rocks don't speak). Rocks highlight certain things about God while hiding others. McFague points out that metaphors become dangerously powerful when we forget that they are indeed metaphors, when we focus so much on the similarities that we forget that there are also differences. This happens when we overuse a metaphor and forget that it is one among many metaphors. It is because metaphors are "risky, uncertain, and open-ended" that "many metaphors are necessary"[57] especially when talking about God. When we overuse one metaphor to the exclusion of others, the "is not" quality of the metaphor tends to get lost.

At their best, metaphors have the capacity to widen the scope of who we imagine God (in this case) to be. However, when metaphors for God become literalized, they lose this function and instead narrow the scope of what we see and make an idol of a particular God-concept. This is, again, easy to see in patriarchal concepts of God. That is, when we consistently call God "Father" and refer to God as "he," it becomes very difficult to remember that God is not male. This is sometimes harder to recognize in metaphors for salvation even though the same

---

53. Waters, "Punishing the Immoral Other," 541.
54. On the dominance of penal-substitutionary atonement in churches, see Baker and Green, *Recovering the Scandal of the Cross*, 161; Love, *Love, Violence*, 3; Van Dyk, *Believing in Jesus Christ*, 87; Sonia Waters, "Punishing the Immoral Other," 534.
55. McFague, *Metaphorical Theology*, 42.
56. McFague, *Metaphorical Theology*, 13 (italics in the original).
57. Sallie McFague, *Speaking in Parables*, 5th ed. (Augsburg Fortress, 2000), 44.

concept is at play. When we consistently use the same metaphor to talk about salvation in churches (in sermons, songs, liturgies, prayers, etc.), it becomes very difficult to remember that we are using metaphors rather than literal language.

This is the case with penal-substitutionary atonement. In many circles this metaphor for atonement has become the only metaphor available to talk about atonement and more importantly has lost its metaphorical capacity, so that it is seen as a literal description of what happens in the atonement as opposed to one metaphor among many. In other words, it is not just that this metaphor is ubiquitous and influences the way we think about God and ourselves in relation to God but that it has become, in some circles, a literal description of the atonement. It then makes sense to view ourselves as criminals who deserve punishment. In this sense, the judicial model becomes an idol. As McFague notes, when metaphors become literalized, "we become imprisoned by dogmatic, absolutistic, literalistic patterns of thought."[58] In this case, God becomes a literal judge who deems humans to be criminals, to which the only proper response is punishment.

For those with addiction, this notion of God as a literal judge who must punish someone in order to forgive is damaging because it takes the notions of blame and punishment, the very things from which those with addiction need redemption, and makes them part of the character of God.[59] Thus, this system of penal-substitutionary atonement surrounds, ensnares, and entraps the person with addiction both by naming her as shameful and by offering her a solution (Jesus taking on the punishment) that is, in essence, a confirmation of the logic of shame and punishment. Hence, this model for atonement imprisons the addicted person in the very shame/addiction cycle from which she seeks liberation.

Beyond entrapping the person with addiction in a shame cycle, the God concept offered in this model also creates a stumbling block to recovery. Recovering persons often have to undo their beliefs about God in order to recover. Within the logic of penal-substitutionary atonement, God is easily seen as angry and punishing. While the intention of this model of atonement is to highlight God's love for us, in fact, people often experience God through this model of atonement as judgmental, angry, and out to punish. This can easily become an obstacle to recovery for people who have addiction, such that they must overcome not only their own shame but also the shame imposed by their religious tradition.

I often hear newcomers to Twelve-Step groups talk about God as a barrier to recovery, not because they weren't church-goers growing up, but precisely because they were. Memoirs and stories of addiction and recovery show a similar tendency. A recovering person in Narcotics Anonymous, for instance, shares, "At first, I did not like the word *God*. It made me think of people and

---

58. McFague, *Metaphorical Theology*, 74.
59. Waters, "Punishing the Immoral Other," 541.

institutions that judge others, like churches that would ban me because I am gay."[60] Another member similarly shares: "The problem was that my idea of a Higher Power was an old man with a long beard who had a scorecard of my life in one hand and a lightning bolt in the other. He was definitely going to send me to hell. How could I possibly make a decision to turn my will and my life over to him?"[61] As I described above, Heather King talks about a similar problem of struggling with a conception of God that is based in judgment: she says, "I did, of course, *believe* in God—judgment, eternal damnation: these were ideas that came easily to me."[62] Likewise, Cupcake Brown talks about God as a God of punishment: "I didn't know much about God, 'cep that if you pissed Him off, He'd getcha one day."[63]

In *Addiction and Pastoral Care*, Sonia Waters offers a particularly strong example of how these notions of God become a stumbling block to recovery when she talks about a lesbian woman in addiction recovery who experienced God as "'hateful, punishing, vengeful, rejecting.'" Rather than being a refuge, the God-image she had imbibed created an additional barrier that she had to overcome in order to recover from addiction.[64] Her unmanageable life in addiction made sense to her because it aligned with how she understood God and God's punishment. Recall Potter-Efron's observation (see chapter 3) that people often continue using almost as a validation of their own worthlessness.[65] In the cruelest reversal of all, the "God" she was offered in church, rather than being a refuge from harm and a source of comfort, became a tool with which she beat herself. Her sense of God as punishing and hateful kept her trapped in the addiction cycle.

CONCLUSION

Thus, from all sides, the logic of penal-substitutionary atonement functions to keep the person with addiction trapped in the very prison from which they seek freedom. It keeps them mired in shame by naming them "criminal" and by offering a solution to brokenness that stays within the logic of shame and punishment. Further, it communicates a punishing and angry God who becomes a hindrance to recovery rather than a help. In the next chapter, I demonstrate that the logic of penal-substitutionary atonement has implications that go far beyond the church's walls because this metaphor for salvation shapes a culture that sanctions shame and criminalization of addiction.

60. *Narcotics Anonymous*, 6th ed. (World Service Office, 2008), 205.
61. *Narcotics Anonymous*, 243.
62. King, *Parched*, 41.
63. Cupcake Brown, *A Piece of Cake: A Memoir* (Broadway Books, 2006), 15.
64. Sonia Waters, *Addiction and Pastoral Care* (Eerdmans, 2019), 86.
65. Ronald Potter-Efron, "Therapy," 223.

Chapter 5

Penal-Substitutionary Atonement and the Making of a Criminal

In the last chapter, I described how metaphors function to describe and prescribe reality and how the judicial metaphor upon which penal-substitutionary atonement is based functions to keep those with addiction locked in the shame cycle from which they so desperately seek redemption. In this chapter I expand the discussion of metaphors and how they function, and I discuss further the implications of the judicial metaphor that undergirds penal-substitutionary atonement; I focus on the societal implications of this metaphor and demonstrate that the war on drugs utilizes the same logic as penal-substitutionary atonement.

METAPHORS AND MODELS

As I explained in the last chapter, metaphors are complex and pervade much more of our thinking than we might be aware of. Sallie McFague points out that some metaphors have a far broader impact than others. She calls these metaphors "models." These are metaphors with "'staying power' . . . that ha[ve] gained sufficient stability and scope so as to present a pattern for relatively comprehensive and coherent explanation."[1] In other words, two things must happen for a metaphor to become a model. First, it must have "staying power": that is, the metaphor must be somewhat common. There are many religious metaphors that fit this first criterion. For instance, the metaphor "God is a rock" is common enough in Christian discourse to fit this description. We find this metaphor in Scripture, hymns, liturgy, sermons, and even common speech about God. "God, the father" is another metaphor that fits this description. It is also a pervasive metaphor in Christian speech.

The second criterion of a model, however, is that it has to be "a sustained and systematic metaphor." For metaphors to become models, they have to become "grids or screens for interpreting [the] relationship between the divine and the human." In other words, "theological models are dominant metaphors with systematic, comprehensive potential for understanding the many facets of this relationship."[2] This is where the metaphor "God is a rock" falls short of being a model. "God is a rock" certainly says something about the human relationship with God. It implies that God is stable, reliable, and unchanging. However, this metaphor does not have systematic potential. We do not tend to infer anything else about the human-divine or human-to-human relationship from this metaphor. The metaphor "God, the father" is very different in this way. This metaphor has systematic potential. It has tendrils, so to speak. The metaphor says something about who God is, but it also says something about who the second person of the Trinity (Son) is in relation to the first (Father), who humans are in relation to God (children), and who humans are in relation to each other (siblings). In other words, the metaphor "God, the father" is a model because it is pervasive and because it generates a system of ideas. Similar to metaphors, good models should retain the "is" and "is not" quality that all metaphors have.[3]

The term "model" is not simply a technical term for a pervasive metaphor with systematic appeal, however. Models also literally model how we are to live. They function as role models do for children, for instance. Role models (e.g., superheroes) function as "systematizing, organizing grids or screens, offering complex and detailed possibilities for analogical transfer to another life."[4] To give an example, I loved New Kids on the Block when I was in seventh and eighth grade. One of my friends had a much-coveted VHS tape of one of their concerts. Along with two friends, I spent many hours in front of the TV, attempting to follow their dance moves. New Kids on the Block became models for us. Their influence went far beyond their music and dance moves, however. We learned all we could about them and liked the things they liked. I even made a cookbook for a school project once based on foods New Kids on the Block indicated they liked.

1. Sallie McFague, *Models of God: Theology for an Ecological, Nuclear Age* (Fortress, 1987), 34.
2. Sallie McFague, *Metaphorical Theology: Models of God in Religious Language* (Fortress, 1982), 67, 125.
3. McFague, *Metaphorical Theology*, 13.
4. McFague, *Metaphorical Theology*, 68.

They modeled a way of living for us that went far beyond their musical abilities. I absorbed everything they did and liked that I could map onto my life. I began to see myself through the grid of New Kids on the Block. McFague helpfully points out that "much of our journey toward defining the self consists of a long series of partial, inadequate, and rejected models which we try on for size."[5]

Theological models have a similar function. They are not only pervasive metaphors with tendrils that affect how we think about a range of ideas, but they also tell us something about who we *should* be in relation to God and each other. Their influence often reaches beyond the specific thing they focus on. Thus, just as I took on New Kids on the Block as models for more than just music and dance, the models we use to talk about God or salvation influence more than just the way we think about who God is or what salvation means. That is, models, like metaphors, both describe and prescribe reality and do so in much more expansive and complex ways.

Part of the complexity is that models become pervasive because we use them. That is, we have some sense of agency in the models and metaphors we choose to use. At the same time, however, we are (much like the concept of the bondage of the will I described in chapter 2) parts of systems that are already at play. My choice to take on New Kids on the Block as model, for instance, was in some ways a free choice, and yet I was also heavily influenced by a marketing campaign directed at my age group (and gender). I didn't have free reign to choose whoever I wanted to be my model. Rather, I was gently pushed by my peers, teen magazines, news stories, products, and so on in the direction of New Kids on the Block. The same is true for the metaphors and models we use to talk about God. We have choices. Metaphors and models only work because we choose to use them. However, our choices are not neutral. We are born into systems where these metaphors and models are already at play. This is, again, most obvious in the model of "God, the father." We could choose not to use this metaphor, and yet the system of patriarchy we are born into makes it extremely difficult to choose otherwise. An added layer of complexity is the fact that the system of patriarchy, for instance, makes it easy for us to use male metaphors for God in churches; and at the same time, our use of these metaphors is at least partly what sustains patriarchy.

Models are thus incredibly important in human thought. McFague demonstrates that we rely on them in almost all fields of knowledge and could not function without them in theology. It is, after all, difficult, if not impossible, to talk about God without the use of metaphors and models. Hence, "a theologian . . . does not have the luxury of deciding between models and no models," but rather must decide, "which models?" Theology, then, is "principally a network of dominant and subsidiary models."[6] Models, in other words, are broadly shared metaphors with far-reaching systematic implications that are necessary for theological thought.

---

5. McFague, *Metaphorical Theology*, 68.
6. McFague, *Metaphorical Theology*, 105, 139.

Penal-substitutionary atonement is both a metaphor and a model for how God saves humanity. It is a model because it is ubiquitous and has broad systematic implications. That is, penal-substitutionary atonement tells a widely accepted story about how salvation is won through the death of Christ. Beyond that, however, it also tells a story about who God is and who we are in relation to God and each other. Because it is a model, it has systematic implications and has the ability to say something about more than just atonement. In the last chapter, I pointed out that this metaphor says something about the human-divine relationship, naming that relationship as one between a criminal and a judge. By doing so, it adds divine sanction to the shame many with addiction already suffer from. As a model, it has even further implications than that, because it says something about what justice looks like. Penal-substitutionary atonement relies on a retributive model of justice, whereby crimes must be met with punishment. While Jesus takes on the punishment in our stead, the need for punishment itself is not alleviated. There is no world in which no one is getting punished for sin. Retribution in the form of punishment is a necessity before forgiveness can be bestowed. This raises all sorts of questions about what forgiveness is and who God is. If God exacts the full punishment before "forgiving" us, is that actually forgiveness? Further, is a God who exacts payment still truly an extravagantly loving God?

Theologians and philosophers have critiqued substitutionary atonement and penal-substitutionary atonement for centuries for precisely these reasons.[7] Keith Ward points out, for instance, "it says little of the love of God that he is alleged to be unable to forgive men until they, or others, have paid for their offenses." He goes on to say, "It hardly seems to be 'forgiveness' to insist on the payment of the due penalty first; certainly, a criminal would think it an odd use of the word if a judge said, 'I forgive you for your crime, but you must still serve twenty years.'"[8] Eleonore Stump also points to this problem when she says, "Contrary to what it intends, this version of the doctrine does not, in fact, present God as forgiving human sin," because "to forgive a debtor is to fail to exact all that is in justice due," but in the (penal) substitutionary model, "God does exact every bit of the debt owed to him by human beings; he allows none of it to

---

7. Peter Abelard, for instance, criticizes substitutionary atonement theology in his *Commentary on the Epistle to the Romans*. He says that Jesus's death could not have been a payment to God for our sins because it would make God less moral than human beings: "How very cruel and unjust it seems that someone should require the blood of an innocent person as a ransom, or that in any way it might please him that an innocent person be slain, still less that God should have so accepted the death of his Son that through it he was reconciled to the whole world!" (Peter Abelard, *Commentary on the Epistle to the Romans*, trans. Steven R. Cartwright [Catholic University of America Press, 2011], 167). In his implicit critique of Anselm, Abelard points to the cruelty of God in Anselm's substitutionary atonement and, therefore, finds it untenable.

As I indicated in chapter 4, penal substitutionary atonement is a more specific version of substitutionary atonement that focuses specifically on punishment and relies on a judicial metaphor. Anselm's version of substitutionary atonement relies, instead, on a marketplace metaphor that centers on payment of (monetary) debt. The critiques leveled against substitutionary atonement also apply to penal substitutionary atonement.

8. Keith Ward, *Ethics and Christianity* (Routledge, 2014), 241.

go unpaid." Of course, one could argue in response that it is God who pays the debt. However, as Stump notes, "what it shows is only that God himself arranged for the debt to be paid in full, not that he has agreed to overlook any part of the debt."[9] She demonstrates this point by giving an example. Suppose someone owes another person $1,000. Should the debtor be unable to pay this amount, and the creditor's son or daughter pays it in the debtor's stead, the payment is still made in full, and none of it is actually forgiven. Sharon Baker makes a similar point in *Razing Hell* and helpfully recognizes that substitutionary atonement functions on an "economy of exchange in which God forgives sin only because Jesus somehow pays the debt incurred." Baker points out that this matters because "if we believe God's forgiveness trades in exchange, we will imitate it and withhold grace from those we are commanded to love."[10]

Importantly, for our purposes, this model for atonement models what justice looks like. Many theologians have pointed out that the concept of justice used in this model is retributive as opposed to restorative. J. Denny Weaver, for instance, notes that "satisfaction atonement assumes the violence of retribution."[11] In *The Nonviolent Atonement*, Weaver argues that substitutionary atonement functions on the logic of retributive justice. Retributive justice is then given divine sanction, which deeply impacts our sense of what justice is. The justice system works on "the assumption that justice means punishment," which Weaver defines as a kind of violence. He demonstrates that "a very pervasive use of violence surrounds us in the criminal justice system, a use of violence whose commonness renders it virtually invisible."[12] For Weaver, penal-substitutionary atonement functions to perpetuate retributive justice, which is problematic because of its insistence on violence and punishment as a solution to, ironically, the problem of violence. This God-ordained form of justice has become a standard by which we live and around which we form societal norms. In the next section, I unpack how this model functions to shape how the United States, in particular, dealt with and, despite efforts to the contrary, often still deals with the problem of addiction.

THE MAKING OF A CRIMINAL

In 1971 Nixon famously used the metaphor of war to talk about the problem of addiction. This metaphor would have far-reaching consequences for the way the United States saw and dealt with those suffering from addiction. In his famous speech, Nixon said, "America's public enemy number one in the United States is drug abuse. In order to fight and defeat this enemy, it is necessary to wage a new

---

9. Eleonor Stump, *Aquinas* (Routledge, 2003), 428.
10. Sharon L. Baker, *Razing Hell: Rethinking Everything You've Been Taught about God's Wrath and Judgment* (Westminster John Knox, 2010), 46, 47.
11. J. Denny Weaver, "Violence in Christian Theology," in *Cross Examinations: Readings on the Meaning of the Cross Today*, ed. Marit Trelstad, 1st ed. (Fortress, 2006), 231.
12. J. Denny Weaver, *The Nonviolent Atonement*, 2nd ed. (Eerdmans, 2011), 8.

all-out offensive."[13] Nixon called for "both enforcement and treatment" and allocated significant funds ($155 million) to the effort to eradicate drug use. In his speech, he frequently used words related to war. For instance, he named drug use as an "enemy" and "danger" and planned to "fight and defeat" this enemy by "wag[ing] an offensive" and called for the support of the entire country.[14] In fact, if you left out all the references to drug use, this would sound exactly like a call to actual war.

As I explained in chapter 4, George Lakoff and Mark Johnson note that we live by conceptual metaphors that underlie the language we use.[15] Nixon's speech relies on a root conceptual metaphor that equates dealing with drug abuse with waging war. The problem with the metaphor of war is that wars entail sides and violence. There are enemies, and the goal is to annihilate that enemy. Wars have winners and losers, and in the process of waging them, casualties occur, and sometimes there is even collateral damage. Villages and cities get blown up, structures are destroyed, enemies are imprisoned, and people die. This metaphor of war did not just describe what happened in America's dealing with drug abuse but also prescribed it.

As Michelle Alexander indicates in the film *13th*, where Nixon declared a metaphorical war on drugs, Reagan's drug policies demonstrate a shift from a metaphorical to a literal war on drugs.[16] While Nixon initially proposed both treatment and policing as a strategy to control drug use, "by 1986 roughly 80 percent of the federal drug budget went to policing and prosecuting people."[17] That is, in the Reagan era the war on drugs became a literal war, not just on drugs, but on drug users.

This is indeed one of the problems with the use of the war metaphor. While the initial target of the war was drugs and drug use, it easily shifted over time from drug use to drug users. As Leslie Jamison notes in *The Recovering*, "When Nixon launched the original War on Drugs in June 1971, he called drugs 'public enemy number one.' But it was actual human beings who were imprisoned."[18] The focus shifted from drugs to drug users. While the American drug war efforts were certainly also geared toward stemming the tide of incoming drugs and the distribution of those drugs, the people most impacted were drug users, and particularly drug users in Black communities.

The war metaphor allowed for, and even encouraged, mass incarceration. The judicial system became the primary tool for dealing with the problem of addic-

---

13. Richard Nixon, "President Nixon Declares Drug Abuse 'Public Enemy Number One,'" posted April 29, 2016 by Richard Nixon Foundation, Youtube, 0:0:29, https://youtu.be/y8TGLLQlD9M?feature=shared.
14. Nixon, "President Nixon Declares Drug Abuse 'Public Enemy Number One.'"
15. George Lakoff and Mark Johnson, *Metaphors We Live By* (University of Chicago Press, 2003).
16. *13th*, directed by Ava DuVernay (Kandoo Films, 2016), 0:25:15, https://youtu.be/krfcq5pF8u8?feature=shared.
17. "American Rehab Chapter 5: Reagan with the Snap," *Reveal* (podcast), 0:21:06, accessed October 6, 2020, https://www.revealnews.org/episodes/american-rehab-chapter-5-reagan-with-the-snap/.
18. Leslie Jamison, *The Recovering: Intoxication and Its Aftermath* (Little, Brown, 2018), 80.

tion. Given the war metaphor, it makes sense that Reagan spent much more on eradicating drug users from the streets than on treating drug use. In 1986, for instance, Reagan passed the Anti-Drug Abuse Act, which included mandatory sentences for drug possession. This act allowed for the infamous discrepancy between crack cocaine, smoked mostly by Black people, and powder cocaine, used mostly by white people. This law dictated that people possessing five grams of crack cocaine would be put away for the same amount of time as people possessing five *hundred* grams of powder cocaine.[19] This discrepancy is one of the factors that caused the mass incarceration of Black people, such that "one in three black men had a felony record in 2010."[20] Alexander points out that those who eventually leave prison continue to be beholden to the system through parole, making it impossible to vote and difficult to find homes and jobs. She argues that through the war on drugs and mass incarceration of Black people, the United States created an underclass out of which people could never arise. The devastating and lifetime impact of incarceration in the United States is such that it creates a virtual caste system in which Black people are disproportionately targeted and kept down.[21]

Alexander says that the idea that this war was waged in order to rid "the nation of drug 'kingpins' or big-time dealers" is a myth. Rather, four out of every five drug-related arrests were for possession (not sales), largely of marijuana. She indicates that incarceration levels increased due to the war on drugs between the years 1980 and 2007 from 300,000 to more than 2 million.[22] Gabor Maté makes a similar argument in *In the Realm of Hungry Ghosts*. He says, "In any war there must be enemies." And as in most wars the enemies are not "the generals" or "the masterminds, or the profiteers." Rather, they are "the foot soldiers, the ones who live in the trenches." As a doctor who works with those suffering from addiction in Canada, Maté is well aware of whom the war on drugs targets. He says,

> The man with severe ADHD and learning disabilities, post-traumatic stress disorder, and deeply entrenched drug addiction; with no employment skills; with no history of successful human relationships—this is one of the culprits the police devote their time, skills, and energy to investigating and arresting; about whose misdeeds prosecutors versed in law gather evidence;

19. Al Letson, host, *Reveal*, podcast, "American Rehab," Chapter 5, "Reagan with the Snap," The Center for Investigative Reporting, July 20, 2020, 0:22:10, https://www.revealnews.org/episodes/american-rehab-chapter-5-reagan-with-the-snap.
20. Many, including Leslie Jamison, argue that this was actually the point of the War on Drugs. Referencing the Nixon era in particular, Jamison quotes an interview with "Nixon's domestic policy chief, John Ehrlichman" in which "he said the Nixon administration couldn't make it illegal to be black, but they could link the black community to heroin" and as Ehrlichman is reported to have said "'We could arrest their leaders, raid their homes, break up their meetings, and vilify them night after night on the evening news.'" Apparently Ehrlichman went so far as to say, "'Did we know we were lying about the drugs? Of course we did'" (Jamison, *The Recovering*, 81). As Jamison also clarifies, Ehrlichman's family has denied the ever said these things (Jamison, 469–70). Quotation from Michelle Alexander, *The New Jim Crow: Mass Incarceration in the Age of Colorblindness*, 10th anniversary ed. (New Press, 2020), xxi.
21. Alexander, *The New Jim Crow*.
22. Alexander, *The New Jim Crow*, 76–77.

whom socially conscious and poorly recompensed legal aid defenders assist; and whom learned judges admonish and repeatedly incarcerate. Such is the War on Drugs.[23]

The war on drugs, while intended to wage war against drug abuse, devolved into a war against drug users.

Thus, the war metaphor for dealing with drug use created space for a literal battle to be waged, particularly geared toward Black communities. Beyond the racial discrepancy, however, the war on drugs also proved to be profoundly ineffective in dealing with the problem of drug use. Maté says, "If the goal of the War on Drugs is to discourage or prevent drug use, it has failed. Among young people in North America, drug use has reached unprecedented levels and enjoys unprecedented tolerance."[24] The roughly 440 percent increase in drug overdose deaths between 1999 and 2022 is one indicator of the failure of the war on drugs. Where fewer than 20,000 people died annually from drug overdose deaths in 1999, more than 107,000 people died of drug overdose deaths in 2022.[25] While COVID-19 profoundly affected the number of drug overdose deaths, the CDC noted that US life expectancy declined for the first time in decades long before the pandemic in 2015 and again in 2017. This decline was due in large part to opioid overdoses.[26]

Beyond a failure to curb drug use among those in North America, the war on drugs also failed to end drug trade. Maté notes that "in Afghanistan the production of opium increased nearly 50 percent from 2005 to 2006."[27] Maté argues the war on drugs has not deterred substance use in any way. In fact, the current opioid crisis demonstrates quite the opposite. If anything, all the war on drugs seems to have really achieved is an astronomical prison population. Maté points out that "the United States contains less than 5 percent of the world's population but houses nearly a quarter of the world's prisoners." This astonishing number

23. Gabor Maté, *In the Realm of Hungry Ghosts: Close Encounters with Addiction*, illustrated edition (North Atlantic Books, 2008), 283, 285.
24. Maté, *Realm of Hungry Ghosts*, 289.
25. "Drugs Overdose Deaths: Facts and Figures," National Institute on Drug Abuse, updated August 2024, "U.S. Overdose Deaths by Sex, 1999–2022, Fig. 1," https://nida.nih.gov/research topics /trends-statistics/overdose-death-rates#Fig1. Recent news reports put the 2022 figure a little higher at 111,0000 (Brian Mann, "U.S. Drug Deaths Declined Slightly in 2023 but Remained at Crisis Levels," May 15, 2024, https://www.npr.org/sections/health-shots/2024/05/15/1251239829/us -drug-overdose-deaths-provisional-2023). While these numbers are certainly skewed as a result of the pandemic, these numbers had already risen to unprecedented heights before 2020. By 2019 over 70,000 people died annually of drug overdose deaths. Thankfully, these numbers are currently decreasing. The CDC indicates that drug overdose deaths declined by 24 percent in the period from Oct. 2023 to Sept. 2024. Where Oct. 2022 through Sept. 2023 had approximately 114,000 drug overdose deaths, the period from Oct. 2023 through Sept. 2024 had 87,000 ("CDC Reports Nearly 24% Decline in U.S. Drug Overdose Deaths," CDC, February 25, 2025, https://www.cdc.gov /media/releases/2025/2025-cdc-reports-decline-in-us-drug-overdose-deaths.html#:~:text=New%20 provisional%20data%20from%20CDC%27s,steep%20decline%20in%20overdose%20deaths).
26. "CDC Director's Media Statement on U.S. Life Expectancy," CDC, Nov. 29, 2018, https:// archive.cdc.gov/#/details?url=https://www.cdc.gov/media/releases/2018/s1129-US-life-expectancy.html.
27. Maté, *Realm of Hungry Ghosts*, 291.

is largely due to the war on drugs. As Maté says, "Drugs do not make the addict into a criminal; the law does." He goes on to say that "neither the methods of war nor the war metaphor itself is appropriate to a complex social problem that calls for compassion, self-searching insight, and factually researched scientific understanding."[28] The metaphor of war proved to be an incredibly powerful yet wholly ineffective way to deal with and talk about the issue of drug addiction. It functioned to justify the eradication of those suffering from addiction but did little to actually deal with the issue of drug addiction.

One of the perplexing aspects of the war on drugs is that this large-scale effort to eradicate drug use through the mass incarceration of drug users seemed (and to some still seems) logical to people. As Michelle Alexander and others have pointed out, this is due in large part to rampant racism within the United States. The fact that people responded with much more compassion to the opioid epidemic, which initially affected mostly white communities, than the crack epidemic, which affected mostly Black communities, demonstrates that racism certainly played a central role in the war on drugs. Most people do not like to admit to their own racism, however blatant it may be, and, therefore, need an argument to support racist practices that at least seems logical, even if the main thrust is racist ideologies. Why did the war metaphor make so much sense to people? Pastoral theologian Sonia Waters asks the question this way: "Why would a drug epidemic not inspire other care and justice practices such as healing or reconciliation rather than justify the devaluation of human life?"[29] Waters argues that beyond racist ideologies, this is the case because "the necessity of punishment in the Christian faith is one thread among many that makes punitive responses to drugs seem commonsense and morally appropriate." She points out that penal-substitutionary atonement and the war on drugs are "wound upon similar theological thread," by which "sin must be followed by punishment, whether enacted by God or by God's representatives on earth."[30] Once retributive justice is attributed to God through the metaphor of penal-substitutionary atonement, this form of justice easily takes on divine status.

This happens in part because metaphors tend to work in two directions. As McFague indicates, when we use the metaphor "father" to talk about God, "the feelings we have about fatherhood influence our consequent feelings about God and vice versa."[31] The former is easy to see and, indeed, the point of the metaphor. However, beyond the concept of fatherhood influencing how we see God, our concept of fatherhood is also changed by applying it to God. Mary Daly makes this argument more succinctly: "If God is male, then the male is

---

28. Maté, *Realm of Hungry Ghosts*, 290, 293, 299.
29. Sonia E. Waters, "Punishing the Immoral Other: Penal Substitutionary Logic in the War on Drugs," *Pastoral Psychology* 68, no. 5 (October 1, 2019): 539, https://doi.org/10.1007/s11089-018-0836-y.
30. Waters, "Punishing the Immoral Other," 534.
31. Sallie McFague, *Speaking in Parables* (Augsburg Fortress, 2000), 44.

God."[32] That is, "If God in 'his' heaven is a father ruling 'his' people, then it is in the 'nature' of things and according to the divine plan and the order of the universe that society be male-dominated."[33] Similarly, using the metaphor of the judicial system to talk about atonement gives almost divine power to the retributive judicial system, such that it is hard to imagine it being *un*helpful in dealing with just about any problem. Attaching retributive justice to God gives it divine status. It, therefore, makes sense that this seemingly divinely inspired judicial system was used to deal with the intractable problem of drug addiction.

Penal-substitutionary atonement and the war on drugs work on a similar logic and are equally destructive to those suffering from addiction in that both rely on a punitive response to dealing with the problem of addiction. Waters notes that one of the reasons this metaphor for atonement was so "effective" in the war on drugs is due to its ubiquity. Similar to Van Dyk in *Believing in Jesus Christ*, and Baker and Green in *Recovering the Scandal of the Cross*, Waters recognizes penal-substitutionary atonement as "the most popularized understanding of atonement."[34] She says, "A Christian does not have to possess a well-articulated version of Penal Substitution to be formed through music, sermons, confessional seasons, and songs claiming they are sinners, and that sin is connected to punishment." This retributive version of justice assumes that "one must pay a penalty proportionate to the crime and pay it in full in order to be free from the penalty." Waters notes that a logic of necessity is at play here where a connection "between crime and punishment seems commonsense and implacable."[35] As I pointed out in the last chapter, Ricoeur makes a similar argument in "Interpretation of the Myth of Punishment," where the link between crime and punishment appears divinely ordered. He says that "the sacred sacralizes the juridical," such that retributive justice seems divinely ordered, entirely rational, and necessary.[36]

As Waters argues, if we apply the logic of retributive justice to God, such that even God cannot forgive without some kind of satisfaction, "we have internalized the penal system into God's character and reified it as the essence of justice. God is essentially just, and the essence of justice is penal retribution." Thus, "by logical extension, a just society must also punish crime in order to uphold the order of justice, which is inexorably and inevitably retributive."[37] This is, in fact, exactly what happened in the war on drugs to disastrous effects.

---

32. Mary Daly, *Beyond God the Father: Toward a Philosophy of Women's Liberation* (Beacon Press, 1973), 19.

33. Daly, *Beyond God the Father*, 13.

34. Leanne Van Dyk, *Believing in Jesus Christ* (Geneva, 2002), 86; Mark D. Baker and Joel B. Green, *Recovering the Scandal of the Cross: Atonement in New Testament and Contemporary Contexts* (IVP Academic, 2011), 161; Waters, "Punishing the Immoral Other," 539.

35. Waters, "Punishing the Immoral Other," 539, 540.

36. Paul Ricoeur, "Interpretation of the Myth of Punishment," in *The Conflict of Interpretations: Essays in Hermeneutics*, ed. D. Ihde, trans. Robert Sweeney (Northwestern University Press, 1974), 357.

37. Waters, "Punishing the Immoral Other," 541.

What is important about this for theologies of addiction is that within the Christian faith it is easy to name addiction as sin.[38] After all, where else would one place such a problem that causes people to act in such reckless and often immoral ways (e.g., stealing money or dealing drugs in order to support the addiction)? As I pointed out in chapter 3, many theologians name addiction as a manifestation of original sin. While these theologians would be vehemently opposed to prescribing retributive justice as the antidote to addiction, the fact that they name addiction as a version of sin keeps the door open to this possibility.

This is one reason I shy away from the language of sin in relation to addiction and focus instead on just one aspect of original sin: namely, the bondage of the will. Many people in the pews today no longer have a good sense of what sin is and conflate it with immorality. When I teach adult Sunday school or even seminary classes on sin, I often begin by naming a variety of issues and conditions and ask students whether they would consider these to be sin or not. Most students agree that "stealing" is sin, but when I ask about "kleptomania," they are hesitant to call that sin. When we unpack why this is the case, most argue that stealing is a choice while kleptomania is not. As we delve deeper into a variety of issues, asking whether each is sin or not (e.g., murder, killing in self-defense, killing in war), we usually uncover that students consider things to be sinful only when a person has free will and agency to act otherwise. For most of these students, sin is conflated with immorality. Of course, as I discussed in chapter 2, the Christian notion of sin is far more complicated, driven by the bondage of the will. Original sin does not assume full free will or agency to act otherwise. Theologians who write about sin often offer these nuanced versions of what sin is, and many pastors, especially in the Reformed tradition, when pushed would also likely offer a more complex definition of what sin is. Despite these efforts, however, Christians in the pews largely seem to conflate sin with immorality. Thus, naming addiction sin, even a very nuanced version of sin, leaves the door open to harmful possibilities because people largely hear "immorality" when they hear "sin." This then makes the step from "addiction is sin" and "sin is a crime" to "the addict is a sinner" and "sinners are criminals" an easy one to make. Again, none of the theologians I mention

---

38. Many theologians, in fact, do call addiction sin. Reinhold Niebuhr, for instance, places addiction in the "sensuality" category of sin. He says, "Sensuality represents an effort to escape from the freedom and infinite possibilities of spirit by becoming lost in the detailed processes, activities and interests of existence, an effort which results inevitably in unlimited devotion to limited values" (Reinhold Niebuhr, *The Nature and Destiny of Man*, vol. 1, *Human Nature* [Charles Scribner's Sons, 1964], 185). He treats the question of "drunkenness" specifically and says that "drunkenness is merely a vivid form of the logic of sin which every heart reveals: Anxiety tempts the self to sin; the sin increases the insecurity which it was intended to alleviate until some escape from the whole tension of life is sought" (Niebuhr, *Nature and Destiny of Man*, vol. 1, 235). As I described in chapter 3, other theologians, such as Linda Mercadante, James Nelson, and Kent Dunnington, speak directly about addiction as a type of sin. In each of their cases they do not mean that addiction is a type of moral failure. Rather, they argue that addiction is a manifestation of original sin (Linda Mercadante, *Victims and Sinners* [Westminster John Knox, 1996], James Nelson, *Thirst* [Westminster John Knox, 2004], and Kent Dunnington, *Addiction and Virtue*, [IVP Academic, 2011]).

in chapter 3 (e.g., Mercadante, Nelson, and Dunnington) would advocate for making such a leap, but the fact that they call addiction sin allows this possibility.

As Waters indicates, invoking the judicial metaphor as an appropriate, God-ordained way to deal with sin then makes it easy to punish those with addiction (both literally and figuratively) rather than offer them the care they actually need to heal. In our conception, people with addiction then become guilty, shameful, and in need of punishment. Importantly, the judicial metaphor does not allow for a system in which sin might simply be forgiven or in which sin might be offered the balm of healing. This is partly due to the way metaphors function.

Max Black explains that metaphors (the justice system in this case) create a grid or frame through which we see the target (atonement in this case). This frame highlights certain things about the target and blocks others from view.[39] In other words, the metaphor of the court frames our thinking about sin and sinners, and addiction and those suffering from addiction by extension, in such a way that it highlights punishment and makes it difficult to imagine interacting with sinners or people with addiction in any other way than punitively. The notions of healing and care fall outside the frame and become unthinkable when the driving metaphor is the judicial system. If this were one metaphor among many, this wouldn't be as big of a problem as it is now, because other metaphors would highlight other aspects of salvation, including healing and care.

As has already been demonstrated in the war on drugs, punishing people with addiction is not at all effective in dealing with substance use disorders. And yet, penal-substitutionary atonement is such a pervasive way of thinking about dealing with the problem of sin that we have a theology that doesn't allow us to think about seeing someone with addiction as anything other than a criminal and dealing with addiction in any other way than punishment.

A CACOPHONY OF METAPHORS

As I have already demonstrated in both this chapter and the last, arguments against penal-substitutionary atonement are numerous. Some of those arguments focus on the problematic notion of the necessity of abuse and trauma within the model or the necessity of punishment. Other arguments focus on the deification of surrogacy and sacrifice, and still others on the glorification of violence. There are many issues with this model for atonement, and yet it persists.[40]

McFague makes the radical claim in *Models of God* that "no matter how ancient a metaphorical tradition may be and regardless of its credentials in Scripture, liturgy, and creedal statements, it still must be discarded if it threatens

---

39. Black, *Models and Metaphors*, 41.
40. Portions of this section were previously published in Jennifer Carlier, "Penal Substitutionary Atonement and the Problem of Shame in Addiction," *Pastoral Psychology* 72, no. 5 (July 17, 2023): 659–73, https://doi.org/10.1007/s11089-023-01089-5. Used with permission.

the continuation of life itself."⁴¹ Thus, she argues that metaphors such as, "God, the father" should be eliminated. Further, she notes that the necessities of our time and culture should become the center around which we build models of God. That is not to say that all past models and metaphors are ineffective. Many still speak to the needs of our time. While I would see great value in eliminating the penal-substitutionary model of atonement, I don't think that is likely or even possible. This metaphor is so entrenched in our collective thinking that eradicating it would be akin to asking someone not to think of an elephant. Similar to the metaphor of "God, the father," this metaphor, while demonstrated to be harmful by many theologians, continues to have a hold.

Despite the many critiques against penal-substitutionary atonement, this version of atonement still has staunch support, especially among evangelical Christians.⁴² Further, in my teaching on models of atonement in theology classes at mainline seminaries and churches, I have also found that people often find tremendous comfort in penal-substitutionary atonement and see in it a God of love. Thus, while I find penal-substitutionary atonement harmful for the reasons outlined in this chapter and the last, I recognize that despite the many critiques leveled at it, this version of atonement will likely continue to hold significant power in the Christian faith.

Thus, here I propose something far more modest: I advocate not for eradicating this model altogether but rather for severely limiting its use, recognizing that it is not a literal description of God's work of salvation and that it is not the only or even best way to think about salvation or justice. If it continues to be a prevalent model for thinking about atonement, it is important to recognize that it is simply one model among many others to talk about the mystery of salvation.

Delores Williams poignantly notes that it has always been a "practice . . . to use the language and sociopolitical thought of the time to render Christian principles understandable" in theology.⁴³ Since models and metaphors for salvation are rooted in particular contexts, none is the only way to talk about salvation. Unfortunately, in some circles, penal-substitutionary atonement has become a literal description of what happens in the atonement rather than a metaphor. In that sense, it has become an idol. Because it has become literalized, it is important to limit its use and perhaps abandon its use altogether for a time in public worship in order to remind ourselves that God's salvation is beyond human understanding and that many attempts are necessary to name what happens in salvation. To be clear, I am not suggesting that all versions of substitutionary atonement have become literalized. Anselm's version, for

---

41. McFague, *Models of God*, 68–69.

42. Oliver Crisp, "The Logic of Penal Substitution Revisited," in *The Atonement Debate: Papers from the London Symposium on the Theology of Atonement*, ed. D. Tidball, D. Hilborn, and J. Thacker (Zondervan Academic, 2008), 208; Thomas R. Schreiner, "Penal Substitution View," in *The Nature of the Atonement: Four Views*, ed. J. Beilby and P. R. Eddy (IVP Academic, 2006), 67.

43. Delores Williams, "Black Women's Surrogacy Experience and the Christian Notion of Redemption," in *Cross Examinations: Readings on the Meaning of the Cross Today*, ed. M. Trelstad (Augsburg, 2006), 29.

instance, is not a literalized metaphor. It still has metaphorical power because it is not so prevalent as to be the only way we talk about atonement. I am arguing that the judicial version of substitutionary atonement has become a literalized metaphor.

A first and admittedly incredibly difficult step is, therefore, to limit its use, especially in public worship. Churches can, for instance, limit the use of liturgies and hymns that draw on judicial images of salvation. A second equally important and difficult step is to embrace the fact that many metaphors for atonement and salvation are necessary to name the complexity of God's salvific power. This is, of course, not a new proposition. After all, there are many theologies of salvation to choose from. Among these are the many varieties of *Christus Victor*, including ransom theory; (non-judicial) varieties of substitutionary atonement; moral influence theory; solidarity with and vindication of the oppressed; and the many metaphors that do not focus on the cross (e.g., the exodus story and the metaphor of "making a way out of no way").[44] What I argue, however, that is different from some theologians who write about salvation is that *all* these theories reach for ways of talking about the truth that God redeems and frees those in bondage. Some of these theories are, in our current climate, more harmful than others, and some must be limited, if not eliminated, yet all of them, at different moments in history and in different circumstances, spoke and speak to their communities of the redemptive power of God.

We don't have to choose a single metaphor for salvation as *the* correct way of viewing atonement or salvation. In fact, we have to do the opposite. Like the Bible itself, we must embrace the multiplicity of metaphors available to talk about salvation. That message—that God redeems those who feel irredeemable, frees the bound, and heals the broken—is a message worth speaking in as many metaphors as necessary so that those who need it most are able to take it in. *How* exactly salvation works and what the role of the cross is or isn't in God's acts of redemption are beyond human knowledge. Hence, I propose that all we

---

44. For examples of *Christus Victor* including ransom theory, see Aulén, *Christus Victor*; James Cone, *The Cross and the Lynching Tree* (Orbis Books, 2013); Gregory of Nyssa, "The Great Catechism" in *Nicene and Post-Nicene Fathers: Second Series, Vol. 5 -- Gregory of Nyssa: Dogmatic Treatises,* ed. Philip Schaff and Henry Wallace, trans. William Moore and Henry Austin Wilson (Christian Literature, 1893), I.24; Weaver, *Nonviolent Atonement.* For an example of non-judicial substitutionary atonement, see Anselm, *Cur Deus Homo,* in *Anselm: Basic Writings,* ed. and trans. Thomas Williams (Hackett, 2007), 237-326. For examples of moral influence theory, see Abelard, "Commentary on the Epistle to the Romans"; JoAnn Marie Terrell, *Power in the Blood* (Orbis Books, 1998). For examples of theories that rely on solidarity with and vindication of the oppressed, see (beyond those already named) Kelly Brown Douglas, *The Black Christ* (Orbis Books, 1994); Kelly Brown Douglas, *Resurrection Hope: A Future Where Black Lives Matter* (Orbis Books, 2021); Jacquelyn Grant, *White Women's Christ and Black Women's Jesus: Feminist Christology and Womanist Response* (Scholars Press, 1989); Jon Sobrino, *Christ the Liberator: A View from the Victims* (Orbis Books, 2001). For examples of theologies of salvation that don't rely on the cross, see Monica Coleman, *Making a Way Out of No Way* (Fortress, 2008); Delores Williams, *Sisters in the Wilderness: The Challenge of Womanist God-Talk* (Orbis Books, 1993). Note that many of the above-mentioned theologians cannot be pinned down to a single theology of salvation and while they are illustrative of the theories named, they often also move beyond them.

can do is reach with as many metaphors as necessary toward the truth that God does redeem the broken. The Bible and the Christian tradition at large have a plethora of metaphors to rely on to speak about atonement and salvation, and each of these metaphors and models has explanatory power, and each uses the symbols and language of its current context to render God's redemption to a new generation. Further, with McFague I argue that it is also necessary to continue to create metaphors. Many metaphors are necessary to reach toward the truth that God redeems the broken.

CONCLUSION

Since I have just dedicated two chapters to unpacking how the penal substitutionary metaphor for salvation is harmful both in content and by its ubiquity for those with addiction (and for a host of other people), I am keenly aware that not all metaphors for salvation are equally useful and that we need some way of evaluating our metaphors. As has always been the case for theologians, I too rely on Scripture, the work of those who have come before me, communities of accountability, as well as my experiences and the experiences of those around me to get a sense of whether a metaphor is likely to cause harm or not. Further, I listen as best I can to how those around me, and those not around me, to hear and absorb the metaphors we use to talk about God. This is one of the reasons I cannot make the argument that penal-substitutionary atonement must be fully eradicated. It clearly helps some people experience God's love and redemption. At the same time, I am hesitant to use such a metaphor in public worship as it has great potential to cause harm to at least some sitting in the pews. With feminist, queer, womanist, and liberation theologians, I look for metaphors that promote the flourishing of all creation.

McFague provides a powerful model for this process of using and evaluating metaphors and models to talk about God in her third work on metaphor, *Models of God*. She argues that metaphorical theology is heuristic in nature. The main thrust of this theology is that it "supports the assertion that our concept of God is precisely that—*our concept* of God—and not God." Mistaking our concept of God for God is the very definition of idolatry. A heuristic theology takes an "adverbial" approach to thinking about God and is concerned more with "how we relate to God" than with "defining the nature of God."[45] McFague describes this heuristic approach as one that is based on experience and investigates which metaphors are most appropriate for our time. For McFague, and for me, the Bible is authoritative insofar as it is a "model of how theology should be done, rather than an authority dictating the terms in which it is done."[46] That is, I do not have to resonate with all the images the Bible uses to talk about God.

45. McFague, *Models of God*, 37, 39.
46. McFague, *Models of God*, 43.

Some are more harmful in my context (e.g., God as judge) than they perhaps were in previous contexts. The question we should be asking is, therefore, not "What does the Bible say?" but rather "What should we be doing for our time that would be comparable to what Paul and John did for theirs?"[47] As Delores Williams poignantly points out, this is the way theology has always been done. We rely on Scripture and at the same time ask what it means to say that God redeems the broken in our current time and place. This approach is, of course, not a watertight approach that ensures all metaphors we choose and use speak equally well to the profound mystery of salvation. Some will fall flat, and some may even cause unintentional harm. This is a process of reflection and praxis and like all theologies will sometimes fail. However, the more we rely on the wealth of metaphors available to us to talk about salvation, the more likely the web of metaphors we retrieve, create, and use will reach toward the truth of this mystery, recognizing that we never fully arrive. In the next chapter, I explore one such metaphor in hope that it may add to the many voices and metaphors that speak to the power of redemption, especially for those with addiction.

---

47. McFague, *Models of God*, 30.

Chapter 6

Salvation Is a Journey through No-Man's-Land

In her memoir *Lit*, Mary Karr describes a moment in her recovery when "suicide as an idea seeps into [her] lungs like nerve gas." She says, "Picking up a drink would betray everybody who's poured effort into my sobriety . . . but death—now, there's a one-stop-shopping idea." Suicide slowly becomes a fixation. "It becomes the one rabbit hole that will hide me,"[1] she says. Instead, Karr drives herself to the hospital and checks herself into a psychiatric ward. That first night, she "tiptoe[s] to the bathroom, and bend[s] onto the cold tiles" and prays: "If you're God . . . you know I feel small and needy and inadequate. And tonight I want a drink."[2]

Karr's prayer echoes the prayers of many people with addiction. Many find themselves at some moment so overwhelmed by the anguish of addiction that whether they believe in God or not, they pray for God's help. I demonstrated in the last chapters that penal-substitutionary atonement does not offer the balm to heal these wounds. After all, what magnificent cruelty would it be if God had told Karr that she is indeed inadequate, so much so that she is a criminal deserving of God's wrath? Even the good news that Jesus takes on her punishment seems a

---

1. Mary Karr, *Lit* (Harper Perennial, 2009), 261.
2. Karr, *Lit*, 275.

flawed response to the vulnerability she offers God. In this chapter, I propose that the response Karr needs is that God heals the broken and frees those in bondage, and I provide a sustained reflection on the story of the exodus as an extended metaphor that offers hope to those with addiction and resonates with experiences of recovery. Before diving into the exodus story, however, I want to clarify a few terms that I rely on heavily in this chapter.

CLARIFYING TERMS

Salvation

In the last two chapters, I focused on one prevalent way of thinking about salvation that is encapsulated by the term atonement. In this chapter I focus instead on the broader category of salvation. Relying on the language of "at-one-ment," atonement suggests that the problem that salvation seeks to address is one of a breach or rift between God and humans. While it is true that many people *feel* separated from God, I strongly disagree with the notion that people are, in reality, ever separated from God. While it is often difficult to recognize God's presence, as we will see in the story of the exodus, God is still present. The term "atonement," with its emphasis on reconciliation or bridging a gap between humans and God, is unhelpful because it keeps the harmful myth alive that it is possible for humans to be separated from God (because of sin, for instance).

Since I have framed the problem of addiction as one of bondage, I rely instead on terms that connote freedom, such as redemption, liberation, and salvation. Further, I use these terms instead of atonement because atonement is often (though not exclusively) associated with the death of Jesus Christ on the cross and focuses primarily on justification. While salvation is centered in the work of Jesus Christ in Christian theology, it includes all of God's redemptive acts and encapsulates both the theological categories of justification and sanctification. It is important to recognize this, lest we limit metaphors of salvation to be interpretations solely of the life, ministry, death, and resurrection of Jesus Christ. The Hebrew Bible is, after all, full of stories of salvation.[3]

Finally, it is important to note that when I talk about salvation, liberation, and redemption in this and the next chapter, I am concerned primarily with salvation in the here and now. As many liberation, feminist, and womanist theologians have argued, if salvation simply signifies a hope for an afterlife, it becomes easy to maintain cycles of oppression. As James Cone notes in *A Black Theology of Liberation*, if "the 'hope' that is offered the oppressed is not the possibility of changing their earthly condition but a longing for

---

3. These include (among many others) the stories of Noah (Gen. 6–9), Hagar (Gen. 21:8–21), the exodus (Exod.), Ruth (Ruth), David (1 Sam. 17), Esther (Esth.), Shadrach, Meshach, and Abednego (Dan. 3:19–30), Daniel (Dan. 6), and Jonah (Jonah).

the next life," then "with the poor counting on salvation in the next life, oppressors can humiliate and exploit without fear of reprisal."[4] It becomes far too easy to accept the status quo, even if that status quo is harmful, when salvation is pushed off to the eschaton. Kelly Brown Douglas, for instance, demonstrates in *The Black Christ* that uncoupling the Jesus of history from the Jesus of salvation made it possible for enslavers to preach salvation without freeing the enslaved people. Salvation was seen as abstract and otherworldly. Thus, "Jesus's salvation had nothing to do with historical freedom," or so the enslavers reasoned.[5] It is precisely to prevent this kind of reasoning that it is important to recognize salvation as being intimately connected to the present moment even as it points to the hope of things to come. Thus, for Cone, Douglas, and many other Black, liberation, and womanist theologians, salvation, while it includes the hope of eternal life, must primarily be about liberation in the here and now.[6]

Similarly, when I talk about salvation in the coming section and next chapter, I am talking primarily about a present reality. It is not enough to tell people with addiction that there's hope in the afterlife. There must be hope in the present moment as well. In the conclusion of the book, however, I also focus on salvation beyond the here and now. The hope of salvation speaks to both our present and future realities.

Extended Metaphors

As I am reading the exodus story as an extended metaphor, it is important to pause and gain clarity on what exactly I mean by this term, especially since extended metaphors are variously defined within the literature on metaphors. I use it in this context to refer to a story that functions as a metaphor. As I indicated in previous chapters, metaphors are living entities that change their shape and meaning all the time. Similarly, extended metaphors are complex. They are

---

4. James H. Cone, *A Black Theology of Liberation*, 40th anniversary ed. (Orbis Books, 2010), 126.

5. Kelly Brown Douglas, *The Black Christ*, 25th anniversary ed. (Orbis Books, 2019), Adobe Digital Editions, 32.

6. Monica Coleman, for instance, says that salvation brings about "survival, quality of life, and the holistic transformation of the world" (Monica A. Coleman, *Making a Way Out of No Way: A Womanist Theology* [Fortress, 2008], 12). More specifically, Jacquelyn Grant sees salvation as enacting "freedom from sociopsychological, psychocultural, economic and political oppression of Black people" (Jacquelyn Grant, *White Women's Christ and Black Women's Jesus: Feminist Christology and Womanist Response* [Scholars Press, 1989], 215). Likewise, Jon Sobrino argues that Jesus Christ's bodily resurrection shows a commitment to "the values of *corporeality*" as opposed to "a soul liberated from the body" as would have been the more common interpretation at the time (Jon Sobrino, *Christ the Liberator: A View from the Victims*, trans. Paul Burns [Orbis Books, 2001], 12, [italics in the original]). Given this commitment it would be odd to presume that the "eschatological had come about in history" through Jesus Christ's bodily resurrection "but that it had no effect on our present life—except in hope" (Sobrino, *Christ the Liberator*, 14). All these theologians point to the recognition that salvation is not just a hope for a better afterlife but also a commitment to the redemption and sanctification of life in the here and now.

not allegories in which "this" in the story represents "that" in theology. In other words, you can't read it in the way you would read *The Pilgrim's Progress*.[7]

My reading of the exodus story as an extended metaphor is heavily influenced by Sallie McFague's notion of how extended metaphors function. In *Speaking in Parables* she focuses on parables as extended metaphors and says, "To say, then, that a New Testament parable is an extended metaphor means not that the parable 'has a point' or teaches a lesson, but that it is itself what it is talking about (there is no way *around* the metaphor to what is 'really' being said)."[8] She goes on to argue, "The parables accept the complexity and ambiguity of life as lived here in this world and insist that it is in *this* world that God makes his gracious presence known."[9] Again, this is different from an allegory. That is "the story is 'thick,' not transparent; like a painting, it is looked *at*, not through."[10] We do not look *through* the story in order to find the deeper meaning. Rather, the story takes you into itself and *is* the deeper meaning. The exodus story functions as an extended metaphor in that it takes us into the story and allows us to see salvation anew.

In exploring the exodus story, I offer what Sallie McFague calls an "intermediary theology." This is not a systematic account of salvation nor a robust exegetical exploration of the exodus story. Rather, I seek to weave together contemporary experiences of recovery with the story of the exodus to come to a greater understanding of what it means to say that we believe in a God who redeems the broken and frees those in bondage. McFague names her indebtedness to Michael Novak, who, in a letter to her, describes what she names intermediary theology. He says, "In between imaginative literature and academic theology there is a form of intelligence which is precise, discursive, and analytical, but also in touch with concrete experience and with the imagination. *That* is the model for academic intelligence." McFague is concerned that when theology becomes purely theoretical and systematic, it divorces itself from lived experiences, "making it more difficult if not impossible for us to believe in our hearts what we confess with our lips." Instead, she argues for a theology "which relies on various literary forms—parables, stories, poems, confessions."[11] This is the kind of theological reflection I aim to offer in this section. Thus, as I have done throughout the book, I rely on a mix of theological explorations of bondage and salvation, stories of addiction and recovery, and theories of addiction as I read the exodus story to come to an understanding of what it means to say that God saves.

To say that the exodus story is an extended metaphor for salvation is to say that it is in reading the story that salvation is revealed. In the following sections, I engage this story alongside the stories of recovery in the memoirs, in part to

---

7. John Bunyan, *Pilgrim's Progress*, rev. ed. (Wordsworth Editions, 1999).
8. Sallie McFague, *Speaking in Parables* (Augsburg Fortress, 2000), 5.
9. McFague, *Speaking in Parables*, 7.
10. McFague, *Speaking in Parables*, 5.
11. McFague, *Speaking in Parables*, 2–3.

demonstrate that this is a particularly apt metaphor for those with addiction and in part to demonstrate that these stories, as they interweave with one another, show us the complexity of what salvation looks like in this world. Together, these stories draw us into themselves, engage us at a deeper level, and name those places where God's salvific power is at work, even in the midst of the complexities and heartbreak of life. As with all metaphors, this metaphor does not name the full breadth of God's saving power. However, I offer it as one metaphor that aptly takes into account some of the concerns I've raised thus far. That is, it offers a helpful solution to the problem of bondage and resonates with experiences of addiction and recovery, thereby validating these experiences while removing some of the shame and stigma associated with addiction. The stories do not offer a clear and systematic theology of soteriology but rather draw us into these experiences to see for ourselves what it means to be saved.

After a brief reflection on the complexity of the narrative of the exodus itself, I offer a reflection in three parts. In the first part (Exod. 1–14), I explore the themes of seeing rightly and being seen as metaphors for salvation. In the second (Exod.15–18), I focus on the metaphor of salvation as a journey away from bondage, and in the last (Exod. 19–40), on salvation as a journey toward freedom. While each of these parts highlights a different facet of salvation, they all flow into each other. That is, the Israelites aren't done with journeying *away from* bondage in the last section. The focus just shifts *toward* living in freedom.

THE EXODUS STORY AS EXTENDED METAPHOR

As we explore each of the three parts of the story and the broad themes therein, it is important to pause and take note of the biblical book's complexity. On the one hand, this story is the story of God's freeing of the Israelites from slavery. Indeed, God is demonstrated to be the God of freedom in this story in powerful ways. James Cone points out in *God of the Oppressed* that in the exodus story "God discloses that he is the God of history whose will is identical with the liberation of the oppressed from social and political bondage."[12] Likewise, Kelly Brown Douglas makes the important point in her work *Stand Your Ground* that this story (among others) attests to God as being fundamentally the God of freedom. She notes that God's act of seeing and then freeing the Israelites attests to God's "preferential option . . . for freedom."[13] Douglas explains that enslaved people in the antebellum period relied on spirituals that attested to freedom in the exodus story, in particular, as both "God's presence in their lives as well as God's very nature."[14] Where white American enslavers saw themselves as God's

---

12. James Cone, *God of the Oppressed* (Harper & Row, 1975), 65.
13. Kelly Brown Douglas, *Stand Your Ground* (Orbis Books, 2015), 162.
14. Douglas, *Stand Your Ground*, 143.

chosen people, those who were enslaved recognized that this could not possibly be the case as God is, in God's nature, a God of freedom.

At the same time, this story and the notion that God is a God of freedom is far from straightforward. As Delores Williams notes in *Sisters in the Wilderness*, while God frees the Israelites from slavery in Egypt, "the end result of the biblical exodus event . . . was the violent destruction of a whole nation of people, the Canaanites, described in the book of Joshua."[15] She also points out that "there is no clear indication that God is against . . . [the] perpetual enslavement" of non-Jewish people. "Likewise, there is no clear opposition expressed in the Christian testament to the institution of slavery."[16] She is, therefore, cautious of theologies that link themselves too closely with the exodus event while ignoring the oppression that occurs at the hand of the Israelites at God's instruction.

Kelly Brown Douglas recognizes these same themes yet says that "it could always be the case that the biblical story of the takeover of Canaan says more about the people telling it than it does about God." This was, after all, certainly the case when the enslavers read the biblical story as being supportive of slavery. Douglas ultimately reads the Bible through the lens of "a belief in the freedom of God,"[17] which allows her to question those parts of the biblical story that do not align with the actions of a God of freedom. What both Douglas and Williams raise is the complexity of reading and interpreting Scripture. We are, for better and worse, always reading the biblical story through the lens of our contexts, experiences, and convictions. With Douglas, I read the story of the destruction of those in Canaan as more indicative of the people's will than God's. I return to this theme again later in this chapter when I talk about God's punishment of the people after the golden calf incident. I raise this here to recognize that the exodus story is by no means a pure story of freedom. It is complex, and I want to be sure to recognize this complexity even as I rely on this story as profoundly liberative for those with addiction.

Further, I want to be careful here to note that the exodus story focuses on the physical enslavement and oppression of a people. The connections that Douglas makes are, thus, literal connections. Where Douglas draws out *literal* parallels between the exodus story and those of enslaved people in America, I am drawing out a *metaphorical* connection, pointing out resonances between the physical enslavement of the Israelites in the exodus story and the metaphorical enslavement of those with addiction in full recognition that these are not identical experiences. As with all metaphors there is an "is" and "is not" quality to this extended metaphor. There are moments when the experiences of the Israelites in slavery resonate with experiences of addiction (the "is" quality of the metaphor) while still being very different experiences (the "is not" quality of the metaphor). In reading the story of the exodus, and in reading Douglas's interpretation of

---

15. Delores Williams, *Sisters in the Wilderness: The Challenge of Womanist God-Talk* (Orbis Books, 1993), 150.
16 .Williams, *Sisters in the Wilderness*, 146.
17. Douglas, *Stand Your Ground*, 162.

it, I am seeing something about who God is that may offer hope to those with addiction. That is, God sees those who are suffering and has a deep concern for and a desire to free those in bondage. This is the message of hope that churches can offer those with addiction.

Part I—Exodus 1–14: Salvation Is Seeing Rightly and Being Seen with Compassion

The story of the exodus begins with a description of the Israelites' descent into slavery.[18] A "new king arose over Egypt, who did not know Joseph" (Exod. 1:8-9), so the story begins. This new king feared the growth and power of the Israelites in Egypt and decided to enslave the people: "The Egyptians subjected the Israelites to hard servitude and made their lives bitter with hard servitude in mortar and bricks and in every kind of field labor. They were ruthless in the tasks that they imposed on them" (Exod. 1:13–14). The repetition of the words "hard servitude" and the use of the words "ruthless" and "bitter" emphasize the desperate plight of the Israelites.[19] They were forced into hard labor, working with mortar and bricks.

The Israelites, crushed in body and spirit by their oppressors, "groaned under their slavery and cried out" (Exod. 2:23). Their cry for help is the beginning of the journey of salvation in the exodus story.[20] In the depths of despair, the Israelites cry out for help. The story in Exodus continues, "Their cry for help rose up to God from their slavery. God heard their groaning, and God remembered his covenant with Abraham, Isaac, and Jacob" (Exod. 2:23–24). And then, there is perhaps the most beautiful verse in all of Scripture: "God *looked* upon the Israelites, and God *took notice* of them" (Exod. 2:25).[21] Terence Fretheim notes in his commentary on Exodus that seeing in this context doesn't just mean "eye contact" but rather "mov[ing] towards the other with kindness and sympathy." God saw their anguish and heard their cry of desperation and took notice. Others translate "took notice" in Exodus 2:25 with "knew." Fretheim notes that knowing here is not referencing

---

18. Critics and commentators disagree on the historicity of the exodus story, with some saying the story is more likely an origin myth than historical account. As a theologian, I cannot do and not weigh into this debate. This question is far outside my field of expertise and interest. Rather, I read the exodus as a narrative in this chapter and see in it what Carol Meyers calls a "core of reality," (p. 10) whether historically accurate or not. (Carol Meyers, *Exodus,* The New Cambridge Bible Commentary [Cambridge University Press, 2005], 1–12.)

19. Terence E. Fretheim, *Exodus,* Interpretation: A Bible Commentary for Teaching and Preaching (John Knox, 1991), 30.

20. Interestingly, this is also the one place where Augustine would claim that we have freedom of the will. That is, while we cannot do or even will the good on our own, Augustine says that we do have the freedom to will the good. We can ask for help. Of course, Reformed theologians such as John Calvin would argue that even the desire to cry out for help is a gift of grace. See chapter 2 for a full exploration of this topic.

21. I have italicized the word "see" ("looked") from the exodus story in several places in this chapter to indicate that these words all come from the same root word in Hebrew (*raah*). Likewise, I have italicized the word "know" ("took notice") in this chapter to indicate that these words all come from the same root word in Hebrew (*yada*).

"'head knowledge,' as if God gained some new information or insight into what is happening," but rather it means "to so share an experience with another that the other's experience can be called one's own."[22]

The beginning of the book of Exodus explores the themes of seeing and knowing at length.[23] When Moses was born, his mother "*saw* that he was a fine baby" (Exod. 2:2) and hid him from Pharaoh, who was killing all male babies. As he gets bigger and his mother is unable to continue hiding him, she puts him in a basket in the river. Eventually, Pharaoh's daughter "*saw* the basket" (Exod. 2:5) and "when she opened it, she *saw* the child" (Exod. 2:6) and took him in as her own. Moses's life is a miracle in that he should have been killed at Pharaoh's hand, and yet he survives because he is seen at crucial moments and looked after by both the women in his family and Pharaoh's daughter. Moses is saved through acts of seeing. Thus, the implication of God seeing the Israelites and their suffering and taking notice (Exod. 2:25) is that it will likewise bring about their salvation.

We often underestimate the power of being seen. Even without a solution, being seen can, in and of itself, provide a healing balm. I remember the first time someone in recovery listened to my story and then reflected back a particular feeling of anguish I had felt that I had not even fully acknowledged for myself. It felt as if she had reached her hand inside me and touched my very soul. In recognizing my pain, she communicated to me that I was no longer alone. In a society that focuses on fixing things, we often overlook the importance of simply seeing and hearing another person.

People who are suffering often struggle with friends who offer advice yet fail to sit with them and truly see the anguish of living with the condition that they are suffering from. Advice is often given as a way of *not* being present, of *not* having to see another person's pain. This happens to Job, for instance, when his friends sit with him after he loses everything. They offer explanations and advice and fail to take notice of their friend who is in pain. Being seen is crucial.

Parker Palmer talks about the importance of being seen in one of his blog posts. He says, "The human soul doesn't want to be advised or fixed or saved. It simply wants to be witnessed—to be seen, heard and companioned exactly as it is. When we make that kind of deep bow to the soul of a suffering person, our respect reinforces the soul's healing resources, the only resources that can help the sufferer make it through."[24] Palmer is talking specifically about the healing friends can offer those who are struggling. In that particular context (of friendship) his notion that we do not want to be fixed or saved seems correct. Instead, we want to be seen, and there is something deeply meaningful and healing about having another person witness our suffering.

---

22. Fretheim, *Exodus*, 48.
23. I am indebted to Christine Roy Yoder for this insight. She helped me see it, if you will.
24. Parker Palmer, "The Gift of Presence, The Perils of Advice," *On Being*, April 27, 2016, https://onbeing.org/blog/the-gift-of-presence-the-perils-of-advice/.

This is especially important for those with addiction because they are so often *not* seen. As I pointed out in chapter 3, part of the problem that those with addiction face is that of being stigmatized and "othered." Stigmatization happens when we are not fully seen. Timothy McMahan King writes about the way people see those with addiction in *Addiction Nation*. He says when others see someone with addiction, they often see the person as *only* an "addict." He says, "We become aware of the way we are being seen, but also of all the ways that we are *not* being seen."[25] The person suffering is seen through a particular lens and then categorized as "addict." Healing begins when the person with addiction is seen in their fullness, and part of that fullness for someone with an addiction is being seen as someone who is not just engaging in maladaptive and perhaps even illegal behaviors but also seen as someone who has and is enduring profound suffering. This is the healing balm that God offers the Israelites in Exodus 2:25—God bears witness to the suffering of the Israelites. I take note of this moment of God's recognition of their suffering, not because it is the only thing the Israelites needed, but because it the very thing we often fail to do. We tend to go straight to fixing a problem without taking the time to truly see the person first.

Of course, the story doesn't end here. God's act of seeing is the beginning of the story of Isreal's salvation. Expanding on the theme of seeing, the book of Exodus shows that God first teaches Moses to see clearly. Early in the story, Moses, a Hebrew boy, secretly raised by Pharaoh's daughter, has an encounter with his own people and "*saw* their forced labor" (Exod. 2:11) While out walking, "He *saw* an Egyptian beating a Hebrew, one of his own people," and in an effort to help him, Moses "looked this way and that, and *seeing* no one he killed the Egyptian and hid him in the sand" (Exod. 2:11–12). This brief interlude is interesting in that it completely backfires. When Moses sees "two Hebrews fighting" the next day and asks why they are fighting each other, one of them turns to him and says, "Who made you a ruler and judge over us? Do you mean to kill me as you killed the Egyptian?" (Exod. 2:13–14). Moses, recognizing that they saw him, goes into hiding. Word even gets to Pharaoh, who "sought to kill Moses" (Exod. 2:15). While this interlude spans just four verses, it raises an interesting theme that is prevalent in addiction literature around the capacity of others to step in and "save" the person with addiction.

As a person with addiction, I have many friends who suffer from addiction, some of whom have long-term sobriety, and some of whom continue to suffer from sometimes lengthy and dangerous relapses. A common impulse for me and most who love people with addiction is to attempt to step in and "fix" the problem, whether by housing the person with addiction in order to keep an eye on their use or compelling the person to go to rehab. It is painful to watch another person suffer, and the impulse to "fix" the problem is normal. However,

---

25. Timothy McMahan King, *Addiction Nation: What the Opioid Crisis Reveals about Us* (Herald, 2019), 46 (italics in the original).

as I have learned through many failed attempts to help friends, I cannot fix this for another person, and attempting to do so often creates messy situations, not least because addiction is a complex problem, of which I often only see a part. I have learned that I can point toward resources, encourage the person to seek help, tell my own story, and walk alongside the person as they seek help.

In this brief episode, Moses takes things into his own hands without full recognition of the scope of the problem he is trying to fix and creates more problems for himself and perhaps also for the Israelites, though the passage does not say anything about this. Over time, Moses learns that he cannot simply step in and save his kinfolk. He has a role to play in their salvation, as do the Israelites themselves, but salvation is ultimately God's work. Our attempts to single-handedly save others, whether from addiction or other afflictions, is one more example of the condition of brokenness that we live in, whereby we sometimes think ourselves to be like God. This short interlude in Exodus reminds us that we are not God.

While Moses saw the suffering of his people rightly, he did not appropriately see his role in their salvation. God then teaches Moses to see rightly, by appearing in a burning bush. Moses "*looked*, and the bush was blazing, yet it was not consumed. Then Moses said, 'I must turn aside and *look* at this great sight and see why the bush is not burned up. When the LORD *saw* that he had turned aside to *see*, God called to him out of the bush . . ." (Exod. 3:2–4). God then tells Moses, "I have *observed* the misery of my people who are in Egypt; I have heard their cry on account of their taskmasters. Indeed, I *know* their sufferings, and I have come down to deliver them from the Egyptians . . ." (Exod. 3:7–8). Exodus 3:7–8 sounds similar to Exodus 2:25 in that God does not only see the suffering (as Moses does), but rather both sees *and* knows their suffering. Moses sees from the outside, but God sees from the outside and from the inside. That is, God doesn't just see it from a distance but knows it intimately and, beyond that, has the power to act. God has seen the same suffering that Moses saw and, unlike Moses, has the power to free the people. God chooses to use Moses to free the Israelites and sends Aaron and Moses to Pharaoh to negotiate their freedom on God's behalf.

What follows is a negotiation between Moses and Aaron and Pharaoh, in which all parties must learn to see appropriately. When Moses's initial request to Pharaoh to "let [God's] people go" (Exod. 5:1) falls on deaf ears and Pharaoh instead increases the labor of the enslaved people, the "Israelite supervisors *saw* that they were in trouble" and said to Moses and Aaron, "'The LORD *look* upon you and judge! You have brought us into bad odor with Pharaoh and his officials and put a sword in their hand to kill us'" (Exod. 5:19, 21). Moses and Aaron arrive to bring salvation, and yet instead of freedom, they bring the people even more hardship.

Where atonement theologies often present salvation as a once-and-done event that happens outside the human realm (e.g., Jesus dies on the cross as a substitute for humans), the exodus story paints a picture of salvation that is far more complicated. Salvation doesn't just happen to the Israelites. They are, for better or worse, involved in and affected by the process of salvation itself. When Moses's first attempt fails, the stronghold of evil on the Israelites' lives becomes even more intense, and their lives become significantly worse. This notion that the beginning of salvation initially brings about more hardship resonates with the experiences of those with addiction as well. Those suffering often find that the moment they seek to disentangle themselves from the addiction, it reaches out and pulls them in even further. Indeed, the rest of the story of Moses's negotiation with Pharaoh exemplifies the difficulty of disentangling oneself from captivity.

What follows Moses's initial request to "let the people go" is a lengthy negotiation between Moses and Pharaoh. Time and time again, Moses and Aaron demonstrate God's intention to free the Israelites and God's power to do so through a series of death-dealing signs and miracles. Each of these mighty acts (e.g., turning the Nile to blood, the plague of frogs, the killing of livestock, covering the land in darkness, etc.) is a sign of death because Pharaoh will not let go of those in captivity until he is shown again and again that failure to let go will result in death. Through these signs, Moses attempts to train Pharaoh to see rightly.

Throughout the story, Pharaoh, overwhelmed by the plague of the day, has a moment of remorse, agrees to let the people go, and asks Moses to intercede on his behalf. Yet, time and time again, "when Pharaoh saw that there was a respite, he hardened his heart and would not listen to them" (Exod. 8:14). Salvation, it seems, is not easily won. Indeed, most metaphors for salvation seem to agree on this theme. Jesus' passion and horrific death on the cross paint a grueling picture of what salvation requires. It seems that the forces of evil (whether they be the forces of empire, an evil king, or evil itself) tenaciously cling to us.

When I read the story of the exodus through the lens of addiction, I tend to see those with addiction as most similar to the Israelites. Yet, there are also moments when I see resonances with Pharaoh. Recall that intermediary theologies are not clean and tidy. This is not an allegory where we can tidily match the experiences of those with addiction to the experiences of the Israelites. Rather, I read this story as a complex metaphor. It is in seeing the story in all its messiness that we come to see who the God of salvation is.

This process of making promises to release the Israelites and of bargaining is very similar to the process of early recovery. Terrible things happen to people who suffer from addiction. Many find themselves living from crisis to crisis, much like Pharaoh. They are confronted time and time again with signs of unmanageability, and often, these painful signs lead them to make promises of sobriety, only to break them once there is respite from the current crisis. Mary Karr describes such a crisis moment when she has six beers, puts a pot roast in the oven, and leaves the house with her young son, only to find the oven smoking and the fire alarm on when she gets home, having forgotten all about the roast. In the process of dealing with this crisis, she yells at her son and lies to her husband once he comes home. She says, "The night ends with a black smudge, and come dawn, I stand in a cloud of shower steam, the former night's conviction to quit solid, though it's daunting to face unmedicated whatever's beyond the plastic curtain I'm scared to draw aside." She goes on to say, "By afternoon, I can't abide Mr. Rogers asking me to be my neighbor without a cocktail."[26] Each new mini-crisis leads to a conviction that it is time to stop drinking. Yet, with each moment of respite after the crisis is over, the conviction loses its potency, and she picks up another drink. Heather King describes a similar process in *Parched*: "Every once in a while, I'd resolve to go on the wagon," she says, "but this never lasted very long." This happened once "after a particularly vicious bender." She says, "I ended up at Mass General with strep throat and a finger I vaguely remember having slashed on a bottle . . . that needed stitches." After this experience she thought, "That's it . . . I have *got* to cut down."[27] Of course, she begins drinking again within a few days. This stage of making promises to change and yet going back on those promises is very common in addiction.

A common model for talking about this is the preparation stage in James O. Prochaska and Carlo D. DiClemente's transtheoretical model.[28] DiClemente and Prochaska propose five stages of change. In the first stage, the precontemplation stage, the person has no intention to make a healthy behavioral change. The second stage, however, is where change begins. In this contemplation stage, people begin to see the benefits of making a healthy change and yet experience a significant amount of ambivalence. The preparation stage is one in which people are determined to make the change in the near future and may make incremental changes, while still taking steps backwards. It isn't until the action and maintenance stages that real change takes place. Many people with addiction struggle with feelings of ambivalence about change (contemplation stage) and with making small changes only to go back to old behaviors (preparation stage) before they make the actual step toward recovery. In her memoir, *Stash*, for instance, Laura Cathcart Robbins recognizes she needs help and thus decides to go to rehab. Yet, as she's packing for rehab, she thinks, "I'm going to need to sneak in some drugs" and carefully cuts open her individually wrapped tampons and stashes a pill in each one.[29] She then replaces her six pack of water with vodka and uses a glue gun to close the bottles back up.[30] Robbins fully recognizes she needs to stop using Ambien and alcohol and demonstrates her commitment by deciding to go to rehab. Yet, the lure of addiction is too strong to stop her from sneaking alcohol and pills into rehab.

The process of making promises, only to go back on them once there is respite from the current crisis, is a common part of addiction recovery and

---

26. Karr, *Lit*, 175.
27. Heather King, *Parched: A Memoir* (New American Library, 2006), 148 (italics in the original).
28. See, e.g., James O. Prochaska and Carlo C. DiClemente, "Transtheoretical Therapy: Toward a More Integrative Model of Change," *Psychotherapy: Theory, Research and Practice* 19, no. 3 (Fall 1982): 276–88; see also James O. Prochaska, Carlo C. DiClemente, and John C. Norcross, "In Search of How People Change: Applications to Addictive Behaviors," *American Psychologist* 47, no. 9 (September 1992): 1102–14.
29. Laura Cathcart Robbins, *Stash: My Life in Hiding* (Atria Paperback, 2024), 96.
30. Robbins, *Stash*, 95–100.

apparently of the process of salvation described in Exodus. There are moments in the story when Pharaoh even attempts to bargain with God (through Moses) and suggests that just the men go with Moses (Exod. 10:11). Bargaining is a common strategy in the contemplation and preparation stages of addiction recovery. At one point, Mary Karr attempts to quit drinking after a couples therapy session with her husband, during which her therapist suggests she stop drinking. For a moment, Karr sees what she must do. However, "Full sobriety as a concept recedes with the holidays," she says, and she decides instead to "cut down."[31] Her attempts at cutting down fail terribly, and soon she is back to drinking as usual again. In different ways, both Pharaoh and those with addiction are struggling to hang on to the illusion of power and control. Pharaoh is afraid to relinquish his power and profit. His identity is attached to his strength as a leader. Through the plagues, Pharaoh learns to see his own powerlessness. Likewise, those with addiction often struggle to let go of the illusion that they can control their drinking or substance use. The first step of recovery in the Twelve-Step program is, therefore, about recognizing our own powerlessness: "We admitted we were powerless over alcohol—that our lives had become unmanageable."[32] Of course, this is not unique to Pharaoh or those with addiction. We spend much of our lives living under the illusion that we have control over what happens to us. It's one of the reasons we are so keen to place blame on people when bad things happen. If we can blame a person's lung cancer on the fact that they smoked, for instance, we can continue living under the illusion that we couldn't possibly get lung cancer ourselves. The alternative is too terrifying. Much of adulthood is learning to accept the fragility of life and learning to live with the fact that we have little control. Many current harmful theologies, such as the prosperity gospel, for instance, play on the illusion of control by saying that if we just believe hard enough and pray hard enough, we can control our financial destiny. The salvation story in Exodus beautifully and painfully describes the powerful hold evil has over us and how tenaciously we want to hold on to our sense of power and control.

Interestingly, the exodus story is never clear about who is in control of Pharaoh's will. At times, we read that Pharaoh "hardened his heart" (Exod. 8:15, 32). In those moments, he is seen as responsible for his intentions. At other times, however, we read that "Pharaoh's heart was hardened" (Exod. 8:19), which leaves open the question of who hardened his heart. Most troublingly, there are also moments when Exodus recounts that "the LORD hardened the heart of Pharaoh" (Exod. 9:12), making God the agent of Pharaoh's will. Some scholars point to the gradual shift from Pharaoh hardening his own heart to God hardening it for him. This would imply that God is not doing anything that Pharaoh has not already determined for himself. God is simply allowing Pharaoh to go where Pharaoh is already going. Fretheim notes that where Pharaoh had some agency and freedom at the beginning, over time, his actions become more determined. Fretheim

---

31. Karr, *Lit*, 180.
32. *Alcoholics Anonymous: The Big Book*, 4th ed. (Alcoholics Anonymous World Services, 2002), 59.

likens this shift from freedom to determinism to a boat as it approaches a waterfall. The closer the boat gets, the harder it is to turn away from the waterfall. At a certain point, so many decisions have been made in a certain direction that it is hard, if not impossible, to make a shift.[33] As I showed in chapter 2, Augustine makes a similar point in the *Confessions* when he says,

> I was bound not with the iron of another's chains, but by my own iron will. The enemy held my will; and of it he made a chain and bound me. Because my will was perverse it changed to lust, and lust yielded to become habit, and habit not resisted became necessity. These were the links hanging one on another . . . and their hard bondage held me bound hand and foot. . . . Habit had grown stronger against me by my own act, since I had come willingly where I did not now will to be.[34]

The more we act in a certain direction, the more bound we become. Augustine notices something important about the human condition in this passage and makes the theological claim that bondage is, in some ways, our own doing, though we are not always cognizant of the process.[35] In recent years, neuroscientists have demonstrated that the brain actually works this way. The more we repeat behaviors and thoughts, the more the brain creates strong synaptic links and pathways that make it more and more difficult to do and think otherwise.[36]

The notion that Pharaoh has agency at the beginning but limits his freedom the more decisions he makes in the direction of evil is complicated by the fact that God tells Moses he will harden Pharaoh's heart in Exod. 4:21.[37] Indeed some scholars say that it is clear that "Yahweh is in every case the prime mover in this matter."[38] As I described in chapter 2, John Calvin has a similar theology. Calvin is so concerned with God's sovereignty that he cannot imagine anything happening outside of God's will. Thus, he comes to the deeply problematic conclusion that "God willed, not only permitted, Adam's fall and the rejection of the reprobate."[39] As I have made clear, I do not hold to such a view of the human will. The human will is deeply complicated, and we are not nearly as free as we often imagine ourselves to be. The will is co-opted and bound, yet we experience ourselves as having limited freedom. The hardening of Pharaoh's heart in Exodus names this complexity of the will without coming to a tidy conclusion. Sometimes, it seems as if Pharaoh hardens his own heart; at others, his heart is simply hardened; and at still others, it seems as if God hardens Pharaoh's heart.

---

33. Fretheim, *Exodus,* 100–101.
34. Augustine, *Confessions,* ed. Michael P. Foley, trans. F. J. Sheed, 2nd ed. (Hackett, 2006), 8.v.10–11.
35. As I explain in chapter 2, Augustine has a far more complex notion of the human will in relation to God's grace than is here demonstrated.
36. See chapter 1 for a fuller description of this process.
37. William H. C. Propp, *Exodus 1–18,* The Anchor Bible (Doubleday, 1998), 353.
38. John I. Durham, *Exodus,* Word Biblical Commentary (Word Books, 1987), 123.
39. John Calvin, *Institutes of the Christian Religion,* ed. John T. McNeill, trans. Ford Lewis Battles (Westminster, 1960), 3.23.8.

Eventually, when God kills "every firstborn in the land" (Exod. 11:5), Pharaoh cannot help but see his own powerlessness and relents. He lets the Israelites go. However, he changes his mind one more time at the last minute, follows the people to recapture them, and is finally drowned in the Red Sea. This could have been the end of the story. Indeed, some might argue that the entirety of the journey from bondage to freedom takes place in these first fifteen chapters of Exodus. After all, once Pharaoh and his army are drowned, the Israelites are technically no longer enslaved. However, the beauty of this story is that it doesn't end here either. Instead, it demonstrates over the coming chapters that the Israelites are still very much enslaved. The remainder of the story is the story of the people slowly shedding their identities of enslavement and taking up their new identities of free people. Like Moses, the Israelites must learn to see themselves anew. The exodus story is both tremendously hopeful and relentlessly realistic about what the process of freedom looks like.

Part II—Exodus 15–18: Salvation Is a Journey Away from Bondage

When I was a teenager in Taiwan, I went to an American Evangelical missionary school where we had spiritual life week twice a year, in which we would start every day of that week with a sermon of sorts given by a speaker, usually flown in for this purpose from the United States. The week would invariably end with an altar call, in which the preacher would ask any of us who wanted to give our lives to Jesus to come forward so that he could pray for us. The synthesizer would play some droning minor chords while the preacher prayed and called us forward. Like clockwork, something in me would break, and I would find myself getting up from my chair, yet again, turning my life over to Jesus. During my years at that school, I converted and gave my life to Jesus on a semiannual basis. Each time, I would confess my sins and ask for forgiveness and each time I would walk away from the experience feeling lighter and different. I would feel redeemed. Of course, within a week, that feeling would pass, and I would go back to being the somewhat morose teenager that I was. Even at the time, I recall being confused about what exactly redemption was supposed to enact in me. Each time I went up to the altar, I thought this time would be different. I was hoping that I would leave my sinful life at the altar and walk out of the sanctuary renewed. Of course, this never happened because salvation is not an event so much as a process.

Many of the dominant metaphors for salvation, including penal-substitutionary atonement, reflect the religious education of my youth. That is, God promises to redeem people and then simply does. Christ takes on the punishment in our stead (penal-substitutionary atonement), pays off the debt we owe to God (substitutionary atonement), offers up himself as ransom in our stead to Satan (ransom theory), or perhaps wages a cosmic battle on our behalf (*Christus Victor*), and then we are freed. There is a once-and-done quality to these metaphors. They present a picture of salvation in which the price is paid or the battle is won in a moment, and we ought not to experience anything but massive relief. There's something incredibly enticing about a once-and-done transformation. Yet the reality of salvation is that it doesn't take place in a single moment. It is a painful journey from a life of slavery toward an unknown yet promised better future.

I still struggle, at times, with the temptation to see change as an event rather than a process. I'm easily seduced by the idea of going away and coming back renewed and "fixed" of whatever needs fixing. This was certainly my mindset when I went to rehab. In fact, in the weeks leading up to it, I had included "go to rehab" on one of my to-do lists as if this was just one more task to complete, similar to doing the dishes, cleaning the house, or completing a project at work. I would go away for three months, do this "rehab thing," and then I would go back home, and everything would go back to normal except that I would be sober and happy. Of course, this is not what ended up happening because recovery, much like salvation, is not an event but a process. The first year after rehab was painful in ways I couldn't have imagined. Recovery turned my life upside down, and the great cruelty of recovery is, of course, that you have to deal with all these changes without the soothing balm of the drug of "choice."[40] Transformation is an ongoing process. While certainly not as raw and painful as it was in that first year after rehab, recovery continues to shape and transform me in unexpected, sometimes painful, sometimes joyful, and often beautiful ways.

The beauty of the extended metaphor of the exodus story is that it highlights the fact that salvation is a slow and often painful process. The exodus story recognizes that salvation includes what theologians often call justification *and* sanctification and that it is impossible to have one without the other.[41] While most theologians, including Calvin, closely pair theologies of justification with theologies of sanctification, churches have a tendency to overemphasize justification at the expense of sanctification, giving the impression that the work is done

---

40. As I have indicated before, while "drug of choice" is a common phrase to refer to the substance a person with addiction primarily uses, I put the word "choice" in quotation marks as a reminder that people are not nearly as free as we often assume they are in addiction.

41. While I recognize that "justification" is a term we often use in theology to talk about redemption more broadly, I don't use this term as much, because of its etymological roots in the legal system. It literally means "to be made just." Justification, thus, implies that salvation is a judicial process (e.g., penal-substitutionary atonement) in which the human condition is one of moral failure and the solution is being made righteous. As I've already argued, I see the human condition as a more complicated mix of brokenness and bondage that often, though not always, includes moral failure. What humans primarily need is not to be absolved from punishment by being made just but to be healed and made whole. Some theologians would see justification as implying all of these (i.e., being absolved, healed, and made whole) and more.

If justification is to be made just, sanctification is to be made holy or to be set apart. It is the work of God in us that brings about transformation. If justification frees us *from* the bondage of evil, sanctification frees us *for* a life in alignment with God's will. Sanctification is the process by which we become more Christlike. It is, to put it in Exodus terms, the process the Israelites go through of letting go of their identities as enslaved people and living into their identity as God's chosen people. The process involves both the work that God does in them and for them as well as the work they must do to live into the freedom they have already received.

once we are justified.[42] Theologies of atonement often also make it easy for us to separate justification from sanctification. In penal-substitutionary atonement, for instance, the work of redemption seems to be complete once Jesus takes on the punishment for our sins. What more does a criminal need than to be absolved of punishment? At most, the criminal may also wish to *feel* absolved of guilt over past actions, but sanctification doesn't really address that problem.

The problem is that from a human perspective, justification without sanctification is meaningless, especially if salvation is to mean something in the here and now. It is akin to imagining a scenario in which God convinced Pharaoh to set the Israelites free, but the Israelites, failing to believe it, show up to make bricks out of straw again the next day. In such a scenario, Pharaoh, having done his part of letting the people go, could happily let the people make bricks for him for all eternity. Technically, the Israelites would be free to leave Egypt and their life of slavery behind, but unless they believed that to be true and actually left, that freedom would be utterly meaningless. While justification without sanctification is meaningless from the perspective of the person being freed, sanctification without justification is impossible. That is, the Israelites couldn't leave without God's intervention. Pharaoh letting the people go and the people leaving are two parts of the same process. The one without the other is meaningless. Theological constructs that cleanly delineate these two aspects of soteriology give the impression that one can happen without the other, but as noted above, from a human perspective, that is a meaningless proposition, especially if salvation is to have any bearing on the here and now.

The story of the exodus paints a picture of salvation that holds together justification and sanctification, recognizing that salvation is often a painful process. Once the Israelites leave Egypt, they go on a literal and metaphorical journey through no-man's land, and it is on this journey that they slowly learn to let go of their old identities as enslaved people.

When they first cross the Red Sea, the Israelites are ecstatic and celebrate their freedom. Right after Pharaoh and his army are drowned in the Red Sea, "the prophet Miriam, Aaron's sister, took a tambourine in her hand; and all the women went after her with tambourines and with dancing. And Miriam sang to them: 'Sing to the Lord, for he has triumphed gloriously; horse and rider he has thrown into the sea'" (Exod. 15:20–21). All of Exodus 15 consists of two songs of praise to the Lord. The people are full of hope and full of a sense of God's goodness.

---

42. Calvin holds justification and sanctification together. He says, for instance, "Christ was given to us by God's generosity, to be grasped and possessed by us in faith. By partaking of him, we principally receive a double grace: namely, that being reconciled to God through Christ's blamelessness, we may have in heaven instead of a Judge a gracious Father [i.e. justification]; and secondly, that sanctified by Christ's spirit we may cultivate blamelessness and purity of life" (Calvin, *Institutes,* 3.11.1). He makes a similar point when he says, "man is justified by faith alone, and simple pardon; nevertheless, actual holiness of life [i.e. sanctification], so to speak, is not separated from free imputation of righteousness [i.e. justification]" (*Inst.,* 3.3.1). Thus, for Calvin justification and sanctification are closely tied together. They are, as he says, a "double grace."

However, this confidence in God does not last very long. Indeed, three days later, failing to find water, "the people complained against Moses" (Exod. 15:24). Then, six weeks later,

> On the fifteenth day of the second month after they had departed from the land of Egypt . . . [t]he whole congregation of the Israelites complained against Moses and Aaron in the wilderness. The Israelites said to them, "If only we had died by the hand of the LORD in the land of Egypt, when we sat by the pots of meat and ate our fill of bread, for you have brought us out into the wilderness to kill this whole assembly with hunger" (Exod. 16:1–4).

This sentiment is repeated in chapter 17, when they say, "'Why did you bring us out of Egypt, to kill us and our children and livestock with thirst?'" (Exod. 17:3). I have often heard pastors and teachers speak disparagingly of the Israelites' lack of faith and how quickly they seemed to lose hope after all that God had done for them. While this view of the Israelites makes sense with the benefit of hindsight, this lack of faith is actually understandable if viewed from the perspective of the Israelites. The Israelites were hungry and thirsty. In those moments of extreme hunger and thirst, their lives were legitimately better in Egypt.

Henri Nouwen describes the difficulty of leaving a familiar, though harmful, place and stepping into the unknown toward new freedom in his journal, *The Inner Voice of Love*. He says,

> You have an idea of what the new country looks like. Still, you are very much at home, although not truly at peace, in the old country. You know the ways of the old country, its joys and pains, its happy and sad moments. You have spent most of your days there. Even though you know that you have not found there what your heart most desires, you remain quite attached to it. It has become part of your very bones.[43]

Nouwen beautifully describes the reality that old ways of being, even those that are painful, are extremely difficult to shed. There is comfort in the familiar.

William Cope Moyers describes this attachment to old habits in his memoir *Broken*. Moyers says, in early recovery, "I was suddenly feeling emotions that I hadn't felt with any sort of purity for my entire adult life." He says, "They were pouring out of me, a thick sludge of emotional gunk. I didn't know what I was feeling because I was feeling everything, and I couldn't separate the guilt from the shame, the grief from the fear, or the anger from the despair." In the midst of the pain of early recovery, of feeling all his feelings without the barrier of mood-altering substances, he says,

> I was desperate to ease the pain. I had been taking drugs for years to avoid my feelings, but now I was in the psych ward, almost two weeks sober, and I

---

43. Henri J. M. Nouwen, *The Inner Voice of Love: A Journey Through Anguish to Freedom*, reprint edition (Image, 1999), 21.

was feeling what any human being would feel in such a situation. My life was broken into bits and pieces and I couldn't handle that reality. How could I handle it? For a decade I'd been taking drugs to handle life. How do you do this thing called life? How do you do this thing called feelings? I didn't have a clue. If I knew how to do life or how to do feelings, I wouldn't have started taking drugs in the first place.[44]

The constant desire to return to old ways of being is normal. It is one of the reasons relapse rates are incredibly high.

Gene Heyman illustrates this point well in his book *Addiction: A Disorder of Choice*. As I explained in chapter 1, Heyman argues that "*individuals always choose the better option.*" This statement seems incorrect at first glance, given the fact that some people continue to use drugs or alcohol despite clear negative consequences. These individuals are clearly not choosing the better option. Heyman explains, however, that "*given a series of choices, there is more than one way to frame the possible options.*" That is, it's possible "to choose between the available items one at a time" (he calls this "local choice") or "to organize the items into sequences and then choose between the different sequences" (he calls this "global choice").[45] In the case of a person with addiction, she can look at her use as a daily choice (local choice) or look at her drug use as sequential (global choice). How she views her drug use (local or global) will determine which she will see as the better option (continuing drug use or stopping respectively).

To understand why addiction makes sense from a local choice perspective, imagine that a person who is using loses her job after repeatedly showing up to work late due to hangovers. Further, in her fifth year of excessive use, she experiences some legal issues as a result of drinking and driving. By the tenth year, her spouse has had enough of the daily chaos of living with an alcoholic person, asks for a divorce, and threatens to pursue legal action to take away her rights to parent her children. While each of these consequences is devastating to the person using, living with these consequences without the use of alcohol would be even more difficult. That is, it would legitimately be more difficult to deal with the anger of her spouse the day after she receives her DUI without alcohol than with. The moment she decides to stop drinking, her life takes a dive, because now she has to deal with all the negative consequences (losing a job, legal problems, divorce, etc.) without the soothing balm of alcohol. Hence, as Heyman points out, the value of living with the drug is, in every moment, always higher than the value of living under those same circumstances without the drug.

In other words, for a time, life in recovery is legitimately worse than life in addiction. Of course, the longer one remains in recovery, the better life becomes, and eventually, the value of life in recovery far exceeds that of life in addiction.

---

44. William Cope Moyers, *Broken: My Story of Addiction and Redemption* (Penguin Books, 2007), 143.

45. Gene M. Heyman, *Addiction: A Disorder of Choice* (Harvard University Press, 2010), 119 (italics in the original).

Part of persevering in recovery means taking a long view and being willing to suffer the momentary (though often excruciating) pain of early recovery with an eye toward future gains. As many recovering people can attest, however, this is extremely difficult, and the temptation to go back to a life of addiction is very real, which is, in part, why so many people relapse, especially in the first year.

Part of the beauty of the exodus story is that there is a recognition of precisely this difficulty.[46] As James Nelson notes in *Thirst*, "recovery is . . . a journey through the desert with a 'cunning, baffling, powerful' adversary lurking never far away."[47] As Nelson notes, this was certainly the experience of the Israelites, who complained regularly to Moses and Aaron about the difficulty of their new lives. When they suffer extreme hunger and thirst, their lives are legitimately more difficult than they were in Egypt.

At the same time, the Israelites also seem to forget, at times, just how difficult life in Egypt was. After God provides food in the form of manna and the immediate hunger pangs are over, the Israelites grow tired of the mundanity of eating manna day after day. The book of Numbers indicates that the Israelites and those who joined them started to develop "strong craving[s]" and again complained to Moses, saying, "'If only we had meat to eat! We remember the fish we used to eat in Egypt for nothing, the cucumbers, the melons, the leeks, the onions, and the garlic, but now our strength is dried up, and there is nothing but this manna to look at'" (Num. 11:4–6). They seem to have forgotten about the earlier crisis of not having any food and now complain that "there is nothing but this manna to look at" (Num. 11:6). Reading the text with the benefit of hindsight, the Israelites seem ungrateful and petty. Don't they recall how dire their situation in Egypt was? Don't they remember how desperate they were to have food at all? In this moment, the Israelites seem to paint a brighter picture of their time in Egypt, forgetting about the hardships that went along with the varieties of food on offer.

This, too, is very similar to how people experience early recovery. Once the initial crisis point that sparked the move away from the addiction recedes into the background, and the newness of recovery wears off, it is easy to fall back into old patterns. I have certainly experienced this in my own recovery. The terror of hitting a new low, of almost getting seriously hurt, or the jolt of getting caught, or of being on the brink of losing something important (like a relationship)—these things could and often did shock me into change. And for a time, I would be fully on board. I would attend a Twelve Step meeting every day, get a sponsor, and do the work. The sheer relief of having survived the latest crisis would drive me to cling to recovery, sure that I would never go back to a life of addiction. But

---

46. Gerald May sees the exodus experience as one in which the Israelites "expressed all the characteristics of addiction" in that they "experienced the stress and fear of withdrawal symptoms, longing for the old days of slavery" along with other modes of being indicative of addiction (Gerald May, *Addiction and Grace* [HarperSanFrancisco, 1980], 133).

47. James B. Nelson, *Thirst: God and the Alcoholic Experience* (Westminster John Knox, 2004), 170.

then, the memory of the crisis would recede into the background, the newness of recovery would wear off, I would forget how bad life in addiction was, and without even being fully aware of it, I'd inch my way closer and closer to a relapse.

Nic Sheff describes this process well in his memoir *Tweak*. He says that one of the counselors who ran the recovery program he was in "describes addiction as a disease of amnesia." At the beginning "it's not hard to stay sober." Sheff says, "Sure, it's hard as hell to *get* sober—to pull yourself out of the cycle of getting high every day and going through the horrors of detox. But honestly, once the drugs are out of my system it isn't too difficult to genuinely feel like I never want to go through that . . . again. Staying sober right after coming back from a relapse is no struggle." The problem for Sheff and many people with addiction is that sense of amnesia: "As the months go by, I always seem to forget why I needed to get sober in the first place. . . . I tell myself that I wasn't really that out of control." Similar to the Israelites in the story of the exodus, it's easy to forget the hardships of the past in the face of current realities. Sheff says, "I swear, every time I've relapsed has been the same story. And, each time, I get a little closer to being dead."[48]

In early recovery, I often felt foolish when I'd relapse. Boredom with the day-to-day of recovery would make it hard for me to remember how painful addiction was, and this amnesia often led to relapses in early recovery. I felt frustrated with my forgetfulness about the suffering that addiction brings with it. How could I fall for the same thing over and over again? The exodus story helps to normalize the difficulty of the journey of recovery for those with addiction and reminds us that living into freedom is a lifelong process; that it is tremendously difficult, especially early on; and that slipping back into old patterns is common.

The same is true for salvation. God assures us that we are free, yet living into that freedom is also a lifelong process. It is not easy to live as free people. It is not easy to step outside the systems of bondage and oppression (e.g., racism, heteronormativity, capitalism, etc.) that we are born into. And thus, we often find ourselves caught in webs not of our own making in which we are nevertheless complicit and sometimes even active agents of harm. It is easy to get complacent, to lose hope. The exodus story powerfully speaks to this part of the human condition, reminding us that we are not the first to struggle with finding our way through the wilderness.

The theme of salvation as a journey is carried through the rest of the story of the exodus. While this second part of the exodus story focused on how difficult it is to extricate oneself from bondage, the third part shifts the focus toward what it looks like to live in freedom, recognizing that even there, the temptation to go back can still be present.

---

48. Nic Sheff, *Tweak: Growing Up on Methamphetamines* (Atheneum Books for Young Readers, 2009), 142.

Part III—Exodus 19–40: Salvation Is a Journey into Freedom

The third part of the book of Exodus describes a time in the Israelites' journey through the wilderness when the crises of extricating themselves from Pharaoh's clutches, outrunning Pharaoh's army through the Red Sea, and dealing with hunger and thirst begin to recede to the background. They enter a new phase and begin to form a community at the foot of Mount Sinai (Exod. 19:2). In other words, while still in the wilderness, they are no longer constantly on the move. The third part of the book of Exodus is an account of what it means to live in this new kind of community.

The Israelites are centered around their relationship with God, who tells the people through Moses, "You have seen what I did to the Egyptians and how I bore you on eagles' wings and brought you to myself. Now, therefore, if you obey my voice and keep my covenant, you shall be my treasured possession out of all the peoples. Indeed, the whole earth is mine, but you shall be for me a priestly kingdom and a holy nation" (Exod. 19:4–6). Immediately after God claims the Israelites as God's own, God offers the people (through Moses) the Ten Commandments and a variety of laws. The community is established through God's covenant, which includes the gift of the law.

Laws are likely not what we immediately think of when we think about forming communities, and yet communities are founded and function through common agreements. The law helps shape the community at Mount Sinai and paradoxically also forms the basis of what it means to live in freedom for the Israelites. The community at Mount Sinai has never lived in freedom. They have spent their entire lives in bondage. So, God offers the people guidance on how to live in freedom by giving them the law.

This is true of basement communities as well. Twelve-Step meetings are so named because they center around the Twelve Steps, which, interestingly, do not offer tips on how to stop drinking. Indeed, they only mention alcohol once. Rather, they offer guidelines on how to live in relationship with God and people. They focus on turning "our will and our lives over to the care of God *as we understood Him*," recognizing unhealthy patterns in our lives and rectifying them, admitting wrongdoing and making amends, and daily self-reflection, prayer, and meditation with the goal of having a "spiritual awakening" and then passing this gift on to others.[49] People who come to Twelve-Step groups often have no idea how to live

---

49. *Alcoholics Anonymous: The Big Book*, 59–60. People often point out that Twelve Steps are grounded in Christian principles, which is not surprising given the Christian roots of Alcoholics Anonymous. E.g., see Linda Mercadante, *Victims and Sinners: Spiritual Roots of Addiction and Recovery* (Westminster John Knox, 1996), 51–82. Mercadante offers a brief history of AA's beginnings in the Christian organization the Oxford Group (chapter 4, 51–72) and of AA's split from the Oxford Group (chapter 5, 73–82). AA opted to move away from its original religious affiliation to be accessible to as many people as possible. This is one of the reasons *The Big Book* uses the language of Higher Power. The General Service Office of Alcoholics Anonymous, therefore, explicitly states in its literature that "*A.A. welcomes anyone seeking help for a drinking problem and is not aligned with any religious tradition or beliefs.*" (See "Understanding Alcoholics Anonymous and Spirituality," Alcoholics Anonymous, August 15, 2023, https://www.aa.org/sites/default/files/literature/AA%20and%20Spirituality%20

without the substance of "choice," so the Twelve Steps offer a much-needed guide on how to live in freedom. Where the Twelve Steps teach people how to live in recovery, the Twelve Traditions function as a guide for how to form communities of recovery. Basement communities are thus formed around governing principles and agreed-upon steps.[50]

The Israelites at Mount Sinai begin to settle into a new rhythm and, accordingly, begin to form a community based around a variety of rules, laws, and customs, but living in freedom is hard. When the immediate crisis of leaving Egypt has passed, and things begin to settle down, God calls Moses up to Mount Sinai once again.[51] This time, Moses is delayed in returning back to the people, and faced with the predicament of Moses's delay, the people slip back into older patterns of mistrust and ask Aaron to create gods for them to worship. In essence the Israelites have a relapse of sorts in this moment.

As I explained above, people often relapse in addiction recovery because they seem to forget why recovery was so important in the first place. However, this amnesia is often coupled with a precipitating event that pushes the person in recovery over the edge. Elizabeth Vargas, for instance, worked months on the Amanda Knox story for ABC, only to have Amanda's first interview go to her colleague Diane Sawyer instead of her. Vargas says she was "devastated, plain and simple," and "on top of it, . . . exhausted." Instead of going to a meeting, calling a friend, or praying, she had her "first drink in six months."[52]

Neil Steinberg describes being kicked out of his outpatient rehab program after several relapses in his memoir, *Drunkard*. He is disappointed and feels like his "supports" have been "kicked away." Initially Steinberg's wife is angry on his behalf because the relapses happened weeks ago, and he is actually sober the moment they kick him out. However, several days later his wife calls him at work, certain that he has relapsed. Steinberg does what many people do in this situation. He says, "Edie thinks I'm drinking? Fine, mustn't disappoint her," and relapses.[53] Of course, not every relapse occurs because of a disappointing

---

Press%20Release%20-%20EN_0.pdf; italics in the original.) However, despite the deliberate split from the Oxford Group and its Christian roots, AA still often comes across as Christian to those who encounter it, not least because many AA groups finish their meetings with the Lord's Prayer. The references to "Higher Power" as God, Father (e.g., *The Big Book*, 62), Him, and Creator (e.g., *The Big Book*, 68) also point to AA's Christian background. Beyond these links that exist within AA itself, many writers have also pointed to connections between the Twelve Steps and Christian principles (e.g., Richard Rhor, *Breathing under Water: Spirituality and the Twelve Steps* [Franciscan Media, 2011]). See also Stephen Haynes, *Why Can't Church Be More Like an AA Meeting? And Other Questions Christians Ask about Recovery* (Eerdmans, 2021), where Haynes devotes a chapter 7 to the various ways people and organizations have connected the Twelve Steps to the Bible.

50. See *Twelve Steps and Twelve Traditions* (Alcoholics Anonymous World Services, 1953).

51. Moses is called up to Mount Sinai multiple times in the exodus story. The story's chronology is not always clear in this third part of the book. For instance, the people are given the law in Exodus 20, yet Moses seems to receive the law again, this time on stone tablets, in Exodus 31.

52. Elizabeth Vargas, *Between Breaths: A Memoir of Panic and Addiction* (Grand Central, 2016), 173, 174.

53. Neil Steinberg, *Drunkard: A Hard-Drinking Life* (Plume, 2008), 230, 231.

precipitating event. Sometimes, people just relapse. However, a lot of the time something pushes a person over the edge.

The exodus story describes a similar pattern. As I mentioned above, the Israelites seem to forget how difficult life in Egypt truly was the longer they are away from Egypt. Once their basic needs are met and they have enough food and water, they begin to complain about the lack of variety in available food and paint a picture of Egypt as a land of abundance, forgetting the ruthlessness of their enslavement. The pain of enslavement that initially caused them to cry out to the Lord recedes into the background, eating at their commitment to their newfound freedom, and then an event pushes them over the edge. When Moses takes longer than expected on Mount Sinai, the people become impatient and perhaps are fearful of being leaderless. They ask Aaron, "make gods for us, who shall go before us" (Exod. 32:1), and Aaron concedes and makes them a golden calf, which they worship.[54]

This moment takes place in between two lengthy sections outlining the specific building instructions for the Tabernacle, which Fretheim calls "Israel's wilderness sanctuary." He notes that the general arc of the story of the exodus is the "movement . . . from slavery to worship, from service to Pharaoh to service of God." This can even be seen in the placement of the building instructions in the book. The Israelites move from "enforced construction of Pharaoh's buildings to the glad and obedient offering of themselves for a building for the worship of God."[55] For all intents and purposes the movement from slavery to freedom is going well. And it is precisely at this moment that the Israelites fall back into old patterns of mistrust.

They move from building a place of worship to God to building the golden calf. Fretheim points out the differences between these two sections. Where the Tabernacle is built at "God's initiative" and requires "painstaking preparations," followed by a "lengthy building process," the golden calf is generated at the "people's initiative," with "no planning," and takes very little time to build.[56] Idolatry is pernicious in that way. It smacks of the real thing yet deviates at important points. While some see the act of asking for the golden calf as "an

---

54. Interestingly, when Moses comes back and asks Aaron what happened. Aaron explains that the people made him do it. He says that they begged for him to create gods for them in Moses's absence, and that he gathered their gold and then he "threw it [people's gold] into the fire, and out came this calf!" (Exod. 32:24). William Propp notes that some biblical scholars see connections between Aaron's statement and the "Near Eastern theology of the self-begotten idol." However, Propp thinks this is unlikely to be the case and says that "it is more natural to read this disclaimer as a bald-faced denial of responsibility, such as a child might make: 'It just broke'" (William H. C. Propp, *Exodus 19–40*, The Anchor Bible [Doubleday, 2006], 562). This latter interpretation resonates with my own experiences in early recovery. When I relapsed in early recovery, I would often say things like, "I don't know what happened—all of a sudden, I was just using." At the time, it truly felt as if it just happened to me. Over time, I had to learn to see the signposts that led to the cliff so that I wouldn't be surprised every time I fell off of it. Amnesia about just how bad life in addiction felt was one of the signposts I had to learn to see so that I could put the brakes on long before getting to the cliff. Another signpost I had to watch out for were moments of crisis, real or imagined.

55. Fretheim, *Exodus*, 263–64.
56. Fretheim, *Exodus*, 267.

expression of egotism," in which the people "were essentially saying they could do better than God" in that "they could make their own God,"[57] I see it more as an expression of fear of having to cope with living in the wilderness without Moses. Durham explains in his commentary that "any absences of their leader, the one person who has been their representative to Yahweh from the moment of his return to them in Egypt, would have been unsettling," and the length of Moses's absence compounds this. The people were in "a frenzy, some perhaps assuming Moses had deserted them, others more charitably fearing some tragedy had befallen their leader."[58] Moses was, for them, God's mediator. Thus, the absence of Moses would likely have felt like the absence of God. William Propp similarly notes that while "God interprets the people's repeated backsliding as plain stubbornness . . . [a] more sympathetic assessment would describe Israel, after centuries of enslavement, as pathologically insecure."[59] I'm not even sure if their insecurity and mistrust could be deemed pathological after centuries of abuse. They came by it honestly, after all. Their mistrust of Pharaoh was justified and had, over time, become engrained and habituated such that it was hard to trust anyone else, including God. This is a common occurrence for those who've experienced trauma. Their mistrust was certainly maladaptive, but I wouldn't call it "pathological."

Moses's absence felt like the absence of God, and without Moses, without God, the journey they were on lacked direction and purpose. They were looking for God, or failing that, as close a facsimile as they could muster. They looked for something that was almost like the real thing yet able to meet their need immediately. Of course, what they latched on to didn't ultimately deliver, but the drive for direction and fulfilment is there even in their moments of deepest mistrust. They long to worship.

In many ways, addiction is a similar bid for direction and purpose. I think this is something that those without addiction often don't fully understand. Addiction is not, at its heart, a hedonistic and nihilistic activity. It is a drive for purpose and meaning that invests itself in the wrong thing. As Augustine would say, it is the attempt to get something finite to meet an infinite need. Relying on the likes of Augustine, theologian Edward Farley describes the human condition as one of having an ultimate desire that "no specific entity, no actual person, no event or cause, no instance of value, beauty or reality" has the capacity to satiate. He calls this the "eternal horizon."[60] It's a desire that never finds satiation because it longs for something that no finite good can satisfy. In many ways, addiction is an attempt to satisfy this desire with a finite good (i.e., the drug of "choice"). Because desire is so innate to who we are, pursuing the substance and wrapping one's life around the addiction feels right for a time. As I described in the first chapter, the

---

57. Arlene Kahn, "The Exodus: A Parable of Addiction and Recovery," *Journal of Ministry in Addiction & Recovery* 5, no. 2 (1998): 20.
58. Durham, *Exodus*, 419.
59. Propp, *Exodus 19–40*, 566.
60. Edward Farley, *Divine Empathy: A Theology of God* (Fortress, 1996), 65.

rush of dopamine in the brain helps fuel the notion that an innate need is being met. Those in AA sometimes refer to this pursuit as trying to find God in a bottle.[61]

Beyond the illusion that the substance of "choice" is filling an innate desire, the substance also drives and directs the addicted person's life in meaningful ways. Kent Dunnington says it well: "Foremost among the spiritual goods that addiction pursues is an integrating principle that renders the immanent activities of human persons meaningful in light of some transcendent pursuit." Addiction focuses a person on a single pursuit, for which they will do almost anything. As Dunnington strikingly describes, "The strength of the addiction resides, not primarily in the heroin or in the sensory pleasures that it provides, but rather in the simplicity and beauty of having one's life measured by one standard, harmonized with one melody, directed to one end."[62] There is a seductive beauty in the simplicity of addiction. It centers life around a single purpose. Tragically, of course, the substance cannot ultimately deliver. At a certain point in addiction, most people recognize to their horror that there is no amount of alcohol or heroin or meth that will fill the void.

Recovery is, in many ways, about recognizing the illusion for what it is and then stepping into no-man's-land in hopes that there is something better out there. Importantly, the exodus story as an extended metaphor for salvation offers those suffering from recovery from addiction a sense of validation, recognizing that the journey from bondage to freedom is difficult and long. Further, the exodus story normalizes the cravings and relapses those in recovery often experience.

In *The Inner Voice of Love*, Nouwen recognizes the pull of what he calls "the old country." He says, "It seems that you keep crossing and recrossing the border. For a while you experience a real joy in the new country. But then you start to feel afraid and start longing again for all you left behind, so you go back to the old country." Of course, once a person has experienced freedom it is hard to enjoy bondage again. Nouwen says, "To your dismay, you discover that the old has lost its charm."[63] Similarly, in Twelve Step meetings, people often muse that there's nothing like recovery that ruins the experience of using. The crossing and recrossing of the border between old and new is part of the process of salvation and of recovery. There is no shame in having cravings or in relapses. It is simply part of the process of shedding the identity of being enslaved and living into freedom. This process takes time and has setbacks. The exodus narrative offers a powerful sense of validation for these experiences for those with addiction. Sadly, those struggling through recovery often do blame

---

61. This is likely based on remarks made by Bill W. and Dr. Bob in 1948, where Bill W. said, "An alcoholic is a fellow who is 'trying to get his religion out of a bottle,' when what he really wants is unity within himself, unity with God" (Just for Today Meditations, February 16, 2015, https://www.justfortodaymeditations.com/daily-recovery-quotes-february-16/).

62. Kent Dunnington, *Addiction and Virtue: Beyond the Models of Disease and Choice* (IVP Academic, 2011), 142, 152.

63. Nouwen, *The Inner Voice of Love*, 21–22.

and shame themselves when they experience setbacks and often have a hard time forgiving themselves.

This too, however, appears to be part of the journey from bondage into freedom. Within the exodus story there is a tremendous amount of shaming and blaming. Interestingly, it is usually Moses and God who do the blaming and shaming, often in the form of punishment. After the Israelites worship the golden calf, for instance, the story reads, "The Lord said to Moses, 'I have seen this people, how stiff-necked they are. Now let me alone so that my wrath may burn hot against them and I may consume them" (Exod. 32:9–10). When Moses sees what the people have done, he demands, "'Who is on the Lord's side? Come to me!'" and when "all the sons of Levi gathered around him," he told them, "Thus says the Lord . . . 'kill your brother, your friend, and your neighbor'" (Exod. 32:26–27). In his commentary on Exodus, Fretheim recognizes that "modern sensitivities may get in the way of our interpretation of this method" and notes that killing off those who do not stand for the Lord is consistent with other passages in the Old Testament.[64] The next day, Moses gathers the people and admonishes them for their sin. He makes atonement on their behalf, but the Lord nevertheless "sent a plague on the people" (Exod. 32:35). Whether consistent with other passages or not, Moses and God's reactions to Israel's unfaithfulness seem overly harsh.

Recognizing that I'm not a Hebrew Bible scholar and am not offering an exegetical account of the exodus, I offer below one way that I make sense of these passages that is, admittedly, heavily influenced by my own experiences of shame that often led to an unhealthy need for some of form of punishment in hopes it would undo the shame. I read these passages as yet another moment in which the Israelites cling to their old identity as enslaved people. God's ruthlessness in these passages is very similar to the ruthlessness of the Egyptians. The exodus story begins with a description of the Egyptians as being "ruthless in all the tasks that they imposed on them [i.e., the Israelites]," and as making "their lives bitter with hard servitude" (Exod. 1:14). The Israelites are beaten (Exod. 2:11; 5:14), and the king of Egypt even commands at one point that all the boys born to the Israelites be killed (Exod. 1:16). When God is angry with the Israelites, God acts in similarly ruthless ways by killing some of God's people (through Moses). One way to read these texts is to see them as Israel's interpretation of events. That is, Moses, in his rage, demanded the sons of Levi kill some of the people, and at one point there was a plague, and the Israelites interpreted these events as punishment from God. They were so used to a punishing master that it made sense to them that God would deal with them in the same way.

As I noted earlier in this chapter, Kelly Brown Douglas makes a similar claim (though about a different passage). She recognizes that the exodus story contains both a liberative strand in that God frees the Israelites from bondage and an annihilative strand in that God commands the people to kill an entire nation in order

---

64. Fretheim, *Exodus,* 289.

to occupy the promised land. She helpfully suggests that the annihilative strand in the story may well "say more about the people telling it than it does about God." She harkens back to the fact that in American enslavement, those who were enslaved recognized "that what their enslavers said about God was not true" as it did not align with their understanding of God as a God of freedom. She says, "Inasmuch as claims about God were incompatible with their experience of God, then those claims were rejected . . . [and] did not have theological authority."[65] Likewise, Delores Williams notes that Black spirituals sometimes reinterpreted Scripture in ways that diminished God's apparent harshness. She says, "Perhaps the brutal treatment and near-death beatings that the slaves often received from disobeying their slave owners discouraged them (the slaves) from believing God could be as cruel and vindictive as their slave masters."[66] Douglas contends that for the previously enslaved, "the freedom of God that the enslaved experienced became the adjudicating principle of their very faith claims." Douglas helpfully reminds us that "the claims we make about God may not always be about God."[67] Her analysis of the multiple strands in the exodus story demonstrates that often part of being freed means letting go of toxic claims about God that keep people enslaved.

In the journey of shedding their old identities as enslaved people, the Israelites have to learn to let go of the idea that there is an angry taskmaster ever looking over their shoulder, ready to punish them at a moment's notice. It is almost as if the Israelites are trying to wrestle with their own sense of shame about worshipping the golden calf and then project their own self-punishing narrative onto God.[68]

This is precisely the point Paul Ricoeur makes. It is the notion that punishment is a necessary part of redemption that we need redeeming from.[69] While we may need punishment to feel redeemed, Ricoeur argues that this is not the divine plan for salvation and that the feeling of shame that leads to the need for punishment is the very sin from which we need redemption. This notion is beautifully illustrated in the 1986 movie *The Mission*. Captain Rodrigo Mendoza (played by Robert De Niro) is imprisoned after he kills his brother when he discovers him sleeping with his fiancée. Father Gabriel (played by Jeremy Irons) encourages Mendoza to do penance for killing his brother and for the violence he has inflicted on the very people Father Gabriel seeks to minister to. Mendoza thus joins Father Gabriel on his next mission trip to a Guarani village. On their way up the mountain, Mendoza chooses to drag a large net filled with armor behind him as a way of doing penance. As Mendoza struggles up the mountain, the net gets caught on the rocks. Seeing his predicament, one of the priests who accompanies him cuts

---

65. Douglas, *Stand Your Ground*, 162.
66. Delores Williams, "A Womanist Perspectives on Sin," in ed. Emilie M Townes, *A Troubling in My Soul* (Orbis Books, 1993), 133.
67. Douglas, *Stand Your Ground*, 162.
68. I am indebted to Wendy Farley for this way of reading this text.
69. Paul Ricoeur, "Interpretation of the Myth of Punishment," in *The Conflict of Interpretations: Essays in Hermeneutics*, ed. D. Ihde, trans. Robert Sweeney (Northwestern University Press, 1974), 372–77.

the sack loose from Mendoza so that it falls below, and Mendoza can continue climbing up the mountain. Mendoza, however, is unable to accept this act of grace. He retrieves the net filled with armor, reties it to himself, and carries it the rest of the way up the mountain. At one point in the movie, one of the priests tells Father Gabriel that the brothers all think Mendoza has done enough penance. Father Gabriel, however, says, "*He* doesn't think so. . . . Until he does, neither do I."[70] What strikes me most about this scene is that it is Mendoza who needs the punishment. The priests, on behalf of God, have long forgiven him, but Mendoza cannot accept this forgiveness without seeing the punishment all the way through.

This need to be punished, this inability to forgive ourselves when we fail, is, in essence, a desire to earn redemption and the very thing we need redemption from. Having caused severe harm to those around him, and having taken the lives of others, Mendoza certainly needs to reconcile and perhaps pay restitution to those he has harmed (e.g., the Guarani, his brother's family, and his fiancée). In many ways he does this through the work he does with Father Gabriel in the Guarani village and by ultimately giving his life to protect the Guarani mission. These life changes are ultimately Mendoza's restitution and directly and positively impact those he has harmed. The scene of him carrying the armor up the mountain is much more about self-forgiveness. It is as if Mendoza cannot forgive himself until he is fully punished.

I have certainly experienced this inability to forgive myself in my own recovery journey. Over ten years ago, when I was stuck in what seemed to be a never-ending sobriety-and-relapse loop, I remember a therapist asking me after one of my relapses what I needed from her. I thought about it for a minute and finally said what felt true for me in that moment: "I need you to hurt me." Of course, I knew she wouldn't do that, but what I felt I needed in that moment to forgive myself was punishment. I thought that maybe I could punish and shame myself into sobriety. Over time, I've learned that recovery requires something much more difficult than punishment and shame, namely, self-compassion.

In the exodus story, the punishment continues after the killing of those unwilling to repent and after the plague. The Lord finally commands the people to go and then says, "I will not go up among you, or I would consume you on the way, for you are a stiff-necked people" (Exod. 33:3). Durham offers a poignant translation of Israel's reaction: "*When the people heard this dreadful news, they plunged themselves into deep mourning.*" The people experience God's absence and are rightly grieved. Durham says, "The great narrative of promised Presence and the great narrative of the Advent of Presence are thus to be brought to an abrupt and empty conclusion by a narrative of Absence."[71] Thankfully, Moses intercedes, and God changes God's mind and stays with this people.

Here again, I offer that the Israelites' experience may have been their own fear of and perception of God's absence in light of their sin. Perhaps, blinded

---

70. *The Mission,* directed by Roland Joffé (Goldcrest Films, 1986), 0:36:03.
71. Durham, *Exodus,* 434, 438 (italics in the original).

by their own shame, they were unable to see God and attributed their inability to see rightly as God's absence. I have certainly experienced what seemed to be God's absence, especially in active addiction. Every time I relapsed, I felt a profound sense of self-loathing and, as a result, felt a spiritual emptiness—as if God had abandoned me.

The fourteenth-century mystic Julian of Norwich offers a beautiful description of God as ever-present and merciful in her work *Showings*. While severely ill, Julian experienced multiple revelations in which she saw God in a new light. She says that she had previously understood the "mercy of God" to be "the remission of his wrath after we have sinned."[72] In her visions, however, she learns that what she perceives as God's wrath and absence is simply human blindness that prevents us from seeing God rightly. What we perceive to be God's absence is not caused by sin but is rather the very thing we need healing and freedom from. Julian describes a vision in which she sees "a lord and a servant." She says, "The lord looks on his servant very lovingly and sweetly and mildly . . . [and] sends him to a certain place to do his will." In the servant's eagerness to do the lord's will, he falls in a ditch and is unable to get out of it. While in the ditch the servant suffers because he perceives the lord to be absent. Julian says, "The greatest hurt which I saw him [the servant] in was lack of consolation, for he could not turn his face to look on his loving lord, who was very close to him."[73] I wonder if what the Israelites experienced as God's momentary absence was really their momentary inability to see God. Perhaps learning to see God as loving and ever-present is part of the journey of letting go of identities rooted in slavery and moving toward living into freedom.

CONCLUSION

These moments of self-blame, shame, and imagining a punishing God are all part of the old identity of being enslaved. Even this part of the identity—the part that gets frustrated with relapses and is willing to shame the self into living into a new identity—needs redeeming, because ultimately shaming doesn't work to bring about real change. Needed instead is a sense of self-compassion. The exodus journey is an extended metaphor of what it is to learn to let go of the familiar (however bad that familiar place may have been) and learn to rely on God instead. It is the daily practice of letting go of the past and stepping into an unknown future, trusting that God will provide. Nouwen offers a beautiful image of this in *The Inner Voice of Love* when he says, "Now you have come to realize that you must leave it [the old country] and enter the new country, where your Beloved dwells. You know that what has helped and guided you in the old

---

72. Julian of Norwich, *Showings*, trans. Edmund Colledge and James Walsh (Paulist, 1978), 260 (long text, chapter 47).

73. Julian, *Showings*, 267 (long text, chapter 51).

country no longer works, but what else do you have to go by? You are being asked to trust that you will find what you need in the new country."[74] While the Israelites experience significant setbacks and regularly hang on to their old ways of being, they also keep going and learn to trust that God will provide for their needs.

For one, they literally keep walking. They continue to follow Moses despite setbacks. They never fully lose their trust in Moses and, by extension, in God. Further, when they reach Mount Sinai, the Lord speaks to Moses and says, "If you obey my voice and keep my covenant, you shall be my treasured possession out of all the peoples" (Exod. 19:5). When Moses "summoned the elders of the people, and set before them all these words that the LORD had commanded him . . . the people answered all as one, 'Everything that the LORD has spoken we will do'" (Exod. 19:7–8). While the people clearly do disobey God even after this event, their affirmation of God's words demonstrates that they do intend to follow God. When God commands Moses to build a tabernacle to explicit specifications, for example, "they came, everyone whose heart was stirred and everyone whose spirit was willing, and brought the LORD's offering to be used for the tent of meeting and for all its service and for the sacred vestments" (Exod. 35:21). The people came together, brought what they had, and used what skill they had to make what the Lord had commanded. These moments demonstrate that in and among moments of clinging to their old lives as enslaved people there are moments when they begin taking up their new lives in freedom.

Throughout the Israelites' struggle with disentangling themselves from enslavement, even from the bondage of their images of a harsh God, God demonstrates Godself to be an unrelenting, compassionate presence to them: God *sees* their suffering and acts to bring about their freedom (Exod. 2:25); God physically comforts and protects them in the wilderness in the form of "a pillar of cloud by day" and "a pillar of fire by night" (Exod. 13:21); God consistently shows up for Israel in moments of crisis through Moses's leadership; God establishes a covenantal relationship with Israel; and, finally, God literally takes up residence among them in the tabernacle. God freed them from bondage in order to be with them. God says, "And they shall *know* that I am the LORD their God, who brought them out of the land of Egypt that I might dwell among them; I am the LORD their God" (Exod. 29:46). As God shows Godself to be intimately connected to the Israelites, the Israelites learn to trust in God. This intimacy is solidified in a covenant whereby God gives the commandments and says, "Before all your people I will perform such marvels, such as have not been done before in all the earth or in any nation, and all the people among whom you live shall *see* the work of the LORD, for it is an awesome thing that I will do with you" (Exod. 34:10). Not only do Moses and the Israelites learn to see God rightly, but others will also see the work of the Lord through them.

---

74. Nouwen, *The Inner Voice of Love*, 21.

God's presence in the midst of the people's journey is an important reminder to them that as they work to shed their old identities as enslaved people, and their old notions of God as being harsh and punishing, God is there, seeing their difficulty and drawing them along toward freedom, and through them showing others who God is.

Chapter 7

Finding God in the Basement

Thus far in this book, I have focused primarily on what churches might offer theologically that can both bear the weight of the suffering of addiction and offer hope for healing and recovery. In doing so, I have relied on the experiences of those suffering and recovering from addiction to inform existing theologies of sin, the bondage of the will, salvation, and church practices more generally. In this chapter and the next chapter I turn to focus more directly on the basement practices that formed my understanding of God and ask what the sanctuary might learn from the basement about who God is, what salvation looks like, and who we are called to be in community.[1] Up until now, I have been in conversation with many other theologians and thinkers to talk about models of addiction, theologies of bondage and freedom, theories of metaphor, and various

---

1. My own recovery has been deeply influenced by Twelve-Step programs (e.g., Alcoholics Anonymous and offshoots of AA). Further, most of the memoirs of addiction and recovery describe a process of recovery that happened through a combination of therapy, treatment centers, and Twelve-Step meetings. As indicated in the introduction, however, people recover from addiction in a variety of ways, and many never make use of Twelve-Step meetings at all. I focus here on the journeys of recovery that make use of Twelve-Step programs because it is what I know best and what most of the memoirs center on. However, I do not claim that this is the only or even the best way to recover from addiction.

interpretations of the exodus story. These scholars have shaped my thinking in important ways. In this chapter and the next, however, I move away from this method of doing theology and rely more heavily on the stories of those in recovery (including my own) to talk about how freedom is lived and experienced by those in the basement. In other words, what I offer here is not a retrieval, critique, or reconstruction of a particular interpretation of a doctrine but rather a description of a lived theology in hopes that it might inform how churches think about what salvation looks like when experienced and practiced in the here and now.

In the last chapter I emphasized the extended metaphor of the exodus story as one way of looking at salvation. I highlighted resonances between the exodus story and stories of addiction and recovery. In this chapter I demonstrate that the journey from addiction into recovery is itself a beautiful extended metaphor for salvation. Similar to the exodus story, the journey of recovery captures both the realities of bondage and freedom in the human experience and recognizes that disentanglement from bondage is a lifetime journey. Since I already covered this ground in the last chapter, I focus in this chapter on two other important aspects of salvation that are highlighted by basement communities. First, the metaphor of recovery demonstrates that salvation does not require assent to a story (e.g., the story of Jesus dying on the cross) so much as living into a story. That is, redemption is a practice that demands our participation more than our cognition. Second, the journey of recovery illustrates that salvation happens in community. The community is a powerful source of support and functions to offer alternative glimpses of who God is.

SALVATION IS A PRACTICE

In this book, I illustrate that metaphors are powerful influencers that can both describe and prescribe reality. The words, stories, and metaphors we use to talk about salvation profoundly affect the way we think about not only salvation, but also about ourselves, each other, and God. Language and stories clearly have a powerful impact on thought and action. One of the benefits of the metaphor of the journey from addiction into recovery, however, is that it highlights the importance of practice over thought and language.[2] This is important, especially for those shaped in traditions and cultures which tend to emphasize words. The memoirs and stories of addiction and recovery demonstrate that recovery from addiction does not necessarily require assent to a particular story or set of ideas about what recovery looks like or how it functions, but rather adherence to a regimen of practices. Recovery, in other words, is embodied before it is understood.

---

2. There is, of course, a certain (unavoidable) irony in *writing* about the importance of practice over language and thought, especially since I rely not only on my own words and thoughts to make this point but also on the words of others recorded in their memoirs.

The fact that recovery is seen as a repetitive practice makes a lot of sense given that addiction itself is, in many ways, a practice. That is, addiction demands rituals and acts that keep it alive. Some of these rituals center on procuring alcohol or drugs. Caroline Knapp tells about her friend Meg, who "used to pretend she was shopping for a dinner party. She'd walk up to the wine merchant and ask, thoughtfully, 'What kind of wine would you recommend with duck?' and then she'd exit with a case, plus bottles of Scotch and mixers." Knapp goes on to say, "Lots of us would shop at different stores every day, sometimes going miles out of our way to get to a new liquor store in order to hide the exact levels of our consumption from the salespeople. Two bottles here, two bottles there, a case somewhere else."[3] Beyond being rituals of addiction, these practices are also rituals of shame.[4] They reinforce, time and time again, that the out-of-control nature of the person's use must be hidden, even from strangers.

There are also rituals around the using itself. Jowita Bydlowska talks about developing a ritual in *Drunk Mom*, which "involves going to the grocery store first to get formula, followed by a visit to the liquor store to get sparkly, and then getting a bottle of Sprite in a convenience store." She then goes to a store or coffee shop and pretends she needs to change her baby's diaper so that she can take as long as she needs in there. Then, she says, "In the bathroom, I first fill a couple of baby bottles with formula. Next, I empty the bottle of Sprite in the sink. Then I gently tap the cork of sparkling wine and twist it while holding it . . . I usually remember to flush the toilet at the same time, just in case" it makes a loud noise.[5] She fills the Sprite bottle with the sparkling wine and drinks it in public while caring for her baby.

Heather King describes the development of a ritual in *Parched* of going to a bar that only heavy drinkers frequented daily. She says, "It was like coming together each morning for the administration of a communal anesthetic. . . . We drank silently, methodically, the pace as steady as an I.V. drip. . . . We were like monks or eunuchs, our lives stripped down to a single all-consuming, self-annihilating passion, our focus on the bartender mixing our morning drinks as pure as the gaze of the faithful as the priest raises the consecrated Host."[6] King describes the ritual of drinking as religious and almost sacred. These heavy, daily drinkers at the bar with King remind themselves daily of who they are and whose they are. Their lives are centered around a single purpose in service of a single all-consuming need. Where alcohol was once a substance they used to achieve an end, they now belong to the substance. There's a ritualistic, religious aspect to all kinds of using. Some people with drug addiction describe the ritual of setting out the necessary paraphernalia (e.g., the tourniquet, spoon, lighter, syringe, etc.) before using. There's a kind of comfort in developing a ritual around drug and alcohol use.

3. Caroline Knapp, *Drinking: A Love Story* (Dial Press Trade Paperback, 1996), 103.
4. I am indebted to Lucy Baum for this insight.
5. Jowita Bydlowska, *Drunk Mom: A Memoir* (Penguin Books, 2014), 122.
6. Heather King, *Parched: A Memoir* (New American Library, 2006), 216.

With drinking, in particular, there are also rituals associated with getting rid of the evidence. Caroline Knapp, for instance, says, "Recycling is a problem to the active alcoholic." She says, "I'd slink out of the apartment at night with a pair of great heavy bags" to get rid of the evidence.[7] Bydlowska describes more elaborate rituals of dumping bottles in neighbors' trashcans. All of these little acts of procuring, administering, and getting rid of the addictive substances work to keep the addiction intact. In many ways, they *are* the addiction.

Knapp notes that "the rituals, the little routines, that alcoholics use to break the drinking into segments and minimize its visibility are very preoccupying. You buy, you edge home with your large brown bag, you lock the door behind you, and only then can you relax. All that planning takes energy."[8] The constant preoccupation and busyness of all these small innocuous acts keep the addiction hidden from the outside world, and more importantly keeps the person with the addiction in constant denial, because they are focused on one task at a time, too busy to take note of the larger picture.

Cupcake Brown describes a moment when, after years of using, she is forced to see the impact of those small daily acts. She sees her reflection in a gas station window while outside, hoping to score. She says, "What I saw stopped me in my tracks. . . . My eyeballs were bloodshot and bulging; my sockets seemed to be sunk into my head. My lips were scabbed and burnt from the metal antenna I'd been using for a crack pipe. . . . What shocked me most was the thin figure in the window."[9] Brown had been busy for years—using while trying to keep a job and selling possessions and turning tricks when money ran out to buy dope. The daily rituals of maintaining heavy drug use had kept her so busy that there was no time to take stock of the bigger picture until she literally almost bumped into herself in the window of the gas station and finally saw what years of use had done to her.

The rituals and routines of using keep the addiction alive. Of course, people don't think of them that way because that would be too confronting. Instead, they engage in these acts a single day at a time, slowly building up a routine. Indeed, this is also how recovery works. We stay sober "one day at a time." Knapp says, however, "'the expression *One day at a time*, which they beat into your head in AA, goes both ways.'" She says to a friend, "'One day at a time. You always think you're just doing it this one time, this one night, and tomorrow will be different.'"[10]

While not an addiction for me, I have certainly built up months of unhealthy eating habits by thinking I would go on a diet tomorrow. The same was true for me with addiction. I had this illusion that if I just used one more day, I would "get it out of my system" and then be ready to stop tomorrow. The problem, of

---

7. Knapp, *Drinking*, 103.
8. Knapp, *Drinking*, 115.
9. Cupcake Brown, *A Piece of Cake: A Memoir* (Broadway Books, 2006), 330.
10. Knapp, *Drinking*, 156 (italics in the original), 158.

course, was that there was no moment when I felt satiated enough to stop for good. Slowly, singular acts become rituals and routines that keep the addiction intact.[11]

Just as addiction itself is a practice that is kept alive through repetitive acts and rituals, the process of recovery also demands a kind of training. Action is important because sobriety and living in recovery is a skill that must be learned and practiced. The great cruelty of recovery is not only that it is tremendously difficult but also that it must be faced without the benefit of the recovering person's primary mode of coping with challenges—namely, the substance of "choice."[12] Knapp says, "You take away the drink and you take away the single most important method of coping you have."[13] Laura Cathcart Robbins talks about how unmoored she feels when she first gets out of rehab. She says, "I'm still as scared, sad, and angry as before, only now I'm utterly without any method of soothing myself or buffering the pain."[14] This is one of the reasons basement communities focus so heavily on actions and practices. Knapp says, "The answer in AA is both simple and complex: you just do it, a day at a time. You practice. You ask for help. For a long time you panic and squirm and you live through the discomfort until it eases. And it does ease." Knapp likens this practice to exercise. She says, "Early sobriety has the quality of vigorous exercise, as though each repetition of a painful moment, gone through without a drink, serves to build up emotional muscle."[15] My own sponsor used to call these experiences of staying sober in (situations in which I used to rely on the addiction) sober reference points. Before recovery, a person with addiction lacks historical evidence that they can, for instance, stay sober at a Christmas party. Over time, however, the person builds up a repertoire of sober reference points that serve as evidence that it's possible to go to the office Christmas party and drink sparkling water instead of wine.

People in early sobriety sometimes have to relearn how to do basic things. They might need to retrain themselves to go grocery shopping. How do you go to the grocery store without buying beer? Or perhaps they have to learn how to engage in small talk again. For many people with addiction, the substance of "choice" gave them a sense of confidence in situations that might normally have provoked social anxiety. When Robbins first left rehab, she says she felt "like an alien."[16] She says, "My hand movements felt awkward, flourishy. I balled them

---

11. Augustine would call these the "links hanging one from another," over time creating "a chain [that] bound [him]" (Augustine, *Confessions*, ed. Michael P. Foley, trans. F. J. Sheed, 2nd ed. [Hackett, 2006], 8.v.10–11). See chapter 2 for a more detailed description.
12. As I have said in other chapters, I put the word choice in quotation marks because I don't think people with addiction have as much free will and choice as we often think they do. See chapters 1 and 2 for a more thorough description of free will as it relates to addiction.
13. Knapp, *Drinking*, 254.
14. Laura Cathcart Robbins, *Stash: My Life in Hiding* (Atria Paperback, 2024), 180.
15. Knapp, *Drinking*, 254, 257.
16. Robbins, *Stash*, 169.

up and put them behind me. *What did I used to do with my hands when I talked? How do people just know what to do with their hands? Smile now. Don't say that. Look pleased now.*"[17] It's as if she's relearning how to walk and talk after a major accident. All of these little steps of simply existing in sobriety require practice.

In early recovery, the emphasis is not so much on understanding what recovery is and looks like but rather living into it by engaging in daily rituals so that they eventually become habitual. Mary Karr says that her sponsor told her, "At this point in your life, you don't know how not to drink yet. No alcoholic does. It takes training."[18] In many ways, basement communities coach those in early recovery to engage in the practices that over time bring about recovery and demonstrate by their mere presence that recovery is possible.

In my own early recovery, I wanted to know why I was addicted, why I felt so much shame and self-loathing. I thought that if I could just understand it, I could master it. It took me a long time to realize this was not a problem I could solve in my head. Instead, I had to live into recovery. King puts it this way: "Bring your body, and the mind will follow."[19] This worked surprisingly well for me. At moments when I felt strong cravings, for instance, those in the basement would suggest I get out of the house and take a walk or build some Lego. Invariably, if I did these things, my mind would eventually move away from cravings toward what I saw around me in nature, or toward the Lego set I was building at the time. As they say in recovery, I had to act my way into better thinking. The practices of recovery include going to meetings, talking to a sponsor, working the steps, asking for help, and praying.

Augusten Burroughs, for instance, describes the importance of engaging in the practice of going to a meeting every day when a friend asks how he stays sober. He says, "'You're supposed to go to a meeting. I mean, as much as you hate them or if they feel stupid or you just don't want to go. The thing is, if you go to a meeting, you won't drink that day. It's like a minibrainwash. It kind of fixes you for a little while.'"[20] Burroughs doesn't particularly like meetings, and yet the mundane act of going helps. He talks about his life in recovery as an "almost monastic process of waking up, taking a shower, going to an AA meeting and then doing this again and again, day after day until an amount of time had passed and it became not a struggle, but a routine."[21] The importance of developing this routine is that it becomes a kind of buffer between him and alcohol and drugs.

Just as the person with addiction kept the addiction intact through singular small habitual acts, so the person in recovery lives into recovery through incremental practices. The notion of not using forever is far too overwhelming for a person in early recovery, so we focus instead on small practices that build toward

17. Robbins, *Stash*, 175, 176 (italics in the original).
18. Mary Karr, *Lit* (Harper Perennial, 2009), 209.
19. King, *Parched*, 260.
20. Augusten Burroughs, *Dry* (Picador, 2003), 293.
21. Burroughs, *Dry*, 292.

a life in recovery. In some ways we leverage the system of denial (that worked so well to keep the addiction intact) in service of recovery. By focusing on small daily or even hourly acts, we train our minds to look at the here and now as opposed to seeing the whole (i.e. the goal of staying sober for a lifetime), because the whole is far too terrifying to fathom. Richard Garrett calls this the difference between doing "the good I *would*" want to do but cannot do "by doing the good that I *can*." Thus, he says in "Addiction, Paradox, and the Good I Would,"

> It [recovery] is a matter of discovering the many things that we *can* do to get our addictions under our rational control. *Right Effort* entails doing whatever we *can* do [i.e., the practices of recovery] in order to do all those good things that we rationally *would do* [i.e., stay sober] but irrationally *do not* do and to stop doing those things that we rationally *would not do* [e.g., drink and drive yet again after having already received a DUI] but irrationally *do* anyway.[22]

To put it differently, it is about finding that small space within the condition of the bondage of the will. For Augustine this small space may only include the ability to ask God for help.[23] As I argued in the second chapter, I see a little more space for doing the good than Augustine does yet also recognize that we cannot, on our own, do the ultimate good (i.e., fully align our will with God's).

The importance of engagement in practices over adherence to a story appears most powerfully in memoirs of addiction and recovery when the authors talk about God and prayer. Many people who start recovery in Twelve-Step groups are dismayed when they hear that Twelve-Step recovery invests heavily in the concept of God and ultimately holds that transformation happens due to a "spiritual awakening."[24] For many people with addiction, this concept of a Higher Power (i.e., God) is a major stumbling block to recovery.[25] As I will describe more fully in the next chapter, this was certainly the case for me.

Mary Karr initially describes those in Twelve-Step recovery as unintelligent people who "fancy some bearded giant staring down from a cloud is gonna zap [them] into shape."[26] Many people with addiction struggle with AA's spirituality. Bydlowska, for instance, wryly remarks, "There is lots of God. Officially there's no religion and no leader, but there's 'one ultimate authority—a loving God as He may express Himself.' And He does tend to be shoved down your throat."[27] Bydlowska also takes note of the fact that AA's concept of Higher Power is "a little

---

22. Richard Garrett, "Addiction, Paradox, and the Good I Would," in *Addiction and Responsibility*, ed. Jeffrey Poland and George Graham (MIT Press, 2011), 259 (italics in the original).
23. As I indicated in chapter 2, while Augustine holds this position in his earlier work, *On Free Will* (Augustine, *On Free Will*, in *Augustine: Earlier Writings*, trans. John H. S. Burleigh [Westminster, 1953], III.xix.53), scholars disagree on his position on limited free will in his later works.
24. *Alcoholics Anonymous: The Big Book*, 4th ed. (Alcoholics Anonymous World Services, 2002), 60.
25. The AA *Big Book* uses God and Higher Power interchangeably.
26. Karr, *Lit*, 126.
27. Bydlowska, *Drunk Mom*, 64. Bydlowska references Tradition Two in this quote (*Twelve Steps and Twelve Traditions* [Alcoholics Anonymous World Services, 1953], 132).

too Christian."[28] The references to a Christian notion of God seem to conjure up images of judgment and hell for many in recovery.

As I described in chapter 4, notions of a God of judgment and punishment seem to come easily to those with addiction. I often hear newcomers to Twelve-Step groups talk about God as a stumbling block to recovery, not because they weren't church goers growing up, but precisely because they were. Many of these people had found in the sanctuary a God of judgment and punishment who inspired guilt and shame, and as much as they were desperate for help, they couldn't imagine turning to this God for help. As someone who is deeply committed to the church, I am saddened that we, the church, have failed so many.[29]

While many in recovery initially struggle with the concept of a Higher Power, a lot of people who stay in a Twelve-Step program find that spirituality, and a reliance on a Higher Power of some sort, becomes an important, if not *the* most important, aspect of recovery. However, many do significant work to shed the toxic God-concept of their upbringing. Slowly, it seems, many people in recovery find a way to integrate AA's concept of a Higher Power into their lives. The memoirs of addiction and recovery demonstrate that for many people in recovery, rather than assenting to a particular story about this Higher Power, or about how recovery comes about, they simply begin living into the story of recovery. It is in practicing spirituality and living into the story that they come to both shed unhelpful concepts of God as punishing and judgmental and form a relationship with a God who truly loves them. Thus, crucially, the journey of recovery as metaphor for salvation highlights that salvation can be a practice long before it is a belief.

When Mary Karr, for example, hits a new low in her addiction, she goes to a "local hospital talk on getting sober," where she meets a recovering alcoholic doctor who tells her, "You have to start giving the higher-power thing a try." When Karr objects and says, "I've never felt anything even faintly mystical in my life," the doctor tells her, "Faith is not a feeling. . . . It's a set of actions."[30] This notion, that faith is "a set of actions" rather than a feeling or even a belief, is pervasive in both AA literature and the stories those with addiction tell about their recovery. The set of actions that constitute "faith" brings about liberation from the bondage of addiction for many of those suffering. Karr articulates and demonstrates this beautifully in her memoir. As such, I want to take a moment to further explore Karr's description of her spiritual transformation and then give several other less detailed examples from other memoirs that demonstrate the same concept.

---

28. Bydlowska, *Drunk Mom*, 64.
29. There are clearly people who experience God as loving, accepting, and redemptive in their churches. In fact, had I grown up in my current church, I likely would have had a very different God-concept. Further, not every person who comes into recovery has a concept of God as punishing and judgmental. Yet, in over ten years in recovery meetings, and in reading many stories and memoirs of recovery, I don't often come across people with addiction who have such a positive concept of God.
30. Karr, *Lit*, 215, 217.

As a result of her talk with the doctor, Karr finally prays, "Higher power . . . where the . . . have you been?" Karr does not immediately experience God after she prays. Rather she says, "The silence envelops me. There's something scary there, some blanket of dread around me that feels like God's perennial absence, his abandonment, if he does exist." Karr parenthetically remarks that she would now see this absence as her "deliberate practiced refusal of his presence." Karr finishes her prayer by saying, "Help me. Help. Me. Help me to feel better so I can believe in you, you subtle bastard."[31] Karr continues to pray every day despite not believing in God. She asks God to keep her sober and thanks God at the end of the day.

Karr continues to experiment with prayer and slowly finds that her craving lifts ever so slightly. Karr prays for specific things (e.g., money) and finds that through odd circumstances, she receives some of these things. She is skeptical and assumes these are coincidences, even though her friends convince her to thank God for them. It isn't so much these "answers" to prayer as the practice of praying that seems to help Karr. She begins "practicing a kind of surrender" by taking suggestions from her sponsor, Joan. She still struggles with an actual belief in God yet continues to pray. At a certain point, her friend Janice convinces her to begin praying on her knees. At first Karr is horrified by this suggestion and says, "What kind of God wants me to get on my knees and supplicate myself . . . ?" Janice responds, "You don't do it for God! You do it for yourself . . . It makes you right size." She continues, "You do it to teach yourself something. When my disease has ahold of me, it tells me my suffering is special or unique, but it's the same as everybody's. I kneel to put my body in that place, because otherwise, my mind can't grasp it."[32] For Karr, prayer allows her to embody and practice her relationship with God rather than trying to articulate it.

As Karr continues to engage in the practice of prayer she finds that "prayers of real desperation . . . are starting to come unbidden," and "sometimes one even leaves a sense of peace—or at least hope that peace is coming." She prays in moments of desperation, "*Please keep me away from a drink*" and finds that she "feel[s] like a calmer human than the one who'd knelt a few minutes before." Karr finds that she is, over time, able to kneel as she prays, "unself-consciously" and discovers that through the act of prayer she feels "spirit," a "vast quiet." She says, "The me I've been so lifelong worried about shoring up just dissolves like ash in water. Just isn't. In its place is this clean air."[33]

For Karr, none of these practices are associated with a particular religion until she goes church-hunting because her son, Dev, decides he wants to go to church "*to see if God's there.*" Interestingly, Karr finds that even though her "half-baked sense of a higher power might resonate with the super-liberal Protestant parishes that shun dogma," these parishes actually turn her off. She finds their messages

31. Karr, *Lit*, 219–20.
32. Karr, *Lit*, 241.
33. Karr, *Lit*, 246, 250–51 (italics in the original), 296.

so bereft of any "mention of God or Jesus" that "the homily" might as well have "come from *Reader's Digest*." It is in the Catholic tradition that she finds her home. She says, "It isn't the ritual of the high Mass that impresses me, but the people—their collective surrender." Where Karr learned the practice of personal surrender through prayer, gratitude, and following her sponsor's suggestions, she learns the practice of collective surrender by participating in the collective prayers and liturgy of the church. Karr eventually gets baptized along with her son, not because she understands or even believes in the crucifixion or resurrection, but because "faith is a choice like any other. . . . You can only try it out."[34]

Karr comes to a belief in God through the practice of prayer, gratitude, and baptism. She chooses to act as though she believes and along the way is given signs that she chooses to see as signs of God's love for her. All of this happens not as a result of a set of beliefs, or adherence to a particular story or theology, but as a result of a daily practice. As the doctor once told her, "Faith is not a feeling. . . . It's a set of actions."[35] Karr articulates and demonstrates this concept beautifully and clearly in her memoir. Other people in recovery, though certainly not all, experience a similar transformation through the practice of prayer.

It seems to be the act of praying, rather than the particularities of who is being prayed to, that works. Patrick Moore describes his spiritual journey in *Tweaked* and says that he initially prayed to his deceased boyfriend, Dino, and then "started praying to the ocean" when he "moved to Venice Beach." When he moves to Los Angeles, Moore sits "in Indian sweat lodges," attends "yoga classes," and sits with "Hollywood wives . . . in a circle around a Kabbalah master." He says, "Though I sometimes ridiculed these experiences, I gained something from each of them."[36] Moore participates in workshops and chanting sessions and ends up praying to the god Ganesh. Moore says, "Something is keeping me sober despite my best efforts to head down another path. That something is, of course, my 'higher power.' Those two words have made millions of newcomers to A.A. cringe because of their religious connotation and their sheer geekiness. It's one thing to wallow in our druggy war stories but quite another to start praying."[37] Moore finds that the act of prayer helps, even when the target of that prayer changes. When he leads a group in a halfway house through the Third Step, he has one of them read from the *Twelve Steps and Twelve Traditions*. While Moore does not comment on this particular passage, he does quote it in full. He quotes, "It is when we try to make our own will conform with God's that we begin to use it rightly. To all of us, this was a most wonderful revelation. Our whole trouble had been the misuse of willpower. We had tried to bombard our problems with it instead of attempting to bring it into agreement with God's intention for us."[38] It is

---

34. Karr, *Lit*, 331, 332, 335, 351 (italics in the original).
35. Karr, *Lit*, 217.
36. Patrick Moore, *Tweaked: A Crystal Meth Memoir* (Citadel, 2017), 124, 126.
37. Moore, *Tweaked*, 124.
38. Moore, *Tweaked*, 136. This quote is taken from *Twelve Steps and Twelve Traditions* (Alcoholics Anonymous World Services, 1953), 40.

through the acts of prayer and ritual that Moore begins to align his will with God's. And it is this that helps him remain sober even "despite his best efforts."³⁹

Elizabeth Vargas does not devote a lot of time to her concept of a Higher Power, but she does describe the spiritual practices that keep her sober. She says,

> Today, when I feel anxiety start to overtake me, I pray. When I feel angry, or resentful, or just cranky, I list everything in my life that is a gift. And now I pray when times are good. I end each day by making a gratitude list—all the things I am grateful for that night. . . . And every single day, I thank God for my family, my health, my home, and a job that I still love.⁴⁰

Prayer and meditation are, for her, "powerful weapons" against the desire and craving she still sometimes experiences. She says that meditation "and prayer have helped slow down the escalation of anxiety into panic. . . . But these tools only work if you use them every single day, several times each day. They are not flimsy tools, as I had thought during that last summer and that terrible relapse. They are powerful weapons. They gave me the power to at last say no to drinking. The power to say yes to life."⁴¹ Prayer and meditation provide stability and sobriety for Vargas, even though she does not seem to have a robust concept of God. It is rather the acts of prayer and meditation that matter.

Karr sums up the importance of spiritual practices in this way: "Therapy rescued me in my twenties by taking me inward, leaching off pockets of poison in my head left over from the past. But the spiritual lens—even just the nightly gratitude list and going over each day's actions—is starting to rewrite the story of my life in the present, and I begin to feel like somebody snatched out of the fire, salvaged, saved."⁴² The practices of prayer, gratitude, and a daily inventory allow Karr to rewrite her story, and it is this rewriting that brings about salvation.

The journey from addiction to recovery is a powerful metaphor for salvation because it demonstrates that salvation demands participation. My education in the Christian faith in my middle and high school years was very much focused on belief and story. The story of Jesus taking on the punishment in my stead was presented as truth and as something I had to assent to. While the Reformed tradition would even see the act of believing and assenting to a story as an act of God's grace, I have, nevertheless, spent significant time, even in this book, excavating stories of salvation, questioning which ones I adhere to and which I do not. One of the benefits of the journey of recovery as metaphor for salvation is that it reminds me that belief is often generated through repeated practice.

---

39. Moore, *Tweaked*, 124.
40. Elizabeth Vargas, *Between Breaths: A Memoir of Panic and Addiction* (Grand Central, 2016), 237.
41. Vargas, *Between Breaths*, 237–38.
42. Karr, *Lit*, 304.

The basement demonstrates that freedom may be found, at least in part, in practices in search of faith. Theology is often referred to as "faith seeking understanding," which comes from the first chapter of Anselm's *Proslogion*. At first read, the *Proslogion* is a reasoned argument that seeks to define who God is. After much deliberation, Anselm determines that God is "that than which a greater cannot be thought,"[43] yet discovers that even that is too small, because I could imagine "a being exists" that is just a touch greater than what I can think, and if I can imagine such a being, then it is not God, because God is beyond human conception. So, Anselm says that God is "greater than can be thought," which, if you think about it, is a meaningless proposition to humans since we cannot think it.[44] And that's precisely Anselm's point. I cannot reason my way into a belief in God. Rather, "I believe in order to understand."[45] That is, theology is not a search for rational proofs for God's existence so that we might have faith. Rather, theology is the heart's desire to know God better through understanding *because* one has faith. In other words, belief comes before understanding, and it is because I believe that I seek to understand. I propose that the basement demonstrates that we might even take this a step further back and say that we practice in order to come to belief and belief seeks understanding. Perhaps salvation is, at least in part, practice seeking faith.

I want to be careful to emphasize that I am not suggesting that salvation is achieved through our own works. There is a mystery at play here. In the basement, people often attribute their recovery to God's grace while also engaging in practices that are conducive to sobriety. Just as with the exodus story, this isn't an either-or situation. The Twelve Steps place a heavy emphasis on turning "our will and our lives over to the care of God."[46] Perhaps, similar to the exodus story, freedom is a gift but must also be lived into to be experienced as freedom. While there would be no possibility for freedom for the Israelites in the exodus story without God's act of freeing them from enslavement, freedom also wouldn't truly exist for the Israelites without their living into it by leaving Egypt. Salvation seems to be a combination of gift and practice, and the recovery practices of those in the basement demonstrate that practices need not follow belief or assent to a story. Rather, practice can lead to belief.

---

43. Anselm, *Proslogion*, in *Anselm: Basic Writings*, ed. and trans. Thomas Williams (Hackett, 2007), chap. 2.

44. Anselm, *Proslogion*, chaps. 2 and 15.

45. Anselm, *Proslogion*, chap. 1. While many see Anselm's argument purely as an attempt to prove the existence of God, I read it as a contemplative work in which Anselm ultimately finds joy in recognizing that God is beyond human reason. The first chapter sets the stage for this interpretation as Anselm introduces the text as a prayer to God. Chapters 2 through 15 contain the so-called ontological argument for God's existence, which most readers focus on. Chapters 16 through 26, however, take on a far more mystical (seeing God as "the unapproachable light" in chap. 16, for instance) and eventually lyrical tone as Anselm finds joy in God's presence.

46. *Alcoholics Anonymous: The Big Book*, 59 (Step 3). Interestingly, the Third Step adds the phrase "*as we understood Him*" to the word "God" (italics in the original). Anselm (and most theologians, myself included) would, of course, balk at this. A god we understand is, after all, precisely not God.

In recovery communities they often call this "acting as if." If you don't believe in God, act as if you do (e.g., pray) and see what happens. If you don't feel like going to a meeting, act as if and show up anyway. When I worked at a bookstore many years ago, I would sometimes find myself feeling incredibly grumpy, but because I worked in sales, I would pretend to be cheerful to customers and would often find that in the pretending, my mood would lift somewhat. A saying in basement communities that gets at the same concept is "move the body and the mind will follow." Acting *as if* relies heavily on recognizing ourselves as integrated, embodied beings. Just as the rituals of using create a groove in the brain that makes it difficult to act otherwise (see chapter 1), the rituals of recovery are meant to create new neural pathways that makes it easier to live into recovery.

Rehab was, in many ways, a giant exercise of acting *as if*. When I went to rehab fifteen years ago, I was appalled to discover that I shared a room with someone else and that my room door was locked for most of the day so that I had to spend time in the common areas with others. I was forced to act as if I was the kind of person who spent the majority of their time in community. We had a schedule that we had to adhere to that included meditation, process groups, exercise, yoga, and therapy, and we had no choice about any of it. Of course, I could choose to leave rehab. I didn't lack agency. Rather, rehab forced me to act *as if* I was the kind of person who meditated in the mornings, talked about feelings, and got regular exercise, and in the acting, I discovered that I might actually *be* the kind of person who values talking about feelings, meditating, and exercising regularly. Before rehab, I was convinced that I was a night owl. Being forced to follow a more conventional schedule of going to bed at 10:00 p.m. and waking up at 6:30 a.m. led me to discover that I actually enjoy the mornings. Acting *as if* is a way of practicing what we aspire to be.

At the same time, it's important to recognize that acting *as if* is not a panacea for all ills. It would be toxic, for instance, to tell a person with depression to just act as if they are not depressed. This is not an exercise of papering over our realities and feelings. Rather, it is an exercise of being clear-eyed about the reality, while practicing within those small spaces where action is possible. I could not, for instance, just act as if I was not addicted. Rather, in recognizing that I was suffering from addiction, I had to find those spaces where there was room for action and do those things despite not wanting to. I also needed mental health specialists to help me see where those spaces were. It would be harmful for me (as someone who is not a mental health professional) to tell a person with depression to act as if they could do the dishes, for instance, without knowing whether that's actually possible for that person or not. If rehab was simply an exercise of going about my regular day at work and acting as if I wasn't suffering from addiction, I would have been set up for failure. Rather, similar to what Richard Garrett described earlier in this chapter, I was given incremental small tasks that I was able to do (e.g., get out of bed at 6:30 a.m., talk to people in the community, notice my feelings, etc.) in order to do the big task (i.e., stop using) that I wasn't yet able to do.

The metaphor of the journey of recovery offers an important counterbalance to theologies of atonement that make it seem as if salvation only happens *to* us and not *with* us. Where the sanctuary sometimes depends too much on our acceptance of a story about how we are saved (e.g., that Jesus won our salvation for us by vanquishing the forces of evil on the cross, or by paying a debt on our behalf, etc.), the basement reminds us that we are also actors in this story. At their best, Twelve-Step communities recognize recovery as a balance of grace and practice. I practiced within the limited realm that I was given. I did not have the freedom, at least not initially, to not ever use again, but I did have the freedom to choose to go to a meeting that day. The memoirs demonstrate that consistent, daily, small choices in the direction of recovery, whether that be the choice to pray, go to a meeting, or pick up the phone, can have exponential effects and literally change lives. Drastic life changes demand not just cognitive consent but also embodied consent.

Part of the beauty of the metaphor of the journey of recovery as a way of thinking about salvation is that it holds the tension between divine mystery and human agency. Mary Karr, for instance, uses her agency to engage in the practices of faith, without actually having faith in God yet. And at the same time, she is given signs, some of her prayers are answered, she stays sober, and slowly she recovers. There's both a sense of agency and a sense of divine mystery. These practices are not identical to going to the gym, where there is a clear relationship between lifting weights and building muscle. There is no logical reason, for instance, that Patrick Moore's prayers to his deceased friend, Dino, or the ocean should help him remain sober, and yet they do. There is grace and a sense of divine mystery.[47] The exodus story similarly demonstrated that liberation and freedom require participation and a reliance on God. This is one of the reasons I struggle with theologies that (often unintentionally) pull justification and sanctification apart.

Justification and sanctification are not two different processes that happen sequentially. They are part of the same process of salvation. Part of the beauty of the metaphor of the journey into recovery is that it holds the processes of justification and sanctification so closely together that you cannot untangle the one from the other. Where in the exodus story, one could say that justification technically happens when Pharaoh and his army are destroyed in the Red Sea, and sanctification begins when they start their journey through the wilderness, in the journey from addiction to recovery there is no moment one can point to as *the* moment when liberation technically occurs. If there's one thing all the memoirs seem to agree on, it is that freedom from addiction is a process. In these stories, living into the freedom of recovery through the engagement of practices of recovery *is* what it means to be freed from addiction. Indeed, it is difficult to point to a beginning moment of the journey, and there is a sense that we also never really arrive. The journey from addiction to recovery happens daily and

---

47. I am grateful to Lucy Baum for offering me this insight.

is always ongoing. It is helpful to have a metaphor for salvation that so closely aligns justification and sanctification that you cannot untangle them because this is how we experience salvation.

SALVATION IS A SOFT LANDING PLACE

The second benefit of the metaphor of the journey of recovery is that it names the importance of community. While I explore basement practices around community more fully in the next chapter, I offer a few observations here.

Creating community is a central principle of Twelve-Step recovery. People in AA often say, "You alone can do it, but you cannot do it alone." What they mean by "you alone can do it" is that no one can make another person recover or stay sober. Practicing sobriety and recovery was up to me. No one could do that for me. This is an important lesson to learn early on, both for the person recovering and the community. Without this recognition, people sometimes take on inappropriate responsibility for another person's recovery. Just as I had to learn that no one could recover or stay sober for me, I also had to learn that I do not have the power to make another person recover, as much as I might want to. At the same time, however, there is also a recognition in basement communities that "you cannot do it alone." For most, recovery is simply too hard to do by yourself. Part of practicing sobriety and recovery entails learning to live in community.

William Cope Moyers articulates the importance of community in AA when he says,

> This wasn't a course of self study, I quickly learned, for the emphasis was never on "I" or "mine" but always on "we" and "ours." "We admitted we were powerless over alcohol and that our lives had become unmanageable" reads the first step of Alcoholics Anonymous. It would take me a long time to realize how critically important that word *we* is to life-long recovery—and how a self-centered focus on *I* can literally be life threatening—but even in those first days at Hazelden I began to glimpse the reality that recovery happens within a community and not in isolation.[48]

Community is embedded in the language of the Twelve Steps. As Moyers notes, the Twelve Steps and the *Big Book* never talk about "I" and "mine," but rather about "we" and "ours." Moyers eventually comes to see community as a primary principle of recovery. He says, "At its heart and in its soul, recovery from addiction is about fellowship—becoming part of a bigger whole. We are all broken, and the only 'cure' for our brokenness is to be broken together."[49] What is it that makes being "broken together" so powerful?

48. William Cope Moyers, *Broken: My Story of Addiction and Redemption* (Penguin Books, 2007), 161.
49. Moyers, *Broken*, 348.

For many people with addiction, AA and NA meetings were the first places they felt a true sense of belonging. Addiction is, in many ways, a disease of isolation. While it may at times seem social, it inevitably makes social circles smaller and smaller. Ultimately, the progression of addiction leads to a diminished existence. Everything becomes smaller. King describes discovering this reductive aspect of addiction in her life in her memoir, *Parched*. When King graduates from law school only to discover that she cannot possibly find a regular job given her dependence on alcohol, she says, "My world was getting smaller by the minute." Eventually, her "existence" literally shrinks "down to a triangle with a quarter-mile border—my apartment, Macy's Liquor and JT's [the local bar]: there were prison yards with bigger perimeters."[50] While I was what people call a "functioning addict," in that I had a job and friends and seemed fine on the outside, I also experienced the isolating effects of addiction in that my interior life became smaller and smaller. My life centered on addiction. When I was with friends, studying, or at work, half my mind was in another world, thinking about how I might create opportunities to use again, or wondering if I had hidden the evidence well enough. It was as if I had another full-time job that I was attending to in the background (and sometimes in the foreground) all the time.

Besides being in another world in my mind all the time, the shame associated with addiction also created a sense of otherness that felt isolating. I came to recovery with an abiding sense of shame. Just as addiction and recovery are practices, shame is a practice as well. Every time I lied about where I had been and what I had been doing to my partner or friends, I practiced shame. Every time I anxiously hid the evidence, I practiced shame. Lies and hiding are practices that engender shame. As I outlined in chapter 3, shame in addiction is not just internal. Those around the person with addiction, often without intending to do so, also bring their own sense of shame to the mix, which adds to the internal shame the person with addiction is already experiencing. All of these elements work together to create an isolating effect.

This is why a sense of belonging is so important for those in recovery. A recovering drug-addicted person, for instance, says, "That feeling of belonging I had at that first meeting was therefore so important—it made certain that I kept coming back." Another shares, "That is when I heard the most profound thing ever told to me by any recovering addict: In the Fellowship of Narcotics Anonymous, you are never alone. I never wanted to believe someone so badly."[51] This sense of belonging is, for many, what they had searched for all along through their addictions. Heather King has her first experience of communities in recovery at a treatment center. She says, "In a sterile meeting room in the middle of rural Minnesota, I began to glimpse the feeling I had looked for all

---

50. King, *Parched,* 212, 228.
51. *Narcotics Anonymous,* 6th ed. (World Service Office, 2008), 204, 237.

those years in sleazy barrooms: a sense of fellowship, belonging, home."[52] This search for belonging is common among those who use. When I was in rehab, for instance, I met many men who engaged in what is known as chemsex or PnP (party and play), which is the use of methamphetamines or other stimulants to have multiple or lengthy sexual encounters. Several of the men I met in rehab described this practice as their way of looking for connection and a sense of belonging. This is one of the reasons rehabs tend to focus on creating a sense of community.

King indicates that the safety of the community she found in rehab allows her to let go of alcohol and grow in recovery. Near the end of her stay in treatment, she says, "Safe in the circle, I was content to sit quietly—pondering the joys and sorrow of the real world, the mysterious resurrectability of the human heart, the strange new life that lay ahead: drinking it all deliriously in."[53] For King, this community allows for the type of healing that brings about redemption. Creating community is, therefore, a central principle of Twelve-Step recovery.

CONCLUSION

The journey of recovery is a helpful metaphor for salvation because it names the importance of community. As demonstrated in this and the last chapter, salvation is a long and arduous journey, with many ups and downs. The metaphor of the journey of recovery offers the crucial reminder that we cannot and should not go on the journey of salvation alone. In the next chapter, I explore the importance of community, mutual sharing, and vulnerability further and suggest ways churches might incorporate some of these basement practices in the sanctuary.

---

52. King, *Parched*, 262.
53. King, *Parched*, 270.

Chapter 8

Basement Practices for the Sanctuary

When I talk about theologies of addiction and recovery in seminary classrooms and with people in churches, I am often asked what churches can and should do to help those with addiction. Some pastors have indicated that they would like a handout or a curriculum that they can easily use in their churches to offer a helping hand to those with addiction. While opinions vary on this, my own sense is that people with addiction don't necessarily need or want programs, liturgies, or even churches catered specifically to them. Basement communities already exist for this purpose. Likewise, as a queer person, I don't need or want a church specifically catered to queer people (again, opinions vary on this). Rather I want to be in the kind of church community where I can show up fully as myself.

Thus, perhaps the more important question than what churches can *do* to help those with addiction is the question of what churches might *become* to be the kinds of communities that those with addiction could call home. I do not mean to imply that churches ought not *do* anything. After all, I argued in the last chapter for the importance of practices. I suggest instead that rather than

---

Large portions of the chapter were previously presented as a TheoEd Talk. Jennifer Carlier, "Finding God in the Basement," September 2022, https://www.theoed.com/jennifercarlier.

focusing on one-off Bible studies, or occasional prayers, we might focus on practices (repeated behaviors) that over time lead to ways of being together in community that allow for more openness and acceptance of people in all the messy ways we show up.

People with addiction need to know that their churches can theologically and socially bear the weight of their existence in all its manifestations—that their churches can bear the weight of profound suffering and offer hope for wholeness even among the wreckage. Indeed, this is what most people need, whether addicted or not. Thus, rather than offering specific liturgies, prayers, and curricula, I use this chapter to describe the authenticity, mutual sharing, and vulnerability that I experienced in the basement and paint a picture of what it might look like to implement some of these basement practices in church settings, recognizing that each church will have to contextualize these practices in their particular setting. Doing this difficult work of building authentic communities in spaces that are not always set up for it will certainly help those with addiction, but far more importantly, it will help all of us in the sanctuary better live into our identity of being a communion of sinners and saints.

Before I delve into these basement practices, I want to take a moment to tell a little of my story, especially as it pertains to what I took away from the churches I attended in childhood and early adulthood so that you might better understand my sense of urgency around creating authentic communities in churches. My understanding of God was formed in the missionary schools and churches I grew up in and is, as such, deeply entangled with parts of my life story that have little to do with addiction. And yet the understanding of God that was forged from these experiences made it easy for me to get lost in addiction and even more difficult to recover. In an odd reversal the fact that I grew up in church ended up being a catalyst for addiction, and more perniciously, a hindrance to recovery. While my story is specific to me, I have met many people in recovery for whom their experience of churches made it more rather than less difficult to recover. I share a little of my story below to demonstrate how I was tutored in the churches I grew up in and how what I learned there affected both the depth of my addiction and my capacity to recover. Before I begin, however, I want to be sure to recognize that the churches I grew up in did the very best they could with the information they had at the time. People in my church community loved me and wanted what was best for me and unfortunately unintentionally also caused deep pain.

I grew up as a missionary kid in Taiwan and while there, between the ages of ten and sixteen, went to a conservative evangelical Christian school. At this school, we were taught math, science, and literature, alongside a host of more conservative theologies around purity, sin, heaven, and hell. I have already talked about some of these theologies (e.g., the moral model of sin and penal-substitutionary atonement) in previous chapters and indicated how they shaped my understanding of God as loving me *in spite of* me.

Within the category of sin, we spent a lot of time at this school talking about dating, learning about the "bases" and how we weren't supposed to get very far around them. And in all of this talk the presumption was that we were talking about partnerships between males and females. The idea of falling in love with someone of the same gender or sex was so unthinkable that it wasn't even mentioned as one of the options on the table. So, for a lot of my childhood, I had no name for what I was experiencing (being gay). And because I had no name for it, it didn't exist. As I've pointed out in previous chapters, language is one way we validate an experience. Being given words to name an experience is one way of acknowledging that the experience exists. As Sallie McFague says, "We can live only within the confines of our language."[1] So, for the longest time, I lived within the confines of a heteronormative reality. And there was no room in that reality for me.

Eventually, the churches I grew up in *did* start talking about "homosexuality." At best, these churches took a "love the sinner, hate the sin" approach, which is complicated when the so-called "sin" is also your identity. Hating the "sin" started to feel a lot like they hated me. When my family left Taiwan when I was sixteen, I went through a long period of hiding my identity. I knew, from sermons, Bible studies, and things my friends said in passing, that the communities I was a part of would not be accepting of me. So, I spent many years hiding my identity to the point that I was essentially living two lives. It was very good training for becoming addicted. I was well-trained in the practice of living a double life by the time my addiction fully developed.

There were many painful things about hiding my identity, but the most destructive was that the hiding itself reinforced the belief that there was something fundamentally wrong with me—so wrong that my church wouldn't be able to accept me if they knew. And if my church wouldn't accept me, then surely God wouldn't accept me either. It wasn't just that I thought I was doing something wrong—I thought my very being was wrong.

That sense of being wrong is, of course, the feeling of shame, and as I've described in chapter 3, shame is inextricably tied to addiction for many people. In early addiction, I often used to escape unpleasant feelings—especially feelings of shame. As many people with addiction know all too well, using doesn't get rid of shame; it only heightens it. So, I often found myself caught in a shame spiral where I would use to diminish shame only to feel more shame because I had used, which would, in turn, generate another binge. As many people with addiction do, I got lost in a vicious downward spiral that circled around shame.

To be clear, I am not suggesting that the experiences of shame in the churches I grew up in *caused* addiction. As I demonstrated in chapter 1, addiction is far too complex a phenomenon to point to one thing as its primary cause. Rather, I'm suggesting that the combination of shame and addiction created a vicious downward shame spiral I could not easily get out of.

1. Sallie McFague, *Speaking in Parables* (Augsburg Fortress, 2000), 22.

More importantly, because my sense of shame was fostered in church, it felt God-ordained. That is, the churches I grew up in said, in so many words (and largely unintentionally), that there was something fundamentally wrong with my identity, and because churches said it, it felt as if it came directly from God. This God-ordained sense of shame, heightened by toxic theologies such as the moral model of sin and penal-substitutionary atonement, became a significant obstacle to recovery.

The theologies churches had spoon-fed me all my life weren't just unhelpful when it came to seeking recovery from addiction. The images of God these theologies engendered in me actively stood in the way of recovery. I know that these churches intended to convey to me that God loved me. While I certainly heard that God loved me, the lesson that I really took in was that God loved me *in spite of* me—that I was fundamentally unlovable, and that God in God's greatness figured out how to love me anyway. And this unintended lesson from these churches that I was fundamentally bad stayed with me. It seeped into my bones. That God-ordained sense of being unlovable made it both easy to get lost in addiction and almost impossible to recover.

I had been going to church most of my life by the time I got to rehab and later Twelve-Step groups in the basements of churches, and yet, the concept that I struggled with the most in Twelve-Step recovery was God. While the Twelve Steps are set up to help people recover from alcoholism and other addictions, these steps only mention alcohol one time. The first step asks the person with addiction to admit that they "were powerless over alcohol." The remaining steps are all about living into a life of spiritual reflection and action. The third step, for instance, reads, We "made a decision to turn our will and our lives over to the care of God *as we understood Him*."[2] As a person tutored in churches, I should have been well-primed to turn my will and life "over to the care of God." Ironically, however, I struggled enormously with this step, not because I had never been to church, but precisely because I *had*.

I discovered in these basement meetings that I wasn't the only person who felt this way. Many people who grew up in churches wrestled enormously with the notion that God is central to Twelve-Step recovery. Again, they resisted the idea of turning their lives over to God, not because they hadn't been to church before, but because they *had*. They, like me, had experienced God through churches that espoused theologies of judgment and shame. For many of them it wasn't about theological stances around sexual orientation as it was for me; for many of them it had to do more with the theologies of sin and salvation that they heard growing up that led them to believe that God was judgmental.

As is true for many people, I sought out more liberative ways of thinking about my gender identity and sexual orientation, and about sin and salvation, in my adult life. Both the seminary and the more progressive churches I later attended offered me a more expansive and nuanced view of God, which allowed

---

2. *Alcoholics Anonymous: The Big Book,* 4th ed. (Alcoholics Anonymous World Services, 2002), 59.

me to see grace and salvation anew; I have shared some of this view in earlier chapters. I was intrigued and over time convinced that these theologies spoke to who I believe God to be. However, I discovered that while I wanted to take in these different theologies of sin and salvation, they couldn't easily penetrate what I believed in my bones about God. It has not been easy to unentangle myself from the theologies of my childhood.

I also noticed that even progressive churches would sometimes inadvertently teach about the God of wrath and punishment in hymns, liturgies, and prayers.[3] For instance, the beautifully haunting hymn "What Wondrous Love Is This" speaks of humans "sinking down beneath God's righteous frown" and of Christ bearing "the dreadful curse for my soul."[4] Years ago, I worked as a volunteer youth group leader at a progressive church. A couple of weeks before Easter, we had a conversation with the youth, all of whom were born into this church, about the meaning of the Lent and Easter seasons. When we asked the youth to tell us what they thought Easter was about, they cobbled together a version of penal-substitutionary atonement. They talked about sin and how God couldn't stand human sin and demanded a punishment, then explained that Jesus took on our punishment in our stead. While these junior high students seemed open to other ways of thinking about the cross and salvation when offered alternative metaphors, I wondered why these kids who had grown up in this very progressive church where we never explicitly talked about punishment still drank from these theological waters. I imagine that this is partly a cultural phenomenon that kids see reflected in the judicial system (see chapter 5) and the ways those around them speak about crime and punishment, and partly the result of unintended theologies that were passed along in hymns and liturgies. I walked away from that experience and others like it, wondering what it would take for me, for these kids, for our broader society that equates justice with punishment to see God differently? How do we allow these other, more liberative ways of thinking about and experiencing God seep into the marrow of our bones so that we might truly believe what we speak with our mouths?

---

3. E.g., see "Alas! And Did My Savior Bleed" (#212) and "O Sacred Head Now Wounded" (#221) in *Glory to God* (Westminster John Knox, 2013). There are many hymns (in a variety of hymnals), especially in sections relating to Jesus's passion and death, that speak of Jesus suffering in our stead. It is often difficult to discern if these hymns are referring to penal-substitutionary atonement or ransom theory. Both theologies of atonement rely on language of sacrifice with the crucial difference being that in the former, Jesus is punished to pay a price that humans owe to God, where in the latter Jesus sacrifices himself in order to free us from Satan, who rightfully owns us until Jesus pays the price. The latter would align more with theologies of freedom from bondage, where the former focuses more on absolution from punishment. People likely hear and take in these hymns in alignment with the theology they are most familiar with, regardless of the intent of the author. Thus, I heard and understood these hymns as referencing Jesus's punishment in my stead, as this was the theology I was most familiar with. Some hymns, however, speak more clearly to a specific theology of atonement, such as "What Wondrous Love Is This" (#215 in *Glory to God*).

4. *Glory to God*, #215.

My most formative education into these more expansive ways of thinking about God happened not in the sanctuary but in the basement, in a room full of so-called drunks and addicts. They taught me the meaning of unconditional love and grace and pointed me to the God of grace, healing, and hope. They showed me, through their own unrelenting acceptance, love, and hope for me, who God is. This book has, in many ways, been a response to the difficulty I and many of my fellows in recovery experienced as a result of the harmful theologies we had been spoon-fed and a recognition of the gift of grace many of us were given in these basement communities.

These basement communities formed me anew and they did so, not through a particular set of teachings (even though they have a particular set of teachings —i.e., the Twelve Steps), but by being a particular kind of community. While I learned a lot about how to live in recovery from the Twelve Steps, the most impactful thing about the basement for me was not the steps but the community. This is why I focus on basement practices churches might engender to become more authentic communities in the rest of this chapter, rather than on curricula or liturgies churches might implement to support those with addiction.

While there are many things I learned in the basement, there are three things that stood out as being especially important in basement communities: the recognition that we are all broken and in need of help, the importance of mutual sharing, and the notion that vulnerability can function as an act of hospitality. It is my hope that these three basement values and practices might continue to make their way up to the sanctuary so that in being a community of faith together, we might come to see even more of the love and grace of God.

BRINGING THE BASEMENT TO THE SANCTUARY

Common Brokenness

One of the first things I learned in the basement is that we are all broken and in need of healing. I learned this almost as soon as I walked into my first meeting. Every time someone opened their mouth in a meeting to share, they said, "My name is 'so-and-so,' and I'm an addict." At first, I struggled with this way of introducing myself. It was counterintuitive to keep harping on the problem in that way. It also seemed unhealthy to bind one's identity so tightly to the problem as to name oneself "an addict."

Some theologians who write about addiction see this practice of naming oneself an addict as unhealthy because it binds the person's identity to a "pathology." Linda Mercadante, for instance, says that a fundamental difference between churches and basement communities is that basement communities create a group identity through common brokenness, while churches are bound together through common grace: "although weakness, finitude, and fallibility are endemic to the human condition, the goal and focus of the church are different. Through the Spirit's power, the church is to envision and actualize the human condition, as it is meant to be and as it is becoming."[5] While I understand the point and agree that over-identification with addiction could become unhealthy, I also recognize that this difference she names between basement communities and churches is precisely what makes it so difficult to talk about brokenness in the sanctuary and keeps people isolated. We are often so eager to show up as we imagine we are "meant to be"[6] in the sanctuary that we fail to show up as ourselves. While churches regularly name that we are broken, we rarely talk about what that brokenness actually entails and the impact it has on each of our lives. Recognizing brokenness in the specific ways it shows for each of us, while perhaps not the first step toward freedom and salvation, is certainly part of the process of salvation and a part that churches often gloss over or only talk about in broad terms. Of course, recognizing brokenness and living in grace are not mutually exclusive propositions.[7]

In theory, we recognize that we are all broken in the sanctuary. This is one of the reasons people often say that "the church is a hospital for sinners, not a museum for saints."[8] Indeed, the late Pope Francis said in a 2013 interview, "The thing the church needs most today is the ability to heal wounds and to warm the hearts of the faithful; it needs nearness, proximity. I see the church as a field hospital after battle."[9] The idea behind seeing the church as a hospital is that we are not a community of perfect people but rather a community of the broken, longing for healing.[10] This sentiment fits well with Jesus's ministry, in which he almost exclusively communes with those society deems sinful and broken. In his ministry, Jesus is, in fact, critical of religious institutions that feign perfection, as his regular arguments with the Pharisees and Sadducees demonstrate. For his own disciples, Jesus gathers twelve deeply flawed men, one of whom denies him on the day he needs him most, and one of whom betrays him, leading to his execution. He purposefully gathers with tax-collectors and sinners—and spends most of his time looking for the broken. When the Pharisees ask why he does

---

5. Linda Mercadante, *Victims and Sinners: Spiritual Roots of Addiction and Recovery* (Westminster John Knox, 1996), 162–63.

6. Mercadante, *Victims and Sinners*, 163.

7. Reformed theologians, like John Calvin, would argue that the recognition of sin only comes once someone is caught by grace. Thus, the recognition of the need for grace often comes, ironically, after grace is already received. Interestingly, a similar pattern is at work in basement communities. People often don't recognize how bad their addiction was until they come to the basement and begin the healing process. While I was certainly aware of being generally unhappy while in active addiction, it was only in recovery and in hindsight that I could see the depth of despair I had lived in for many years.

8. This saying is often attributed to Augustine.

9. Antonio Spadaro, SJ, "A Big Heart Open to God: An Interview with Pope Francis," *America the Jesuit Review* (September 20, 2013), https://www.americamagazine.org/faith/2013/09/30/big-heart-open-god-interview-pope-francis. I'm grateful to my editor, Stacy Davis, for (among many other things) pointing me to this article.

10. In this same interview, Pope Frances is asked, "'Who is Jorge Mario Bergoglio?'" After a pause, he answers, "I am a sinner. This is the most accurate definition" (Spadaro, "A Big Heart Open to God").

this, Jesus says, "It is not the healthy who need a doctor, but the sick" (Luke 5:31 NIV).

Most people in the sanctuary are theoretically in agreement with the sentiment that the church is a hospital for sinners. Yet, for a community that sees itself as a hospital for sinners, we seem oddly surprised when someone in our midst turns out to be an actual sinner. It seems we want to be a place of healing for those who are broken, without having to admit that any of *us* are in fact broken.

In the basement no one is confused about their identity. Everyone—whether they've been in recovery for twenty-five years, or not even twenty-four hours—introduces themselves as an addict. Everyone shares what is going on in their lives and in their minds, admitting to the messiness of it all. It's why we're in the room together. If I walked into a basement meeting full of people who pretended they weren't addicted, I'd be mystified. And yet, this happens in the sanctuary on an almost weekly basis. When I sit next to my fellows in the sanctuary, I do not sit next to them in full recognition of our common brokenness, because brokenness is often merely theoretical in the sanctuary, the details of which are relegated to the realm of the private.

For me, church was a place where our family showed up on our best behavior. We didn't swear at church, and whatever else was going on in my family that day, when we arrived at church, we put on our smiles, stopped fighting, and looked the part. We smoothed out all the rough edges before entering the building, lest people see the messiness of our (and everyone's) lives. To be fair, the churches I grew up in were able to cope with some areas of life's difficulties. For instance, we were great at creating meal trains when there was a death in the family, or someone broke their leg or was diagnosed with cancer. But I don't recall us ever starting a meal train for someone lost in depression, or someone who relapsed on their addiction. These topics were off limits and, therefore, beyond the reach of care. Kent Dunnington writes in *Addiction and Virtue* that the "prevalence of such communities [i.e., recovery communities] can be seen as an indictment of the church." He says, "the massive growth of twelve-step groups has exposed the church's inability to deal honestly and adequately with the brokenness of persons."[11]

I want to be clear here that it is not my intention to conflate issues of morality (what churches often call moral evil or moral sin) with issues of suffering and brokenness. These are clearly not the same, and yet the lines between them can be incredibly blurry, which is why I am concerned about using the language of sin to talk about addiction. Sin, as I have explained (see chapter 2), is often conflated with moral failing. In the Christian tradition, sin is a concept that is so much more expansive and nuanced than moral failing. However, because most people conflate sin and moral failing, I prefer to talk about the condition of the bondage of the will. We are caught in systems not of our own making

---

11. Kent Dunnington, *Addiction and Virtue: Beyond the Models of Disease and Choice* (IVP Academic, 2011), 169, 179.

that cause tremendous suffering and under which we often cause harm to others. Addiction is a prime example of this condition in that it is hard to draw a clear boundary between the condition of addiction and the harms perpetrated under that condition. For instance, is stealing in order to support a daily drug habit part of the condition of the illness or an issue of morality?[12] Churches and American society more generally can sometimes get caught up in trying to parse out moral failing from suffering. This is one of the reasons the war on drugs seemed logical. One of the things I appreciated about the basement is that I could talk about all of it—the condition of addiction that trapped me and the many things I did to cause harm under that condition. Being in a community in the basement where we recognized that everyone is broken was tremendously healing for me.

A small way that churches can begin to name, if not share, the burden of collective and individual brokenness is to speak in our prayers, sermons, and liturgies about the various ways we suffer. Thus, we might include language around addiction or other mental health challenges, such as depression, bipolar disorder, schizoaffective disorder, suicidal ideation, etc., in our extemporaneous and liturgical prayers or sermons. Likewise, we would do well to include those with mental health challenges (with permission, of course) in our efforts to support those in need through cards, visits, or meal trains. Again, I want to be careful here to note that I am *not* saying that the many ways we suffer that I just named are manifestations of sin. As I have clearly stated in chapter 2, I do not see the condition of addiction (or any of the conditions I name above) as sin. I take the notion that the "church is a hospital for sinners" more broadly to mean that we are given permission to show up fully as ourselves. And I also take it as an invitation to treat those things we normally think of as issues of morality (e.g., adultery, lying, stealing, etc.) with a great deal of compassion, recognizing that given the right circumstances many of us would find ourselves doing things we imagined we would never do. As I've talked about throughout this book, language has tremendous power for both good and ill. Naming people's realities is one small act that goes a long way toward destigmatizing and normalizing people's experiences.

Language validates the reality of people's experiences. As I said at the beginning of this chapter, until I had language to talk about being gay, I had no way to fully acknowledge the reality of being gay even for myself. To give a trivial example, when I was thirteen, I had a group of friends, and there was one friend that I really, really liked, but because she was a girl and people in my community didn't talk about sexual orientation, I didn't know what I was experiencing. My feelings, however, were strong enough that I wrote her a song (as you do) that I recorded on my tape recorder, the profound words of which were "I like you in a special way, and . . . I like you in a special way." Growing up in a missionary community, no one had ever told me about same-gender-loving couples, so I had no idea that

---

12. See chapter 3 for a fuller discussion of the complexities of the concepts of disease and sin as it relates to addiction.

what I was experiencing was the feeling of being in love. Without language, I was able to gesture toward what I was experiencing, but it wasn't until I was given language (e.g., same-gender-loving, queer, gay, lesbian, etc.) that I was able to fully recognize myself. Language is powerfully validating. Thus, naming people's realities in sermons, prayers, and conversations is one small step that churches can take toward creating welcoming spaces for those with addiction and other afflictions.

Mutual Sharing

The second thing I learned in the basement is that there is power in mutual sharing. Kent Dunnington rightly notes that "when a member [in the basement] speaks of craving, withdrawal, depression, loneliness, or even relapse, he is not raising an issue that must be dealt with before the group can move on to its business; he is doing the group's business." The church, on the other hand, "has too often been less committed to fostering an atmosphere in which its members feel not only free but indeed expected to publicly recognize their status as sinners and narrate their lives to others within this paradigm."[13] Publicly recognizing one's status as one who is sinful or broken might conjure up images of more conservative churches where some members are asked to share their sin publicly (usually people who commit adultery) while others are not. The decision regarding who must confess publicly and who needn't is usually linked to the perceived gravity of sin, which in turn causes shame. This is not what I'm advocating for. The sharing I'm promoting is reciprocal in nature. That is, in basement communities, I share authentically, because everyone does. I am not made a spectacle or example by being asked to be the lone person sharing my deepest pain or most heinous shortcomings. Rather, the sharing is an open invitation to everyone in the room, and the more people share of their lives, the more shame is reduced for everyone.

As I've indicated in previous chapters, shame is a perennial problem in addiction that often keeps the person locked in cycles of using. While shame may not play exactly the same role in the lives of people who are not addicted, most people hold a good dose of shame about something in their lives, whether that be a past trauma, a perceived failure of parenting, a body image issue, or perhaps a harm caused to another person. Shame thrives in silence and secrecy and often ends up coming out sideways in a hurtful remark, envy, an inability to set boundaries, or an insatiable drive to be perfect. Most people carry a burden of shame about something in their lives.

I came to the basement with a crushing amount of shame. There were things that I thought, did, and experienced that I didn't want anyone to ever know about. These secrets took up space in my life and kept that small (and sometimes very loud) voice alive in my head that would say "if only people knew that I'm an addict, they . . ." wouldn't love me, wouldn't say such complimentary things,

13. Dunnington, *Addiction and Virtue*, 186.

wouldn't want to be around me, and so on. That voice became a self-defeating engine that snatched defeat out of the jaws of victory every time.

When I finally began sharing my story in the basement, the most interesting thing I learned was that I'm not all that interesting. I learned in the basement that most of us are having a fairly standard human experience. There were variations in the way we lived out our addiction, insecurities, fears, and sense of failure, but even in these differences, it quickly became clear to me that we all played to a similar tune. We were not that different from each other. As we say in the basement, "you're just another bozo on the bus." I've been in the recovery community for well over a decade, and while I've certainly heard stories that stood out—in being especially painful, or beautiful, or embarrassing, or sad—I have never heard a story I could not relate to in some way.

When I first came to the basement, I knew in theory that I was not the first or only person who had done some of the things that I did that caused me the most shame. The internet told me that much. Yet it wasn't until I actually said these things out loud and saw the nods of affirmation and smiles of recognition that I really believed it. It wasn't until I recognized my own story in the story of another that I found freedom from isolation and shame.

Mutual sharing becomes especially important in the basement when someone relapses. Basement communities offer a soft landing place when relapses happen. The community is always there to welcome back the person who has relapsed. For instance, Neil Steinberg says that after his relapse "nobody seems critical," and "after the meeting, people linger, come over to" him and "say a few kind words. . . ." They've been there; they know."[14] Almost everyone in the recovery community has gone through a relapse, or at the very least had a close call. There is a sense of understanding and empathy.

Jowita Bydlowska demonstrates this empathy when she talks to her friend Chris from the meetings, who has recently relapsed. Chris is five days sober and having a hard time sleeping. Bydlowska asks, "You think you'll sleep tonight?" Chris finally says, "Thing is, I'm afraid to wake up." Bydlowska immediately knows what she's talking about and says, "You mean you're afraid to be awake." Chris nods in agreement. Bydlowska knows, "It's easier not to wake up. The world goes on. But not with you in it." Bydlowska is able to offer Chris the gift of validation by truly seeing her and recognizing the tremendous pain of early recovery. She says, "This is why we're here together, on this side of addiction. We'll always understand what it's like to be afraid to wake up."[15] By being able to bear witness to Chris's pain without trying to fix it, Bydlowska offers her a soft landing place. She can do this because she knows exactly what it's like to relapse, how difficult those first days of sobriety are, and how hard it is to want to live in those early days.

---

14. Neil Steinberg, *Drunkard: A Hard-Drinking Life* (Plume, 2008), 213.
15. Jowita Bydlowska, *Drunk Mom: A Memoir* (Penguin Books, 2014), 300.

The community is able to offer grace, acceptance, and love. These communities are sacred because they are authentic and because they are built on acceptance and love. A member of AA says, "A.A.'s [i.e., the people in the meetings] had unconditionally loved me until I could."[16] Similarly, a recovering drug-addicted person says, "The emotional pain was intense, and there were moments when I thought I was going to die, but the love and care of other addicts helped me to carry on and to take it a day at a time."[17] The bonds that are forged through authenticity and love are almost familial in nature. Bydlowska, for instance, runs into a member of her group whom she hasn't seen in a long time, and when they part, she says, "We hug each other as if we were a family. As if we were a family and haven't seen each other for decades—as if one of us, or both of us, were at war the whole time. Now we are safe."[18] Members of AA and NA frequently see their fellows in recovery as siblings.[19]

In recovery communities, people bear witness to each other's stories, and in these stories recognize themselves. These stories take on qualities of the sacred. Caroline Knapp articulates this when she says, "When people talk like that about their deepest pain, a stillness often falls over the room, a hush that's so deep and so deeply shared it feels like reverence." People in recovery offer each other the gift of bearing witness, and at the same time receive the gift of recognition. Further, people in these communities also offer each other a tremendous amount of hope through mutual sharing. As Knapp says, "in their very first weeks of sobriety, people . . . are frightened and despairing and not at all sure that meetings are going to help them." And yet, she also says, "AA is like a daily shot of hope: you see people around you grow and change and flower. You hear people struggling, out loud, to get through the days. Meetings keep things in perspective."[20] People in recovery communities share both their brokenness and their growth, and in so doing support each other through the journey of recovery. As Steinberg says, there is "something triumphant in these thousands of bands of disparate individuals, united as best they can in a single purpose, like earth's battered survivors, gathered in caves, courageously fighting back against an overwhelming alien invader."[21] Gathering in communities allows people in recovery to do together what they could not do alone.

In an unexpected way, this mutual sharing taught me more about God and my faith than the churches I had been to up until then ever had. Sharing my story with a community that valued it as sacred, that saw it as part of who I am today and held it without judgment, was a profound experience of grace. My sponsor and fellow recovering addicts gave me the gift of time, of being

16. *Alcoholics Anonymous: The Big Book*, 336.
17. *Narcotics Anonymous*, 217.
18. Bydlowska, *Drunk Mom*, 290.
19. Interestingly, people in churches also often refer to each other as siblings. However, while churches use similar nomenclature, I have found that the familial communities that are created in the basement tend to run much deeper than those in the sanctuary.
20. Caroline Knapp, *Drinking: A Love Story* (Dial Press Trade Paperback, 1996), 256.
21. Steinberg, *Drunkard*, 267.

willing to sit, sometimes for hours, and listen to my story and receive it without judgment. In a culture where we pay for people's time, it was a countercultural experience to meet people who were willing to listen, asking nothing in return. Over time, I also learned to give others the gift of being present and listening, and I discovered resonances between their stories and mine, which lowered my shame. Hearing my story in the story of another and therein finding freedom from isolation and shame—that was salvation for me. Sharing the most painful parts of myself and seeing grace, acceptance, and even love on the faces of those listening was an experience of seeing God in the face of my fellows. A member of AA shares a similar sentiment in the *Big Book*. She shares about her first meeting and says, "Today I believe I saw my Higher Power for the first time in those faces."[22] The gathering of people with addiction in recovery became, for her, the very face of God.

These communities in the basement made grace, freedom from bondage, and unconditional love and acceptance tangible for me in ways the sanctuary had not. They showed me who God is and allowed me to live into more liberative theologies. While I certainly haven't arrived and still regularly revert to the more toxic theologies of my youth, these basement communities helped me to see God as if for the first time. I needed a community that lived these theologies together on a daily basis to undo some of the more damaging theologies I had been given as a teenager. What would it take for people in our churches to begin to not only recognize intellectually but also experience that we are *all* broken, that we are not that different from each other and that there is nothing so shameful that it cannot be redeemed?

The Hospitality of Vulnerability

It's not easy to be a hospital for sinners. If we are serious in the sanctuary about being a community of welcome and healing, then we're going to have to do some hard work. The initial impulse might be to do a sermon series or set up an educational ministry opportunity around mental health and addiction, and those are good impulses. The more we talk about addiction and other mental health issues with each other and from the pulpit, the more we destigmatize addiction. This is crucial work. Stigma and shame thrive in secrecy and silence, so the more opportunities we create for people to talk about this, the better.

At the same time, I think programs still sometimes unintentionally create the impression that things like addiction happen "out there" to other people. If we really want to create space for people to be open about addiction, mental health issues, or any kind of brokenness that they're experiencing, then we're going to have to do something far simpler and far more difficult than starting a new program. We're going to have to show up with our *own* brokenness. It may not be addiction, but we all carry some kind of brokenness. Often when we talk in

---

22. *Alcoholics Anonymous: The Big Book*, 326.

churches about wanting to create space for people to share with openness and authenticity, what we mean is that we want to create space for *other* people to be vulnerable. Most of us would be happy and honored to listen to someone share of themselves. We just don't want to be the person sharing. The problem, of course, is that most of us feel that way, and people don't feel comfortable sharing in a place where that is not the norm. This only works if the majority of us participate. In the basement, I feel safe sharing my brokenness because everyone is sharing their brokenness. I'm not doing something that is out of the norm there. Basement communities are skilled at creating a culture of mutual sharing. Thus, the third thing the sanctuary can learn from the basement is how to begin creating such a culture, through the power of vulnerability. The basement recognizes that vulnerability can be an act of hospitality.

The first time I walked into one of these recovery meetings, I was terrified. I didn't know what to expect. I was worried people would ask me questions, that they would judge me for being too messed up for help, or maybe not messed up enough. I had spent so long just trying to hold it all together, making sure everything looked perfect on the outside, that I had no idea how to even begin talking about the sheer unmanageability of my life. So, I armored up, sat down, looked at the carpet, and hoped that no one would take notice of me. Of course, they did take notice.

Every person in that room could tell I was a newcomer. And they knew from their own experiences of recovery that what I needed most was to get out of the isolation I had lived in for so many years. They knew that I needed to find a way to talk about what was going on, but they didn't ask me questions. Instead, they did the most generous thing.

One by one, every single person in that room told me the story of how they arrived in the basement. They told me about losing jobs, marriages, homes, money, and dignity. They told stories about lying to their loved ones and disappointing their kids. They talked about the pain and shame of addiction. They told me how scary it was for them to come to the basement for the first time, and how over time through mutual sharing and support, this community changed their lives. Every single person there opened up their lives to me, and by sharing so much of themselves, they gave me the courage to come out of isolation, to put down my armor, and to begin telling my own story. Sharing their brokenness with me that day was an act of hospitality. Without it, I would never have opened up. Their vulnerability created a path for me to begin my own journey of healing.

So, if we want the church to be "a hospital for sinners," if we want to create space for people to show up as their whole selves—messiness, brokenness, and all—then *we* need to take the first step in being vulnerable. Taking that first step is an act of hospitality. It is a way of saying, "we expect you to show up as your whole self here, and it's safe for you to do so." If you've read this far into this book, I imagine you care about people with addiction and want the church to be a place where those who are suffering can show up and talk about what's going on with them, but that may not happen unless *you* dare to show up and talk about what's going on with *you*. It doesn't have to be about addiction if that's not what you are suffering from. It can be about whatever you are going through in that moment. The gift of hospitality through vulnerability is a powerful way of opening space for reciprocal sharing, which will also create space for people to share about addiction. That is, in the sanctuary, we can't just create spaces for *others* to share—we have to be willing to be in the messiness of it all too.

People often ask how you start doing that in a place where it isn't really baked into the culture. One generative starting place may be to simply begin taking small risks of vulnerability ourselves. Because sanctuaries have often been spaces where people don't share vulnerably, it will be important to start small, both as a way of protecting yourself and as a way of getting the community used to the idea of being more vulnerable. So, perhaps, the next time the person sitting next to you in church asks how you are doing, you could risk telling them the truth. Depending on the kind of church you go to, this may not be the norm. When I first arrived in the United States from my home country of the Netherlands, it took me some time to discover that "hey, how are you doing?" was not an invitation to share how I was doing. It was just a way of saying hello. In some ways truthfully answering the "how are you doing?" question is so countercultural in the United States it borders on a social faux pas. Perhaps this is not such a bad thing. Churches are, after all, supposed to be countercultural. Part of our calling in the sanctuary is to be set apart. So why not try telling someone at church how you're really doing the next time they ask? I know from experience that the worst that can happen is that they just won't make the mistake of asking you again. Next time they'll just say "hello," like we do in the Netherlands.

Sometimes, though, I think we'll find that people actually *do* want to know, and more than that, they also want to share how they're doing. I think more often than not, we'll discover that people are longing to be seen and heard—and that all they needed was for someone to pave the way for them. *Your* vulnerability can be the act of hospitality that creates room for others to share theirs. Likewise, the next time you are in Sunday school, a Bible study, or a small group, you could practice sharing something a little more vulnerable. Or the next time people ask for prayer requests, you could consider sharing what's going on with you. Small acts of vulnerability can go a long way. They have the capacity to change the culture of a place.

I have seen this happen time and time again in the basement. There are moments, even in the basement, when fellows simply go through the actions of having a meeting and sprinkle their shares with recitations of the *Big Book* instead of sharing about their own lives. I tend to find these meetings rather boring as I can read the *Big Book* by myself. I cannot, however, see how one of my fellows in recovery lives by its principles unless they are willing to tell me about their lives. However, such boring meetings are quickly turned around as soon as *one* person risks being vulnerable. Once this happens, the whole thing changes. One after another, people start sharing what's really going on with them. Vulnerability and authenticity are infectious in that way.

I also recognize that vulnerability is risky business. Every time I talk about addiction and my own story in a church or even in this book, it feels risky. For many years, I did research on addiction and went to various churches to talk about eradicating the stigma around addiction without being willing to share my own experiences with addiction. I was afraid it would ruin my reputation, or that I might not be able to get a job after I finished studying if people knew I was in addiction recovery. Then one day, I decided that I didn't want to live my life guarding my reputation and that I wasn't willing to work at a place that wouldn't hire a person in recovery, so I started sharing parts of my story. To be clear, I didn't decide one day to share *all* of my story with everyone. Not everyone is safe to share with, and not everyone is in a place to hear our stories. So, I'm discerning and ask close friends for advice when I'm unsure if I should share something in a sermon, for instance (or a book!).

CONCLUSION

Sharing parts of my story felt risky, and it still does, every time—even now. And yet I also believe that this is what it means to be the church together. This is what it means to go on this journey of faith with our fellows. The sanctuary wasn't meant to be a tidy place where everyone shows up as their best. The sanctuary was meant to be just that—a sanctuary—a place of refuge, respite, and safety. We have focused so much on the sanctuary as a "holy" and consecrated place that we have forgotten it is also meant to be a place of safety and refuge where people can show up as their full selves, knowing they are safe. The church was meant to be a community of real people, with real problems and a lot of messiness, going on a journey of faith together. The more we are able to live into that in the sanctuary, the more we have to offer those with addiction.

While churches can do a host of things to help those with addiction—including naming addiction in liturgies, sermons, and prayers; offering educational ministry opportunities; giving tangible help to those with addiction; or creating space for basement communities to meet—the most important gift the sanctuary can offer those with addiction is a community that can bear the weight of people's suffering, offer hope for healing, and step into the messiness of it all through reciprocal sharing of brokenness.

Conclusion

In recovery meetings, we often end the meeting by standing in a circle, holding hands, and saying the Serenity Prayer. Before the prayer we often offer up a moment of silence for those who are still suffering. In this final section of the book, I offer my own version of that moment of silence for the person still suffering by sharing an image that speaks deeply to me of who God is when freedom isn't found in this lifetime. The harsh reality of addiction is that not everyone finds the path to liberation, and some who manage to stay sober do not experience the sense of contentment and freedom those of us with addiction long for. Theology must be able to bear the weight of human experience. We must, therefore, find ways to speak to the reality that not everyone recovers. Thus, in this last section, I focus on what it means to find God in the depths. It is not my intention to offer a theodicy, or to offer empty hope; rather, I share an image that speaks deeply to me of God's presence in the midst of suffering.[1]

---

1. I included sections from this chapter in a meditation at one of Columbia Theological Seminary's chapel services. Jennifer Carlier, "Service of Word and Table—Jenn Carlier—April 12, 2024," April 2024, https://www.youtube.com/watch?v=iQSkpy19nrY.

Years ago, I spent three months in rehab with a young man I'm going to name John.[2] For three months, John and I didn't have access to our phones, the internet, or the outside world, and therefore we spent a lot of time with each other and the other people in rehab. Over those three months, as we shared meals, group therapy, outings, and free time together, we came to share our lives with each other. I came to know him as a deeply caring and empathic human being who suffered tremendously from the often lethal combination of depression and addiction. We found resonance in each other's stories, discovered a sense of belonging and love in this odd community of people with addiction, offered each other support at the end of difficult days, and in a sense, became family to each other. When we left rehab, John went home and did all the right things. He went to individual therapy, group therapy, and Twelve-Step meetings, yet as many do, he struggled to stay sober. After a good period of trying to live into recovery, he took his own life. Suicide is perhaps the bleakest thing one can encounter in life. It is the absence of hope—the very absence, it seems, of God and redemption. And yet, suicide is a common end to the struggle with addiction, especially when other mental health issues are present as well, such as depression or bipolar disorder. In my fifteen years in recovery, I have personally known four people with addiction who died by suicide.

A month before he died, John told his boyfriend, who was also in recovery, "No one loves me." Part of the tragedy of addiction and depression is that it robs a person of the ability to see clearly. In the height of his addiction, all John could see was a vast emptiness. "No one loves me." A month later, he died by suicide, firm in the belief that he was alone. Where in the midst of this tragedy is God?

My friend died at the height of the COVID-19 pandemic when quarantine and isolation were the norm. Since no groups could gather at the time, his friends could not attend his funeral. However, on the day of his funeral, as his family drove in a motorcade carrying his body to its final resting place, his friends—over a hundred of them—lined the streets and threw flowers before the limousine carrying his body. His friends, constrained by the pandemic, created a walk of honor to remember their deceased friend. On that day, over a hundred of his friends lined the streets and stood in defiance of his "No one loves me." They covered the road in flowers, and by this act they carried him to his final resting place. In the midst of perhaps the most hopeless of all moments, these friends created a beacon of hope, a sign of redemption.

Their presence demonstrated that they were there for him. They were there the day his body was put in the ground, and they were there a week, a month, a year before he died by suicide. I see glimpses of God in the faces of these friends who not only showed up to send him off but were there all along, who stood and

---

2. To protect the identity of my friend, and more importantly, his family, I have used a pseudonym in place of his real name. I do this *not* because I think suicide is a shameful act but because I do not know what his family would want.

lined the street and said, "We love you—we have *always* loved you." Salvation is being caught in the embrace of a love that holds us—in life *and* in death.

Walks of honor are normally reserved for organ donors. Hospital staff, friends, and family line the halls of the hospital as the deceased person is wheeled toward the place where her organs will be harvested. It is a way of expressing gratitude and deep respect for this moment between life and death, as one life ends, and another is given another chance. Walks of honor are a way of celebrating and honoring the gift this person is leaving behind. It is a celebration of a kind of substitutionary atonement. The death of the one leads to life in many others. It's a beautiful story in which death is demonstrated *not* to be the end of the story. The person lives on in the eyes, kidneys, hearts of another. It's a story of life in the midst of what is often a tragic death. In this sense the walk of honor is an image, or a metaphor for redemption.

Those who offer their organs for donation in many ways "deserve" their walks of honor. The concept of being deserving is rife within organ donation. Not only does the donor deserve honor for their gift of life, but the receiver also has to prove herself deserving of the organ. Due to the scarcity of organs available, doctors carefully weigh who is deserving of organs that become available. It is a matter of controversy, for instance, to give a liver to an alcoholic person in need of a liver transplant due to alcohol induced cirrhosis. After all, didn't the alcoholic person do this to herself? While alcoholic people are not deemed immediately unworthy, their cases (e.g., likelihood of relapse) are carefully studied before they are given the transplant. In that sense the receiver of the organ also has to demonstrate herself to be worthy of it.

What I find so beautiful about my friend's walk of honor is precisely that he didn't "deserve" it. He was not, as far as I know, an organ donor. His death did not bring about new life in others. Nor did he give his life so that others might live, in the way that perhaps a parent protecting a child from a shooter might have. My friend died a lonely death and, in many ways, a meaningless one. He died alone, likely high on his substance of "choice," which as we've seen is not really a choice at all. Enshrouded in the isolation of depression and active addiction, he took his own life. There is nothing redeeming or beautiful about suicide. Suicide is a death caused by illness, yet it is often tragically seen as the least honorable end one can have. We don't tend to commend the person who died by suicide for the way they courageously fought their illness (e.g., depression, addiction, etc.) every day in the way that we commend people who die from cancer, for instance.

And yet his friends lined the streets and threw flowers before his body as if his was a death that had purpose, as if he saved many others in the process of dying. In a regular walk of honor, it is the dying person that demonstrates the beauty of redemption even in the face of death. In this walk, however, it was the friends who brought redemption to a largely purposeless death. They showed up to honor him, to stand in defiance of the meaninglessness of suicide, to tell him that even in his deep despair, he was loved. They brought a kind of gospel reversal to his death, turning his dreadful death upside down, and for a very brief moment created an unspeakable beauty.

The walk of honor doesn't bring my friend back. It doesn't change that he died of depression, addiction, and suicide. It doesn't make it okay. And yet, it does create a small breach in the darkness—a moment of light. It created a moment of hope where there was none. In her book *Though the Fig Tree Does Not Blossom,* Ellen Ott Marshall talks about hope as a practice that holds in tension the realities of loss and the possibilities all around us. She says that hope is not a kind of optimism that asks us to abandon ourselves but rather a practice that asks us to engage deeply with the real, and in it to find the possible. She says that "the practice of hope requires that we discern and join the life-giving movement of God within this death-dealing world." This is what I saw in that walk of honor—a "life-giving movement of God"[3] even in the midst of death. It was an act of defiance of the hopelessness we all felt that day—an offer of redemption, if not for him, then for those of us left behind. This peculiar walk of honor was for me an image of who God is and how God redeems the broken. In that moment God acted through John's friends to demonstrate to all those who saw this act, and to demonstrate to my friend, even in death, that God is a God of fierce love and unconditional acceptance.

The flowers on the street became a kind of red carpet, similar to that rolled out for celebrities and people of high honor. It was as if God, through the act of the friends, was rolling out the red carpet to bring this luminary home. And in true celebrity fashion, people lined the streets to get a glimpse of this son of God who, after a long struggle, was finally coming home.

---

3. Ellen Ott Marshall, *Though the Fig Tree Does Not Blossom: Toward a Responsible Theology of Christian Hope* (Abingdon, 2006), 97.

Bibliography

Abelard, Peter. *Commentary on the Epistle to the Romans.* Translated by Steven R. Cartwright. Catholic University of America Press, 2011.

Alcoholics Anonymous. *Alcoholics Anonymous: The Big Book.* 4th ed. Alcoholics Anonymous World Services, Inc., 2002.

Alexander, Adam C., and Kenneth D. Ward. "Understanding Postdisaster Substance Use and Psychological Distress Using Concepts from the Self-Medication Hypothesis and Social Cognitive Theory." *Journal of Psychoactive Drugs* 50, no. 2 (April 2018): 177–86. https://doi.org/10.1080/02791072.2017.1397304.

Alexander, Bruce K. "Addiction: The View from Rat Park." Bruce K. Alexander. Accessed March 24, 2025. http://www.brucekalexander.com/articles-speeches/rat-park/148-addiction-the-view-from-rat-park.

Alexander, Bruce K., Barry L. Beyerstein, Patricia F. Hadaway, and Robert B. Coambs. "Effect of Early and Later Colony Housing on Oral Ingestion of Morphine in Rats." *Pharmacology, Biochemistry, and Behavior* 15, no. 4 (October 1981): 571–76. https://doi.org/10.1016/0091-3057(81)90211-2.

Alexander, Michelle. *The New Jim Crow: Mass Incarceration in the Age of Colorblindness.* 10th anniversary ed. The New Press, 2020.

American Psychiatric Association. *Diagnostic and Statistical Manual of Mental Disorders: DSM-5-TR.* 5th ed. American Psychiatric, 2022.

Anselm. *Cur Deus Homo.* In *Anselm: Basic Writings*, edited and translated by Thomas Williams, 227–326. Hackett, 2007.

———. *Proslogion.* In *Anselm: Basic Writings*, edited and translated by Thomas Williams, 75–98. Hackett, 2007.

Aristotle. *The Rhetoric and the Poetics of Aristotle.* Translated by W. Rhys Roberts and Ingram Bywater. Modern Library, 1984.

Augustine of Hippo. *The City of God.* Translated by Marcus Dods. Hendrickson Pub, 2016.

———. *Confessions.* Edited by Michael P. Foley. Translated by F. J. Sheed. 2nd ed. Hackett, 2006.

———. *On Free Will.* In *Augustine: Earlier Writings*, edited by John Baillie, John T. McNeill, and Henry P. Van Dusen, translated by John H. S. Burleigh. Westminster, 1953.

———. *On Grace and Free Choice.* In *On the Free Choice of the Will, On Grace and Free Choice, and Other Writings*, edited and translated by Peter King. Cambridge University Press, 2010.

———. *On Nature and Grace.* In *Saint Augustine: Four Anti-Pelagian Writings*, edited by Thomas P. Halton et al., translated by John Mourant and William J. Collinge. Catholic University Press, 1992.

———. *The Spirit and the Letter.* In *Augustine: Later Works*, edited by John Baillie, John T. McNeill, and Henry P. Van Dusen, translated by John Burnaby. Westminster, 1955.

Aulén, Gustav. *Christus Victor: An Historical Study of the Three Main Types of the Idea of Atonement*. Translated by A. G. Herbert. Wipf & Stock, 2003.
Baker, Mark D., and Joel B. Green. *Recovering the Scandal of the Cross: Atonement in New Testament and Contemporary Contexts*. IVP Academic, 2011.
Baker, Sharon L. *Razing Hell: Rethinking Everything You've Been Taught about God's Wrath and Judgment*. Westminster John Knox, 2010.
Baldwin, Jennifer. *Trauma-Sensitive Theology: Thinking Theologically in the Era of Trauma*. Cascade Books, 2018.
Barth, Karl. *Doctrine of God*. Vol. 2.2. Edited by Geoffrey William Bromiley and Thomas Forsyth Torrance. T&T Clark, 1957.
Belin, David, Sietse Jonkman, Anthony Dickinson, Trevor W. Robbins, and Barry J. Everitt. "Parallel and Interactive Learning Processes within the Basal Ganglia: Relevance for Understanding of Addiction." *Behavioral Brain Research* 199 (April 12, 2009): 89–102. https://doi.org/10.1016/j.bbr.2008.09.027.
Berridge, Kent C., and Terry E. Robinson. "Drug Addiction as Incentive Sensitization." In *Addiction and Responsibility*, edited by Jeffrey Poland and George Graham. MIT Press, 2011.
———. "Liking, Wanting, and the Incentive-Sensitization Theory of Addiction." *American Psychologist* 71, no. 8 (2016): 670–79. http://dx.doi.org/10.1037/amp0000059.
Black, Max. *Models and Metaphors: Studies in Language and Philosophy*. Cornell University Press, 1962.
Boudreau, Tyler. "The Morally Injured." *Massachusetts Review* 52, no. 3/4 (Autumn/Winter 2011): 746–54.
Brock, Rita Nakashima. *Journeys by Heart: A Christology of Erotic Power*. Wipf & Stock, 2008.
Brock, Rita Nakashima, and Rebecca A. Parker. *Proverbs and Ashes: Violence, Redemptive Suffering, and the Search for What Saves Us*. Beacon Press, 2001.
Brown, Cupcake. *A Piece of Cake: A Memoir*. Broadway Books, 2006.
Bunyan, John. *Pilgrim's Progress*. Rev. ed. Wordsworth Editions, 1999.
Burroughs, Augusten. *Dry*. Picador, 2003.
Bydlowska, Jowita. *Drunk Mom: A Memoir*. Penguin Books, 2014.
Calvin, John. *The Bondage and Liberation of the Will: A Defense of the Orthodox Doctrine of Human Choice against Pighius*. Edited by A. N. S. Lane. Translated by G. I. Davies. Baker Books, 1996.
———. "The Eternal Predestination of God." In *Calvin's Calvinism: The Eternal Predestination of God and the Secret Providence of God*, translated by Henry Cole. Wipf & Stock, 2019.
———. *Institutes of the Christian Religion*. Edited by John T. McNeill. Translated by Ford Lewis Battles. Westminster, 1960.
Carlier, Jennifer. "Penal Substitutionary Atonement and the Problem of Shame in Addiction." *Pastoral Psychology* 72, no. 5 (July 17, 2023): 659–73. https://doi.org/10.1007/s11089-023-01089-5.
———. "Finding God in the Basement." *TheoEd*. Filmed September 2022. https://www.theoed.com/jennifercarlier.
———. "Service of Word and Table—Jenn Carlier—April 12, 2024." YouTube, 42 min., 27 sec. https://www.youtube.com/watch?v=iQSkpy19nrY.
Castaneda, R., H. Lifshutz, M. Galanter, and H. Franco. "Empirical Assessment of the Self-Medication Hypothesis among Dually Diagnosed Inpatients." *Comprehensive Psychiatry* 35, no. 3 (May–June 1994): 180–84. https://doi.org/10.1016/0010-440X(94)90189-9.
Ceceli, Ahmet O., Charles W. Bradberry, and Rita Z. Goldstein. "The Neurobiology of Drug Addiction: Cross-Species Insights into the Dysfunction and Recovery

of the Prefrontal Cortex." *Neuropsychopharmacology* 47, no. 1 (January 2022): 276–91. https://doi.org/10.1038/s41386-021-01153-9. Centers for Disease Control and Prevention. "CDC Director's Media Statement on U.S. Life Expectancy." CDC, November 29, 2018. https://archive.cdc.gov/#/details?url=https://www.cdc.gov/media/releases/2018/s1129-US-life-expectancy.html.

———. "CDC Reports Nearly 24% Decline in U.S. Drug Overdose Deaths." CDC, February 25, 2025. https://www.cdc.gov/media/releases/2025/2025-cdc-reports-decline-in-us-drug-overdose-deaths.html#:~:text=New%20provisional%20data%20from%20CDC%27s,steep%20decline%20in%20overdose%20deaths.

———. "Drug Overdose Deaths in the U.S. Top 100,000 Annually." CDC, November 17, 2021.https://www.cdc.gov/nchs/pressroom/nchs_press_releases/2021/20211117.htm.

Chilton, Jennifer M. "Shame: A Multidisciplinary Concept Analysis." *Journal of Theory Construction & Testing* 16, no. 1 (Spring 2012): 4–8.

Coleman, Monica A. *Making a Way Out of No Way: A Womanist Theology*. Fortress, 2008.

Cone, James. *The Cross and the Lynching Tree*. Orbis Books, 2013.

———. *God of the Oppressed*. Harper & Row, 1975.

Cook, Christopher. *Alcohol, Addiction, and Christian Ethics*. Cambridge University Press, 2006.

Courtwright, David T. "The NIDA Brain Disease Paradigm: History, Resistance and Spinoffs." *BioSocieties* 5, no. 1 (March 2010): 137–47. https://doi.org/10.1057/biosoc.2009.3.

Crisp, Oliver. "The Logic of Penal Substitution Revisited." In *The Atonement Debate: Papers from the London Symposium on the Theology of Atonement*, edited by Derek Tidball, David Hilborn, and Justin Thacker. Zondervan Academic, 2008.

Daly, Mary. *Beyond God the Father: Toward a Philosophy of Women's Liberation*. Beacon Press, 1973.

Darke, Shane. "Pathways to Heroin Dependence: Time to Re-Appraise Self-Medication." *Addiction* 108, no. 4 (April 2013): 659–67. https://doi.org/10.1111/j.1360-0443.2012.04001.x.

Dearing, Ronda L., Jeffery Stuewig, and June Price Tangney. "On the Importance of Distinguishing Shame from Guilt: Relations to Problematic Alcohol and Drug Use." *Addictive Behaviors* 30, no. 7 (August 2005): 1392–1404. https://doi.org/10.1016/j.addbeh.2005.02.002.

Deykin, E. Y., and S. L. Buka. "Prevalence and Risk Factors for Posttraumatic Stress Disorder among Chemically Dependent Adolescents." *The American Journal of Psychiatry* 154, no. 6 (1997): 752–57. https://doi.org/10.1176/ajp.154.6.752.

Doidge, Norman. *The Brain That Changes Itself: Stories of Personal Triumph from the Frontiers of Brain Science*. Penguin Books, 2007.

Donaldson, David. "What Metaphors Mean." In *Philosophical Perspectives on Metaphor*, edited by Mark Johnson, 200–21. University of Minnesota Press, 1981.

Douglas, Kelly Brown. *The Black Christ*. 25th anniversary ed. Orbis Books, 2019. Adobe Digital Editions.

———. *Resurrection Hope: A Future Where Black Lives Matter*. Orbis Books, 2021.

———. *Stand Your Ground*. Orbis Books, 2015.

Dunnington, Kent. *Addiction and Virtue: Beyond the Models of Disease and Choice*. IVP Academic, 2011.

DuPont, Robert L., and Mark S. Gold. "Comorbidity and 'Self-Medication.'" *Journal of Addictive Diseases* 26, sup. 1 (2007): 13–23. https://doi.org/10.1300/J069v26S01_03.

Durham, John I. *Exodus*. Word Biblical Commentary. Word Books, 1987.

DuVernay, Ava, dir. *13th*. Kandoo Films, 2016. YouTube, 1:40:02. https://youtu.be/krfcq5pF8u8?feature=shared.

Erickson, Carlton K. *The Science of Addiction: From Neurobiology to Treatment.* W. W. Norton, 2007.
Ertl, Verena, Regina Saile, Frank Neuner, and Claudia Catani. "Drinking to Ease the Burden: A Cross-Sectional Study on Trauma, Alcohol Abuse and Psychopathology in a Post-Conflict Context." *BMC Psychiatry* 16 (June 24, 2016): 1–13. https://doi.org/10.1186/s12888-016-0905-7.
Everitt, B. J., A. Dickinson, and T. W. Robbins. "The Neuropsychological Basis of Addictive Behaviour." *Brain Research Reviews* 36, no. 2–3 (October 2001): 129–38. https://doi.org/10.1016/S0165-0173(01)00088-1.
Farley, Edward. *Divine Empathy: A Theology of God.* Fortress, 1996.
Farley, Wendy. *Tragic Vision and Divine Compassion: A Contemporary Theology.* Westminster/John Knox, 1990.
Fauconnier, Gilles, and Mark Turner. *The Way We Think: Conceptual Blending and the Mind's Hidden Complexities.* Basic Books, 2003.
Fisher, Carl Erik. *The Urge: Our History of Addiction.* Penguin Books, 2023.
Fretheim, Terence E. *Exodus: Interpretation: A Bible-Commentary for Teaching and Preaching.* John Knox, 1991.
Garnett, Matthew, and Arialdi M. Miniño. "Drug Overdose Deaths in the United States, 2003–2023." *NCHS Data Brief,* no. 522, National Center for Health Statistics, December 2024. https://dx.doi.org/10.15620/cdc/170565.
Garrett, Richard. "Addiction, Paradox, and the Good I Would." In *Addiction and Responsibility,* edited by Jeffrey Poland and George Graham, 247–68. MIT Press, 2011.
Geppert, Cynthia A. *Addiction and the Captive Will: A Colloquy between Neuroscience and Augustine of Hippo.* T&T Clark, 2024.
Glory to God. Westminster John Knox, 2013.
Gibbs, Raymond W. *Metaphor Wars: Conceptual Metaphors in Human Life.* Cambridge University Press, 2017.
Giordano, A. L., et al. "Addressing Trauma in Substance Abuse Treatment." *Journal of Alcohol and Drug Education* 60, no. 2 (August 2016): 55–71.
Goldstein, Rita Z., and Nora D. Volkow. "Dysfunction of the Prefrontal Cortex in Addiction: Neuroimaging Findings and Clinical Implications." *Nature Reviews Neuroscience* 12, no. 11 (November 2011): 652–669. https://doi.org/10.1038/nrn3119.
Gorringe, Timothy. *God's Just Vengeance: Crime, Violence and the Rhetoric of Salvation.* Cambridge University Press, 1996.
Grant, Jacquelyn. *White Women's Christ and Black Women's Jesus: Feminist Christology and Womanist Response.* Scholars Press, 1989.
Gregory of Nyssa. "The Great Catechism." In *Nicene and Post-Nicene Fathers: Second Series, Vol. 5—Gregory of Nyssa: Dogmatic Treatises,* edited by Philip Schaff and Henry Wallace, translated by William Moore and Henry Austin Wilson. Christian Literature, 1893.
Grisel, Judith. *Never Enough: The Neuroscience and Experience of Addiction.* Vintage, 2020.
Hari, Johann. *Chasing the Scream: The First and Last Days of the War on Drugs.* Bloomsbury, 2016.
Haynes, Stephen. *Why Can't Church Be More Like an AA Meeting? And Other Questions Christians Ask about Recovery.* Eerdmans, 2021.
Heilig, Markus, James MacKillop, Diana Martinez, Jürgen Rehm, Lorenzo Leggio, and Louk J. M. J. Vanderschuren. "Addiction as a Brain Disease Revisited; Why It Still Matters, and the Need for Consilience." *Neuropsychopharmacology* 46 (2021): 1715–23. https://doi.org/10.1038/s41386-020-00950-y.
Henderson, Nicole L., and William W. Dressler. "Medical Disease or Moral Defect? Stigma Attribution and Cultural Models of Addiction Causality in a University Population." *Culture, Medicine, and Psychiatry* 41 (2017): 493. https://doi.org/10.1007/s11013-017-9531-1.

Hepola, Sarah. *Blackout: Remembering the Things I Drank to Forget*. Grand Central, 2016.
Heyman, Gene M. *Addiction: A Disorder of Choice*. Harvard University Press, 2010.
———. "Addiction: A Latent Property of the Dynamics of Choice." In *What Is Addiction*, edited by Don Ross, Harold Kineaid, David Spurrett, and Peter Collins, 159–91. MIT Press, 2010.
Horwedel, Isaac. "Freely Compelled, Compulsively Free: A Critical Pastoral Approach to Addiction." *Pastoral Psychology* 71 (17 July, 2021): 61–78. https://doi.org/10.1007/s11089-021-00965-2.
Jamison, Leslie. *The Recovering: Intoxication and Its Aftermath*. Little, Brown and Co., 2018.
Joffé, Roland, dir. *The Mission*. Goldcrest Films, 1986.
Johnson, Elizabeth A. *She Who Is: The Mystery of God in Feminist Theological Discourse*. Herder & Herder, 2017.
Johnson, Mark. "Introduction: Metaphor in the Philosophical Tradition." In *Philosophical Perspectives on Metaphor*, edited by Mark Johnson, 3–47. University of Minnesota Press, 1981.
Jones, Serene. *Call It Grace: Finding Meaning in a Fractured World*. Penguin Books, 2020.
Julian of Norwich. *Showings*. Translated by Edmund College and James Walsh. Paulist, 1978.
Just for Today Meditations, February 16, 2015. https://www.justfortoday meditations.com/daily-recovery-quotes-february-16/.
"Just Say No." The Ronald Reagan Presidential Foundation & Institute. Accessed March 19, 2025. https://www.reaganfoundation.org/ronald-reagan/nancy-reagan/her-causes.
Kahn, Arlene. "The Exodus: A Parable of Addiction and Recovery." *Journal of Ministry in Addiction & Recovery* 5, no. 2 (1998): 13–32.
Karr, Mary. *Lit*. Harper Perennial, 2009.
Khantzian, E. "Addiction as Self-Regulation Disorder and the Role of Self-Medication." *Addiction* 108, no. 4 (2013): 668–69. https://doi.org/10.1111/add.12004.
———. "The Self-Medication Hypothesis of Addictive Disorders: Focus on Heroin and Cocaine Dependence." *American Journal of Psychiatry* 142, no. 11 (November 1985): 1259–64. https://doi.org/10.1176/ajp.142.11.1259.
———. "The Self-Medication Hypothesis of Substance Use Disorders: A Reconsideration and Recent Applications." *Harvard Review of Psychology* 4, no. 5 (1997): 231–44. https://doi.org/10.3109/10673229709030550.
Khar, Erin. *Strung Out: One Last Hit and Other Lies That Nearly Killed Me*. Park Row, 2020. Kindle.
Khoury, Lamya, Yilang L. Tang, Bekh Bradley, Joe F. Cubells, Kerry J. Ressler. "Substance Use, Childhood Traumatic Experience, and Posttraumatic Stress Disorder in an Urban Civilian Population." *Depression and Anxiety* 27, no. 12 (November 2010): 1077–86. https://doi.org/10.1002/da.20751.
Kime, Katie Givens. "Interpretive Phenomenological Analysis of the Spiritual Characteristics of Recovery Experiences in the Context of the Brain Disease Model of Addiction." *Pastoral Psychology* 67, no. 4 (August 1, 2018): 357–72. https://doi.org/10.1007/s11089-018-0816-2.
King, Heather. *Parched: A Memoir*. New American Library, 2006.
King, Peter. "Chronology." In *Augustine: On the Free Choice of the Will, On Grace and Free Choice, and Other Writings*, xxxiii–xxxiv. Cambridge University Press, 2010.
King, Timothy McMahan. Addiction Nation: What the Opioid Crisis Reveals about Us. Herald Press, 2019.
Knapp, Caroline. *Drinking: A Love Story*. Dial Press Trade Paperback, 1996.
Komline, Han-Luen Kantzer. *Augustine on the Will: A Theological Account*. Oxford University Press, 2019.

Koob, George F., Michael A. Arends, and Michel Le Moal. *Drugs, Addiction, and the Brain*. Academic Press, 2014.
Kovecses, Zoltan. *Metaphor: A Practical Introduction*. Oxford University Press, 2010.
Kuhar, Michael. *The Addicted Brain: Why We Abuse Drugs, Alcohol, and Nicotine*. FT Press, 2015.
———. "Contributions of Basic Science to Understanding Addiction." *BioSocieties* 5, no. 1 (March 1, 2010): 25–35. https://doi.org/10.1057/biosoc.2009.5.
Kunzmann, Kevin. "Nora D. Volkow, MD: Combating COVID-Era Issues in Substance Use Disorder." May 23, 2022. https://www.hcplive.com/view/nora-volkow-md-covid-era-issues-substance-use-disorder.
Lakoff, George, and Mark Johnson. *Metaphors We Live By*. University of Chicago Press, 2003.
Lembke, Anne. *Dopamine Nation*. Dutton, 2023.
———. "Time to Abandon the Self-Medication Hypothesis in Patients with Psychiatric Disorders." *The American Journal of Drug and Alcohol Abuse* 38, no. 6 (August 28, 2012): 524–29. https://doi.org/10.3109/00952990.2012.694532.
Letson, Al, host. "American Rehab, Chapter 5: Reagan with the Snap." *Reveal*, podcast, The Center for Investigative Reporting, July 20, 2020. 0:22:10. https://www.revealnews.org/episodes/american-rehab-chapter-5-reagan-with-the-snap.
Leshner, A. I. "Addiction Is a Brain Disease, and It Matters." *Science* 278, no. 5335 (October 1997): 45–47.
Levy, Neil. "Addiction, Responsibility and Ego Depletion." In *Addiction and Responsibility*, edited by Jeffrey Poland and George Graham. MIT Press, 2011.
Lewis, Marc. *The Biology of Desire: Why Addiction Is Not a Disease*. PublicAffairs, 2016.
———. "Brain Change in Addiction as Learning, Not Disease." *The New England Journal of Medicine* 379, no. 16 (October 12, 2018): 1551–60. https://doi.org/10.1056/NEJMra1602872.
Love, Gregory A. *Love, Violence, and the Cross: How the Nonviolent God Saves Us through the Cross of Christ*. Cascade Books, 2010.
Mandavia, Amar, Gabriella G. N. Robinson, Bekh Bradley, Kerry J. Ressler, and Abigail Powers. "Exposure to Childhood Abuse and Later Substance Use: Indirect Effects of Emotion Dysregulation and Exposure to Trauma." *Journal of Traumatic Stress* 29, no. 5 (September 13, 2016): 422–29. https://doi.org/10.1002/jts.22131.
Mann, Brian. "U.S. Drug Deaths Declined Slightly in 2023 but Remained at Crisis Levels." May 15, 2024. https://www.npr.org/sections/health-shots/2024/05/15/1251239829/us-drug-overdose-deaths-provisional-2023.
Maté, Gabor. *In the Realm of Hungry Ghosts: Close Encounters with Addiction*. Illustrated edition. North Atlantic Books, 2008.
Marshall, Ellen Ott. "Moral Agency under Constraint." *Moral Agency under Constraint*. Accessed April 7, 2025. https://scholarblogs.emory.edu/moralagency2019/.
———. *Though the Fig Tree Does Not Blossom*. Abingdon, 2006.
May, Gerald. *Addiction & Grace*. HarperSanFrancisco, 1988.
McCarthy, Thomas J., dir. *Spotlight*. Participant Media, First Look Media, Anonymous Content, and Rocklin/Faust Productions, 2015.
McFadyen, Alistair. *Bound to Sin*. Cambridge University Press, 2000.
McFague, Sallie. *Metaphorical Theology: Models of God in Religious Language*. Fortress, 1982.
———. *Models of God: Theology for an Ecological, Nuclear Age*. Fortress, 1987.
———. *Speaking in Parables*. Augsburg Fortress, 2000.
McFarland, Ian A. *In Adam's Fall: A Meditation on the Christian Doctrine of Original Sin*. Wiley-Blackwell, 2010.
Mercadante, Linda. *Victims and Sinners: Spiritual Roots of Addiction and Recovery*. Westminster John Knox, 1996.

Meyers, Carol. *Exodus*. The New Cambridge Bible Commentary. Cambridge University Press, 2005.
Moore, Patrick. *Tweaked: A Crystal Meth Memoir*. Citadel, 2017.
Moyers, William Cope, with Katherine Ketcham. *Broken: My Story of Addiction and Redemption*. Penguin Books, 2007.
Narcotics Anonymous. 6th ed. World Service Office, 2008.
National Institute on Drug Abuse. "Drug Misuse and Addiction." Last modified July 6, 2020. https://nida.nih.gov/publications/drugs-brains-behavior-science-addiction/drug-misuse-addiction.
———. "Drugs and the Brain." Last modified July 6, 2020. https://nida.nih.gov/publications/drugs-brains-behavior-science-addiction/drugs-brain.
———. "Drugs Overdose Deaths: Facts and Figures." Updated August 2024. https://nida.nih.gov/research-topics/trends-statistics/overdose-death-rates.
———. "Drug Overdose Death Rates." National Institute on Drug Abuse. Accessed April 9, 2025. https://nida.nih.gov/research-topics/trends-statistics/overdose-death-rates.
———. "NIDA IC Fact Sheet 2025." National Institute on Drug Abuse (NIDA). Last accessed May 2025. https://nida.nih.gov/about-nida/legislative-activities/budget-information/fiscal-year-2025-budget-information-congressional-justification-national-institute-drug-abuse/ic-fact-sheet-2025#:~:text=46.3-million%20people%20in%20the%20United%20States%20had%20an%20SUD%20in%202021.&text=In%202021%2C%20only%206.3%20percent%20of%20people%20with%20SUD%20received%20treatment.&text=In%202022%2C%20about%20110%2C000%20people%20died%20of%20drug%20overdoses.
Nelson, James B. *Thirst: God and the Alcoholic Experience*. Westminster John Knox, 2004.
Niebuhr, Reinhold. *The Nature and Destiny of Man, Vol. I: Human Nature*. Charles Scribner's Sons, 1964.
Nixon, Richard. "President Nixon Declares Drug Abuse 'Public Enemy Number One.'" Posted April 29, 2016, by Richard Nixon Foundation. YouTube, 4 min., 11 sec. https://youtu.be/y8TGLLQlD9M?feature=shared.
Nouwen, Henri J. M. *The Inner Voice of Love: A Journey Through Anguish to Freedom*. Image, 1999.
Palmer, Parker. "The Gift of Presence, The Perils of Advice." *On Being*, April 27, 2016. https://onbeing.org/blog/the-gift-of-presence-the-perils-of-advice/.
Pelagius. "To Demetrias." In *Pelagius Life and Letters*, edited by B. R. Rees, translated by B. R. Rees Ferrante. Boydell, 1998.
Petry, Nancy M., Jessica M. Pierce, and Maxine L. Stitzer. "Effect of Prize-Based Incentives on Outcomes in Stimulant Abusers in Outpatient Psychosocial Treatment Programs." *Archives of General Psychiatry* 62, no. 10 (October 2005): 1148–56. https://doi.org/10.1001/archpsyc.62.10.1148.
Pickard, Hanna. "Addiction and the Self." *Noûs* 55, no. 4 (December 2021): 737–61. https://doi.org/10.1111/nous.12328.
———. "What We're Not Talking about When We Talk about Addiction." *Hastings Center Report* 50, no. 4 (2020): 37–46. https://doi.org/10.1002/hast.1172.
———. "Responsibility Without Blame for Addiction." *Neuroethics* 10, no. 1 (January 7, 2017): 169–80. https://doi.org/10.1007/s12152-016-9295-2.
Potter-Efron, Ronald. "Therapy with Shame-Prone Alcoholic and Drug-Dependent Clients." In *Shame in the Therapy Hour*, edited by R. L. Dearing and J. Tangney, 219–35. American Psychological Association, 2011.
Powers, Brian S. *Full Darkness: Original Sin, Moral Injury, and Wartime Violence*. Eerdmans, 2019.
"Preventing and Reducing Youth and Young Adult Substance Misuse: Schools, Students, Families." *U.S. Department of Education*. Last reviewed March 11, 2025. https://www.ed.gov/opioids/.

Prochaska, James O., and Carlo C. DiClemente. "Transtheoretical Therapy: Toward a More Integrative Model of Change." *Psychotherapy: Theory, Research and Practice* 19, no. 3 (Fall 1982): 276–88.

Prochaska, James O., Carlo C. DiClemente, and John C. Norcross. "In Search of How People Change: Applications to Addictive Behaviors." *American Psychologist* 47, no. 9 (September 1992): 1102–14.

Propp, William H. C. *Exodus 1–18*. The Anchor Bible. Doubleday, 1999.

———. *Exodus 19–40*. The Anchor Bible. Doubleday, 2006.

Reed, Philip L., J. C. Anthony, and N. Breslau. "Incidence of Drug Problems in Young Adults Exposed to Trauma and Posttraumatic Stress Disorder: Do Early Life Experiences and Predispositions Matter?" *Archives of General Psychiatry* 64, no. 12 (December 2007): 1435–42. https://doi.org/10.1001/archpsyc.64.12.1435.

Richards, I. A. *The Philosophy of Rhetoric*. 1st ed. Oxford University Press, 1965.

Ricoeur, Paul. "Interpretation of the Myth of Punishment." In *The Conflict of Interpretations: Essays in Hermeneutics*, edited by D. Ihde, translated by Robert Sweeney, 354–77. Northwestern University Press, 1974.

Robbins, Laura Cathcart. *Stash: My Life in Hiding*. Atria Paperback, 2024.

Rohr, Richard. *Breathing under Water: Spirituality and the Twelve Steps*. Franciscan Media, 2011.

Sanderson, Christiane. *Counseling Skills for Working with Shame*. Jessica Kingsley, 2015.

Satel, Sally, and Scott O. Lilienfeld. "Addiction and the Brain-Disease Fallacy." *Frontiers in Psychiatry* 4 (March 2, 2014). https://doi.org/10.3389/fpsyt.2013.00141.

Schindler, Andreas. "Attachment and Substance Use Disorders—Theoretical Models, Empirical Evidence, and Implications for Treatment." *Frontiers in Psychiatry* 10 (October 14, 2019). https://doi.org/10.3389/fpsyt.2019.00727.

Schreiner, Thomas R. "Penal Substitution View." In *The Nature of the Atonement: Four Views*, edited by J. Beilby and P. R. Eddy, 67–117. IVP Academic, 2006.

Shaffer, Howard J., Debi A. LaPlante, Richard A. LaBrie, Rachel C. Kidman, Anthony N. Donato, and Michael V. Stanton. "Toward a Syndrome Model of Addiction: Multiple Expressions, Common Etiology." *Harvard Review of Psychiatry* 12, no. 6 (December 11, 2004): 367–74. https://doi.org/10.1080/10673220490905705.

Sheff, Nic. *Tweak: Growing Up on Methamphetamines*. Atheneum Books for Young Readers, 2009.

Sobrino, Jon. *Christ the Liberator: A View from the Victims*. Translated by Paul Burns. Orbis Books, 2001.

Spadaro, Antonio, SJ. "A Big Heart Open to God: An Interview with Pope Francis." *America: The Jesuit Review*, September 20, 2013. https://www.americamagazine.org/faith/2013/09/30/big-heart-open-god-interview-pope-francis.

Steinberg, Neil. *Drunkard: A Hard-Drinking Life*. Plume, 2008.

Stitzer, Maxine L., Nancy M. Petry, and Jessica Pierce. "Motivational Incentives Research in the National Drug Abuse Treatment Clinical Trials Network." *Journal of Substance Abuse Treatment* 38, supplement 1 (June 2010): S61–S69. https://doi.org/10.1016/j.jsat.2009.12.010.

Stobbe, Mike. "CDC Says More than 107,000 Americans Died of Drug Overdoses in 2021, Setting 'Staggering' Record." *PBS NewsHour*, May 11, 2022. https://www.pbs.org/newshour/health/cdc-estiates-more-than-107000-americans-died-of-drug-overdoses-in-2021-setting-staggering-record.

Stump, Eleanore. "Augustine on Free Will." In *The Cambridge Companion to Augustine*, edited by David Vincent Meconi and Eleanore Stump. Cambridge University Press, 2014.

———. *Aquinas*. Routledge, 2003.

Substance Abuse and Mental Health Services Administration (SAMHSA). "Naltrexone." Last updated March 29, 2024. https://www.samhsa.gov/medications-substance-use-disorders/medications-counseling-related-conditions/naltrexone.

———. "National Survey on Drug Use and Health (NSDUH)." Accessed April 9, 2025. https://www.samhsa.gov/data/data-we-collect/nsduh-national-survey-drug-use-and-health/national-releases. In the "National Reports and Tables" section, you can click on "view by Collection Year" to select a year and see the reports and data for that year.

Szalavitz, M. *Unbroken Brain: A Revolutionary New Way of Understanding Addiction*. St. Martin's, 2016.

Terrell, JoAnn Marie. *Power in the Blood*. Orbis Books, 1998.

Twelve Steps and Twelve Traditions. Alcoholics Anonymous World Services, 1953.

"Understanding Alcoholics Anonymous and Spirituality." *Alcoholics Anonymous*, August 15, 2023. https://www.aa.org/sites/default/files/literature/AA%20and%20Spirituality%20Press%20Release%20-%20EN_0.pdf.

United Methodist Hymnal. United Methodist Publishing House, 1989.

Van Dyk, Leanne. *Believing in Jesus Christ*. Geneva, 2002.

Vargas, Elizabeth. *Between Breaths: A Memoir of Panic and Addiction*. Grand Central, 2016.

Volkow, Nora. "Drug Addiction." *Vital Speeches of the Day* (June 2006).

Ward, Keith. *Ethics and Christianity*. Routledge, 2014.

Waters, Sonia. *Addiction and Pastoral Care*. Ecrdmans, 2019.

———. "Punishing the Immoral Other: Penal Substitutionary Logic in the War on Drugs." *Pastoral Psychology* 68, no. 5 (October 2019): 533–48. https://doi.org/10.1007/s11089-018-0836-y.

Weaver, J. Denny. *The Nonviolent Atonement*. Eerdmans, 2011.

———. "Violence in Christian Theology." In *Cross Examinations: Readings on the Meaning of the Cross Today*, edited by Marit Trelstad, 1st ed., 225–40. Fortress, 2006.

Wetzel, James. *Augustine: The Limits of Virtue*. Cambridge University Press, 1992.

Wiechelt, Shelly A. "The Specter of Shame in Substance Misuse." *Substance Use & Misuse* 42, no. 2–3 (2007): 399–409. https://doi.org/10.1080/10826080601142196.

Williams, Delores. "Black Women's Surrogacy Experience and the Christian Notion of Redemption." *In Cross Examinations: Readings on the Meaning of the Cross Today*, edited by Marit Trelstad. Augsburg, 2006.

———. *Sisters in the Wilderness: The Challenge of Womanist God-Talk*. Orbis Books, 1993.

———. "A Womanist Perspective on Sin." In *A Troubling in My Soul*, edited by Emilie M. Townes. Orbis Books, 1993.

Index

Page numbers followed by an i indicate an image on that page.

AA (Alcoholics Anonymous). *See* Alcoholics Anonymous (AA)
Aaron (brother of Moses), 114–15, 127–28, 128n54
abortions, 80
abuse, child, 50, 60, 67, 80, 85. *See also* childhood trauma
act as if, 149
Adam's sin. *See* fall of man; original sin
addiction
    definitions of, 10, 13, 29, 33
    disease of (*see* brain disease model of addiction (BDMA))
    experiences of (*see* experiences of addiction)
    God's/church's role in, 87–88, 126–27n49, 130, 143–44, 148, 155–58, 166, 169
    life overcome by, 44, 139–40, 152
    models of (*see* addiction models)
    neuroscience of (*see* neuroscience of addiction)
    recovery from (*see* recovery, addiction; Twelve-Step groups (recovery groups))
    rituals of, 139–41
    sin and, 50–51, 55, 68–69, 99–100, 99n38 (*see also* sin)
    societal responsibility for, 67–68
    statistical trends of, 2–3, 2n2, 3n5, 59, 59n1, 65, 65n35, 96, 96n24
    symptom clusters of, 10
    term use, 2n1
    totalizing effects of, 44–45
Addiction: A Disorder of Choice (Heyman), 15, 123
Addiction and Pastoral Care (Waters), 18, 88

Addiction and Virtue (Dunnington), 32, 161
addiction models
    bondage of the will and, 53–57 (*see also* will, bondage of)
    brain disease model of addiction (BDMA), 29–30 (*see also* neuroscience of addiction)
    choice model, 15–17
    moral model, 13–15
    neuroscience and (*see* neuroscience of addiction)
    self-medication model, 17–21
    spectrums of, 11–13
Addiction Nation (King), 64–65, 113
addiction theology
    addiction models, 9–34 (*see also* addiction models)
    author's story and, 155–59
    churches, recovery group practices for, 159–69
    exodus story, as extended metaphor, 105–36 (*see also* exodus story, as extended metaphor)
    penal-substitutionary atonement, personal harms of, 72–88 (*see also* penal-substitutionary atonement doctrine)
    penal-substitutionary atonement, societal harms of, 89–104 (*see also* models (pervasive and systematic metaphors); penal-substitutionary atonement doctrine; war on drugs)
    recovery journey metaphor, for salvation, 137–53 (*see also* recovery journey metaphor, for salvation)
    shame and, 58–71 (*see also* shame)
    will (human choice) and, 35–57 (*see also* will, bondage of; will, freedom of)

addict vs. person suffering from addiction, 2n1, 113
advice to those with addiction, 112–14
afterlife, oppression and, 106–7
agency. *See* will, freedom of
Alcohol, Addiction, and Christian Ethics (Cook), 50
Alcoholics Anonymous (AA)
  Big Book, The (Alcoholics Anonymous World Services) and, 10, 33, 63, 151, 166
  Bill W. and, 52, 63
  Christian nature of, 126–27n49, 130, 143–44 (*see also under* addiction: God's/church's role in)
  community in, 150–53, 159, 164–65
  on free will, 63n25
  history of, 126–27n49
  "powerlessness" in, 52
  See also Twelve-Step groups (recovery groups)
Alcoholics Anonymous: The Big Book. See Big Book, The (Alcoholics Anonymous World Services)
Alexander, Bruce, 19–21
Alexander, Michelle, 13, 63, 94–95, 97
amnesia, addiction disease of, 122–25, 127–28, 130
Anselm of Canterbury, 83, 84n47, 92n7, 101–2, 148
Anti-Drug Abuse Act, 95
anxiety, prayer and, 147
atonement
  alternative words for, 106
  in hymns, 4–5, 158, 158n3
  justification, sanctification, and, 121
  metaphors, importance of multiplicity, 102–3 (*see also under* metaphors: for salvation)
  in progressive churches, 158
  satisfaction model of, 83–84
  separation of God and humans and, 106
  surrogacy and, 76–77
  theologies of, 5–6, 6n15, 77 (*see also* penal-substitutionary atonement doctrine)
  See also salvation
attachment styles, childhood, 18–19
Augustine of Hippo
  Calvin's interpretation of, 49–50
  free will, changing positions on, 39n15, 48–50

on free will, 38–41, 48–51, 54, 70, 118
on help, freedom of asking for, 48–49, 70, 111, 111n20
on original sin, 56, 66
Pelagius on, 40, 40n18, 48–49
Stump on, 48–51
"Augustine on Free Will" (Stump), 48

Baker, Sharon, 93
balance, brain, 23–24, 24n57
basement communities. *See* Twelve-Step groups (recovery groups)
BDMA (brain disease model of addiction). *See* brain disease model of addiction (BDMA)
behavioral addictions, 2, 2n1, 33. *See also* process addictions
belonging, importance of feeling, 151–53. *See also* communities; Twelve-Step groups (recovery groups)
Berridge, Kent, 15–16
Between Breaths (Vargas), 9, 52, 127, 147
Big Book, The (Alcoholics Anonymous World Services), 10, 33, 63, 151, 166. *See also* Alcoholics Anonymous (AA); Bill W. (William Griffith Wilson)
Bill W. (William Griffith Wilson), 52, 63. *See also* Alcoholics Anonymous (AA)
Black, Max, 74, 100
Black Christ, The (Douglas), 107
Blackout (Hepola), 18
Black Theology of Liberation, A (Cone), 106–7
"Black Women's Surrogacy Experience and the Christian Notion of Redemption" (Williams), 76
blame
  Big Book, The, on, 63
  -blamelessness spectrum, 11–13, 11i, 36, 36i, 55
  elements of, 36
  experiences of, 60, 62
  harm of, to those with addictions, 62–64, 85
  original sin's redemption against, 66–68
  penal-substitutionary atonement and, 85
  sin, free will, and, 40
  See also shame
Bondage and Liberation of the Will, The (Calvin), 46

bondage of the will. *See* will, bondage of
Bound to Sin (McFadyen), 36
brain. *See* neuroscience of addiction
brain disease model of addiction (BDMA)
   about, 29–30
   alternatives to, 31
   bondage of the will and, 53
   disadvantages of viewing addiction as, 32
   on freedom-compulsion spectrum, 11
   neuroscience and (*see* neuroscience of addiction)
   recovery, as outside of medical system, 32, 69
   shame and, freedom from, 85
brain's communication system, 22–23, 22i
Broken (Moyers). *See* Moyers, William
brokenness, in churches vs. Twelve-Step groups, 159–63, 167
Brown, Cupcake, 50, 67, 88, 140
bulimia, 61, 61n13
burning bush, 114
Burroughs, Augusten, 142
Bydlowska, Jowita, 25, 37, 51–52, 60, 139–40, 164

Call It Grace (Jones), 43–44, 55
Calvin, John
   on compulsion, 45, 47–48, 47n2
   on fall of man, 47, 48i, 49, 118
   on help, asking for, 111
   on justification, 120–21nn41–42
   on penal-substitutionary atonement, 78–79
   on salvation, 78–79, 79nn26–27
   on sin, 84, 160n7
   on will (human choice), 41–50
Canaan, destruction of, 110
capitalism, addiction and, 20
caregivers, childhood. *See* parents/parenting, of those with addictions
child abuse, 50, 60, 67, 80, 85
childhood relational experiences, 18–19
childhood trauma, 59–60, 67. *See also* child abuse; trauma
choice model of addiction, 15–17
choices
   choice model of addiction, 15–17
   vs. free will, 45–47 (*see also* will, freedom of)
   global and local, 15–16, 123
   of goodness vs. evil (*see* goodness, choosing)
   human's capacity of (*see* will, bondage of; will, freedom of)
   models and, 91
   recovery and, 69–70
   sin's influence in making, 50–51
   understanding addicts', 28–29, 53
   (*see also* addiction models)
Christ. *See* Jesus Christ
church
   addiction and recovery, role in (*see under* addiction: God's/church's role in)
   author's experience with, 155–59
   bondage of will, responsibility to teach, 70–71
   brokenness acknowledgment in, 159–63
   progressive, 157–58
   recovery group practices for, 159–63
   vs. Twelve-Step groups on grace, 3–5, 7, 159, 165–66
   vulnerability in, 167–68
cleansing, punishment logic and, 82–83
cognitive linguistic theory of metaphor, 75
colonization, of Indigenous peoples, 19–20
communities
   guides for living in, 126–27
   importance of in recovery, 150–53, 159, 164–65
compassion, God of, 135
compulsion, 11–13, 11i, 31, 41, 41i, 45, 47, 47n42
compulsion-volition tension
   in addiction, 56
   as essence of addiction's problem, 46
   experiences of, 9, 37, 45–46, 51–52, 54, 81
   shame and, 52
conceptual metaphor theory, 75
Cone, James, 106–7, 109
Confessions (Augustine), 54, 118
conservative Christian education, 155–56
control/power, 52, 63n25, 117
Cook, Christopher, 50–51
coping, during recovery, 141
COVID-19 pandemic, impact of, 2–3
cravings, 25–26, 26n64, 46, 142
criminalization, of drug possession, 13–14, 63–64, 94–95
criminalization, of humans metaphor, 77, 79–80, 82–85, 92, 98
crisis-induced sobriety promises broken, 115–16

Daly, Mary, 97–98
deaths
  organ donors and, 172
  overdose, 2–3, 2nn2–3, 3n5, 65, 65n35, 96, 96n25
  shame/stigmas in families and, 65
  suicide, 63, 105–6, 171–73
decision-making. *See* choices
depression, 21, 33, 149, 162, 171–73
desires
  acceptance of, free will and, 49
  addiction as need to fulfill, 129–30
  Calvin on, 45
  dopamine as neurotransmitter of, 23–26, 29, 53
  vs. needs, 25–26, 26n64
  temporal vs eternal, 38–39, 53
Diagnostic and Statistical Manual of Mental Disorders (DSM-V), 10
DiClemente, Carlo D., 116
disease, addiction as. *See* brain disease model of addiction (BDMA)
divine-sanctioned shame, 79–80
dopamine, 23–26, 29, 53
Douglas, Kelly Brown, 107, 109–11, 131–32
Drinking: A Love Story (Knapp), 61, 64, 139–41
drug policies, federal. *See* war on drugs
drug possession, criminalization of, 13–14, 63–64, 94–95
drug trade, 96
drug use
  moral model of addiction and, 13–14
  Nixon on, 93–94
  overdoses from (*see* overdoses)
Drunkard (Steinberg), 127–28, 164–65
Drunk Mom (Bydlowska), 25, 37, 51–52, 60, 139–40, 164
DSM-V (*Diagnostic and Statistical Manual of Mental Disorders*), 10
Dunnington, Kent, 7, 32, 53, 69, 161, 163
Durham, John I., 129, 133
Dyk, Leanne Van, 5

eating disorders, 61, 61n13
education, for addiction prevention, 14
"Effects of Early and Later Colony Housing on Oral Ingestion of Morphine in Rats" (B. Alexander), 19
enslavement
  of American antebellum period, 109–10, 132
  of Israelites (*see* exodus story, as extended metaphor)
environment, substance use and, 19–20
Erickson, Carlton, 30
eternal horizon, 129
eternal vs. temporal desires, 38–39, 53. *See also* goodness, choosing
evil
  existence of, 38–39 (*see also* sin)
  will and, 47n42, 48
exodus story, as extended metaphor
  about, 109–11
  as about human nature vs. God's, 131–34
  being seen in (*see* seen (acknowledged in empathy))
  freedom, difficulties for attaining, 127–30
  guides for community living, 126–27
  justification and sanctification in, 120–21nn41–42
  past, longing for, 122–25, 127–28, 130
  process of, 119–25
  punishment, need for and, 131–33
  salvation definition for, 106–7
  shame/blame and, 130–31
experiences of addiction
  about, 10
  abuse, 50, 60, 67, 80–81
  author's, 155–59
  blame, 60, 62
  bondage of will, compared to, 44–45
  change stages and, 116–17
  compulsion-volition tension, 9, 37, 45–46, 51–52, 54, 81
  cravings, 25–26
  crisis-induced sobriety promises broken, 115–16
  loved ones and, 12–14
  multi-addiction cycle, 64
  parenting shame, 60
  physical toll of addiction, 140
  recovery, early, 122–23, 140–42
  recovery, meeting attendance and, 142
  recovery, prayer in, 145–47
  recovery, relationships during, 151, 164–65
  recovery, sense of belonging in, 152–53
  relapses, 28, 52, 125, 127–28
  rituals and, 139–40

self-medicating, 18
shame, 9, 52, 61–63, 65, 80–81
extended metaphors, about, 107–9. *See also* exodus story, as extended metaphor
external conditions
  self-medication model of addiction and, 55
  sin and, 42–45
  of will, 54–55
external shame, 62–66

faith
  as action vs. feeling, 144
  as choice, 146
  Israelites', 122, 131
  as recovery obstacle, 6
  search for, 148
fake it till you make it, 149
fall of man, 39–40, 47, 48i, 49, 118. *See also* original sin
families, of those with addictions
  addiction's impact on, 12–13, 35
  being seen by, importance of, 112–14
  responses of, to those with addiction, 14–15
  saving those with addictions, attempts of, 112–14
  shame, and death from addiction, 65
Farley, Edward, 129
Farley, Wendy, 71
fatherhood, God and, 76, 90–91, 97–98, 101
feminist theology, 76, 106
first- and second-order volitions of will, 48–50
Fisher, Carl, 46
forgiveness, 68–69, 92–93, 131, 133
foster parents, 50, 67. *See also* parents/parenting, of those with addictions
Francis (Pope), 160
"Free Compelled, Compulsively Free: A Critical Pastoral Approach to Addiction" (Horwedel), 20
freedom
  from addiction, 148, 150, 166, 170 (*see also* recovery, addiction)
  from bondage (*see* salvation)
  -compulsion spectrum, 11–13, 11i, 16, 21, 36, 36i, 41, 41i, 47–48, 48i
  difficulties of attaining, 127–30
  from enslavement (*see* exodus story, as extended metaphor)
  as gift and practice, 148
  God of, 109–11, 132
  from shame, 163–64, 166
  of will (*see* will, freedom of)
free will. *See* will, freedom of
Fretheim, Terence, 111, 117–18, 128, 131
friendships, of those with addictions, 14–16, 112–14, 164–65, 171–73. *See also* communities; families, of those with addictions
Full Darkness (Powers), 66

Garrett, Richard, 69–70, 143
global choices, 16, 123
God
  absence of, 82, 106, 128–29, 133–34, 145
  addiction, role in (*see under* addiction)
  addiction as attempt to find, 130
  Alcoholics Anonymous and, 126–27n49, 143–44
  of compassion, 135
  as creator of good and evil, 38–39
  defining, 148
  forgiveness of, questioned, 92–93
  of freedom, 109–11, 132
  grace of, 49, 148
  help, humans seeking, 48–49, 70, 111, 111n20
  human relationship and, 90–92
  of Israelites, 111–13
  as judge, 77–78, 80–81, 87–88, 157
  love of, questioned, 4–6, 155–57, 163–64, 171
  metaphorical language regarding, 76, 78, 80–81, 86–87, 90–91, 97–98, 101
  patriarchal language regarding, 76, 86, 91, 97–98
  penal-substitutional atonement, role in, 78–79
  personal interpretations of, 132
  Pharaoh's will and, 117–18
  of punishment, 81–82, 87–88, 92–93, 131, 158
  seeing of, by humans, 134
  seeing of Israelites by, 111–13
  separation of from humans, 82, 106
  shame and, 157 (*see also* shame)
  sovereignty of, 47
  trust of, 134–35
  wrath of, 4–6, 87, 158

God of the Oppressed (Cone), 109
golden calf, 127–29, 128n54, 131–32
goodness, choosing, 38–40, 39n15, 47–50, 47n42, 53, 55, 143. *See also* will, freedom of
grace
   acceptance of, free will and, 49, 49n50, 70
   Calvin on, 47
   practice with, 147, 150
   recovery and, 148
   from Twelve-Step groups vs. church, 3–5, 7, 159, 165–66
gratitude, 146–47
gray mass, reduction of, 28
Grisel, Judith, 23–24
guides, for freedom living, 126–27
guilt, 85. *See also* shame
guilt, inherited, 41, 56, 69

habits, 26–27, 54, 117–18, 122–25, 128
heart, hardening of Pharaoh's, 117–18
help, seeking
   Augustine on, 48–49, 70, 111, 111n20
   of Israelites in exodus story, 111
   shame as preventing, 64–65
Hepola, Sarah, 18, 85
hereditary guilt, 41, 56, 69
Heyman, Gene, 15–16, 123
hiddenness, 139–40, 156
Higher Power, 126–27n49, 143–47, 166
highs, tolerance and, 24
homosexuality, feelings of identity of as sinful, 5, 88, 156–58, 162
hope, 106–7, 165, 171, 173
Horwedel, Isaac, 20
hymns, 4–5, 158, 158n3

identities
   of Israelites, 119, 120n41, 121, 131–32, 134
   as unacceptable to God, fear of, 5, 155–57, 163–64, 171
idolatry, 38–39, 68, 87, 101, 103, 127–29, 128n54
In Adam's Fall (McFarland), 56
incarceration, 13–14, 63–64, 68, 94–97
incentives, recovery, 16–17, 31
Indigenous peoples, substance use by, 19–20
inherited guilt, 41, 56, 69
injustice, 43, 54–55, 68, 94–95, 95n20, 97

Inner Voice of Love, The (Nouwen), 122, 130, 134
Institutes (Calvin), 46
intermediary theology, 108
internal shame, 62–63. *See also* shame
"Interpretation of the Myth of Punishment," (Ricoeur), 98
isolation
   in addiction, 19–20, 44, 64, 152
   brokenness and, 160
   freedom from, 166
Israelites
   building patterns of, 128–29
   cravings of, for food, 124
   cry for help by, 111
   enslavement of, 109–11
   faith of, 122, 131
   freedom from Pharaoh, 119
   golden calf construction and, 127–29, 128n54, 131–32
   identities of, 119, 120n41, 121, 131–32, 134
   as insecure, during absence of Moses, 129
   laws and, 126
   past, longing for, 122–24, 128
   punishment of for unfaithfulness, 131, 133
   as seen by God, 113
   shame of, 132
   trust of God by, 134–35

Jamison, Leslie, 94, 95n20
Jesus Christ
   as debt payer, 83–84, 84n47
   liberation and, 106–7
   ministry of, with the broken, 7, 160–61
   role of in penal-substitutionary atonement, 76–79, 92–93
   salvation and, 4–6, 6n15
   as surrogate, in womanism, 76–77
Johnson, Mark, 75
Jones, Serene, 43–44, 55
journey metaphor. *See* exodus story, as extended metaphor
judicial metaphor of atonement
   about, 77
   criminals, humans as (*see* criminalization, of humans metaphor)
   as divine inspired, 98
   judge, God as (*see under* God: as judge)
justification, sanctification, and, 120n41

literalization of, 101–2
punishment, shame, and, 79–80, 82, 85–87
retributive justice and, 82–83, 92–93
See also penal-substitutionary atonement doctrine
judicial system, retributive version of. *See* retributive justice
Julian of Norwich, 134
justification, 106, 120–21nn41–42, 150–51

Karr, Mary, 44, 60, 105, 115–17, 142, 143, 144–47, 150
Khantzian, Edward, 17–18
Khar, Erin, 65, 80–81
King, Heather, 44–46, 54, 81–82, 88, 116, 139, 142, 152–53
King, Timothy McMahan, 64–65, 113
Knapp, Caroline, 61, 64, 139–41
knowing, meaning of in Exodus, 111–12, 111n21
Kövecses, Zoltán, 75

Lakoff, George, 75
language
 importance of in brokenness recognition, 162–63
 patriarchal (*see* patriarchal language, in theology)
 as validating, 156
 See also metaphors
lapses, in recovery. *See* relapses
laws/rules, 126–27
learning disorder, addiction as, 31
Lewis, Marc, 15, 17, 28, 31–32
LGBTQ+ population. *See* homosexuality, feelings of identity of as sinful
liberation theology, 106–7
Lilienfeld, Scott, 32
Lit (Karr), 44, 60, 105, 115–17, 144–47
literature, theology and, 108. *See also* exodus story, as extended metaphor
local choices, 15, 123
love, feeling of questioned, 4–6, 155–57, 163–64, 171
loved ones, of those with addictions. *See* families, of those with addictions
Luther, Martin, 78

maleness, divine, 76, 86, 91, 97–98
Manicheism, 38, 41, 41i

marketplace metaphor, 83–84, 84n47
Marshall, Ellen Ott, 56, 173
Maté, Gabor, 95–97
McFadyen, Alistair, 36
McFague, Sallie, 76, 86, 89, 91, 97, 100–101, 103, 108, 156
McFarland, Ian, 56
medications for addiction, 30
meditation, 147
memoirs, of addicts
 Between Breaths (Vargas), 9, 52,
 Blackout (Hepola), 18, 85
 Broken (Moyers) (*see* Moyers, William)
 Drinking: A Love Story (Knapp), 61, 64, 139–41
 Drunkard (Steinberg), 127–28, 164–65
 Drunk Mom (Bydlowska), 25, 37, 51–52, 60, 139, 164
 Lit (Karr), 44, 60, 105, 115–17, 144–47
 Parched (King), 44–46, 54, 81–82, 88, 116, 139, 142, 152–53
 Piece of Cake, A (Brown), 50, 67, 88, 140
 Stash: My Life in Hiding (Robbins), 18, 26, 37, 116, 141–42
 Strung Out (Khar), 65, 80–81
 Tweak (Sheff), 28, 51–52, 125
 Tweaked: A Crystal Meth Memoir (Moore), 146–47
memories, of past pain distorted, 122–25, 128, 130
mental health, 21, 33, 149, 162, 171–73
Mercadante, Linda, 68–69, 99n38, 126n49, 159
Metaphorical Theology (McFague), 76, 86
metaphors
 for atonement (*see* judicial metaphor of atonement; penal-substitutionary atonement doctrine)
 for atonement, importance of multiplicity, 102–3
 bondage of the will, 51–52, 51n56, 54, 56, 65–66, 69–70
 conceptual, underlying language, 94
 criminals, humans as, 79–80, 82–85
 divine-human relationship and, 76–77
 elimination of harmful, 100–101
 evaluation of, 103
 extended, about, 107–9 (*see also* exodus story, as extended metaphor)
 for God (*see under* God: metaphorical language regarding)

metaphors (*continued*)
  judicial (*see* judicial metaphor of atonement)
  literalized, 86–87, 101–2
  models (*see* models (pervasive and systematic metaphors))
  for salvation, 86–88, 107–9, 119–20, 147, 150 (*see also* exodus story, as extended metaphor; penal-substitutionary atonement doctrine; recovery journey metaphor, for salvation)
  theories of, 73–75, 73n2
  war, drug use and, 93–94, 97 (*see also* war on drugs)
Metaphors We Live By (Lakoff, Johnson), 75
Mission, The (Joffé), 132–33
models (pervasive and systematic metaphors)
  choice and, 91
  criteria of, 89–90
  elimination of harmful, 100–101
  as models on how to live, 90–91
  penal-substitutionary atonement and, 92–93
models of addiction. *See* addiction models
Models of God (McFague), 100–101, 103
Moore, Patrick, 146–47
morality and addiction, 36–37, 62–64, 66, 161–62. *See also* moral model of addiction
moral model of addiction, 11, 13–15
Moses
  absence of, 127–28, 128n54, 129
  as God's communicator to Israelites, 126
  negotiations with Pharaoh, 114–15
  and Pharaoh 114–15
  as seen and seeing, 112–14
  shame/blame by, 131
  trust of, 135
motherhood, shame and, 60
Moyers, William
  on addiction as overwhelming, 44–45
  on community in recovery, 151
  on cravings, 25
  on early recovery, 122–23
  on loved ones, blame from, 14
  on loved ones, impact of addiction on, 12–13
  on shame, 61–63
multi-addiction cycle, 64
murder
  of Egyptian by Moses, 113

God's command to Israelites, 131–32
NA (Narcotics Anonymous). *See* Twelve-Step groups (recovery groups)
naltrexone, 30
Narcotics Anonymous (NA). *See* Twelve-Step groups (recovery groups)
National Institute on Drug Addiction (NIDA), 22, 29
needs vs. desires, 25–26, 26n64, 37. *See also* compulsion-volition tension
negotiation/bargaining in addiction, 115–17
Nelson, James, 68–69, 99n38, 124
neural highways, 26–28, 27i
neuroscience of addiction
  brain's system of communication, 22–23, 22i
  cravings, 25–26
  dopamine equilibrium, 23–24, 53
  interpretations of, alternatives to brain disease, 31–33
  long-term effects of substance use, 28–29
  neural highways, habits, 26–27, 54
  will, as limited over time, 54
neurotransmitter dysregulation, 30
neurotransmitters, 22–23, 22i
Never Enough (Grisel), 23–24
New Jim Crow, The (M. Alexander), 63
NIDA (National Institute on Drug Addiction), 22, 32, 33
Niebuhr, Reinhold, 99n38
Nixon, Richard, 93–94
Nonviolent Atonement, The (Weaver), 93
Nouwen, Henri, 122, 130, 134
Novak, Michael, 108

obsession, addiction as, 31
"old country" concept (familiar past vs. unknown future), 122–25, 128, 130
On Free Will (Augustine), 38–41, 48–51
On Grace and Free Choice (Augustine), 49
On the Spirit and the Letter (Augustine), 49
opioid crisis, 96
oppression
  afterlife as relief from, 106–7
  biblical vs. freedom, 110
organ donors, 172
original sin
  addiction and, theologians on, 68–69
  Augustine on, 56
  bondage of the will and, 68–70

collective brokenness and, 66–68
definition of, 41–42
free will and, 39–40, 99
internal corruption by, 44
redemptive capacity of, 66–67
suffering and, 56
See also fall of man
overdoses, 2–3, 2nn2–3, 3n5, 65, 65n35, 96, 96n24

Palmer, Parker, 112
parables, 108
Parched (King), 44–46, 54, 81–82, 88, 116, 139, 142, 152–53
parents/parenting, of those with addictions
abuse by (*see* child abuse)
blame/shame and, 60, 81
foster, 50, 67
relational experiences with, 18–19, 62
past, longing for, 122–25, 128, 130
patriarchal language, in theology, 76, 86, 91, 97–98
Paul (apostle), 52
Pelagian-Manichean spectrum, 41i
Pelagius, 39–41, 41i, 48–49
penal-substitutionary atonement doctrine, 4–6, 6n15
atonement metaphor, multiplicity of, 101–3
Calvin's understanding of, 78–79
critiques of, 92, 92n7
literalization of metaphor of, 101–2
marketplace metaphor and, 83–84
metaphor of, 77, 86–88 (*see also* judicial metaphor of atonement)
as model, 92–93
pervasiveness of, 101, 158
punishment and, 81–85 (*see also* punishment)
retributive justice and, 97–98
sanctification and, 121
shame, as heightened from metaphor of, 79–80, 82, 85–87 (*see also* shame)
Pharaoh, 114–15, 117–19
Philosophy of Rhetoric, The (Richards), 73
physical impact of addiction, 140
Pickard, Hanna, 14, 31–33, 37
Piece of Cake, A (Brown), 50, 67, 88, 140
plagues, 115, 131
pleasure, neuroscience on, 23
post-traumatic stress disorder (PTSD), 17
Potter-Efron, Ronald T., 64

poverty, 68
power/control, 117
"powerlessness" (in addiction), 52, 63n25, 117. *See also* compulsion-volition tension
Powers, Brian, 66–68
prayer, power of, 144–47
prefrontal cortex (PFC), damage to, 28
pre-ingestion rush, 26
preparation state of change, 116–17
prison, 13–14, 63–64, 68, 94–97
process addictions (behavioral), 2, 2n1. *See also* behavioral addictions
Prochaska, James O., 116
promises broken, sobriety, 115–16
Propp, William, 129
Proslogion (Anselm), 148
psychological suffering, 17–18
PTSD (post-traumatic stress disorder), 17
punishment
of Christ, for humans, 78–79, 84 (*see also* penal-substitutionary atonement doctrine; salvation)
equalization of with crime (*see* retributive justice)
free will of sin and, 40
God of, 4–5, 80–82, 87–88
God's as necessary before forgiveness, 92
vs. healing of those with addictions, 97, 100
by incarceration (*see* incarceration)
of Israelites for unfaithfulness, 131
logic of, 82–88
need for, feeling of, 85, 131–33
shame and, 79–80, 82, 85–87, 132–33
purpose/meaning, addiction as need to fill, 129–30

racism
criminalization of drug possession and, 13–14, 94–95, 95n20, 97
societal complicity in, 68
systems of, 43
"Rat Park" experiment, 19
Razing Hell (Baker), 93
Reagan, Ronald, 94–95
Recovering, The (Jamison), 94
recovery, addiction
choices and, 15–17, 28–29, 53, 69–70, 123
community, importance in, 151–53, 159, 164–65

recovery, addiction (*continued*)
  early, 122–24, 140–42, 164
  experiences of, 122–23, 140–42, 145–47, 151–53, 164–65
  God's/church's role in, 87–88, 126–27n49, 130, 143–44, 148, 155–58, 166, 169 (*see also* church; God)
  meeting attendance and, 142 (*see also* Twelve-Step groups (recovery groups))
  prayer in, 143–47
  as process with hardships, 115–17, 120, 125, 137n1 (*see also* recovery journey metaphor, for salvation)
  recovery groups (*see* Alcoholics Anonymous (AA); Twelve-Step groups (recovery groups))
  rehab (*see* rehab)
  relapse and (*see* relapses)
  rituals of, 149
  routine in, 142–43 (*see also* prayer, power of)
  salvation and (*see* salvation)
  self-forgiveness and, 133
  shame preventing seeking, 64–65 (*see also* shame)
  short- vs. long-term value of, 123–24
  sobriety promises broken, 115–16
  training for sober living during, 141–42
recovery group practices for churches
  brokenness acknowledgment, 159–63
  sharing, mutual, 163–66
  vulnerable hospitality, 166–69
recovery groups. *See* Alcoholics Anonymous (AA); Twelve-Step groups (recovery groups)
recovery journey metaphor, for salvation
  act as if in, 149
  community and, importance of, 151–53
  grace and, 147–48, 150
  prayer, power of in, 143–47
  recovery group meeting attendance, 142
  rituals and, 139–41
  training and, 141–42
  See also recovery, addiction
redemption, 6, 106, 171–73. *See also* salvation
Red Sea, 121
rehab
  act as if and, 149
  leaving, 9, 52, 141–42
  as process, 120
  safety in, 153

sneaking substances into, 116
See also recovery, addiction
relapses
  experiences of, 28, 52, 125, 127–28
  of Israelites, 128
  memories of past hardships as distorted, 124–25
  mutual sharing of, 164–65
  from precipitating events, 127–28
  self-loathing and, 133–34
  shame and, 80 (*see also* shame)
  spiritual tools during, 147
relationships, in Twelve-Step groups, 164–65
retributive justice, 82–83, 92–93, 97–98
rewards, 16–17, 23, 31
Richards, I. A., 73–74
Ricoeur, Paul, 82–85, 98, 132
rituals of addiction, 139–41
rituals of recovery, 149
Robbins, Laura Cathcart, 18, 26, 37, 116, 141–42
Robinson, Terry, 15–16
role models. *See* models (pervasive and systematic metaphors)
rosy retrospection, 122–25, 128, 130
rules/laws, 126–27

salvation
  brokenness and, 160
  Calvin on, 78–79, 79nn26–27
  definition of, 106–7
  as deserving, 172
  in earthly vs. afterlife, 106–7, 107n6, 109, 121
  enslavers on, 107
  as God's work vs. human's, 114
  as grace and practice, 147–48
  justification, sanctification, and, 120–21, 150–51
  metaphors for, 86–88, 107–9, 119–20, 147, 150 (*see also* exodus story, as extended metaphor; penal-substitutionary atonement doctrine; recovery journey metaphor, for salvation)
  penal-substitutionary atonement doctrine and, 4–6 (*see also* atonement; penal-substitutionary atonement doctrine)
  as process with hardships, 114–15, 119–21, 125 (*see also* exodus story, as extended metaphor)

progressive thought on, 158–59
shame, punishment, and, 132
theologies of, 102–3 (*see also under* atonement: theologies of)
sanctification, 106, 120–21nn41–42, 150–51
sanctuary. *See* church
Sanderson, Christiane, 62–63
Satel, Sally, 32
satisfaction model of atonement, 83–84, 93
saving those with addictions, attempts to, 112–14
science, of addiction. *See* neuroscience of addiction
Science of Addiction, The (Erickson), 30
second-order volitions of will, 48–50
seeing, meaning of in Exodus, 111, 111n21
seen (acknowledged in empathy)
 vs. "fixing" those with addiction, 112–14, 164
 by God, of Israelites, 111–13
 of God by humans, temporary inability of, 133–34
 Moses and, 112–14
 as process, 114–19
self-compassion, 133–34
self-help groups. *See* Twelve-Step groups (recovery groups)
self-loathing, 52, 61, 64, 80–82
self-medication model of addiction
 attachment styles, childhood and, 18–19
 bondage of will and, 53
 capitalism and, 20
 concerns with, 21
 external conditions and, 55
 for psychological suffering, 17–18
 societal factors and, 19–20
sexism, 43, 55
sexually deviant behavior, 63, 153
sexual orientation. *See* homosexuality, feelings of identity of as sinful
shame
 -addiction cycle, 60–62, 80–81, 85, 156
 bondage of the will, alleviated by, 69–70
 childhood trauma and, 59–60
 church's role in, 156–57
 divine-sanctioned, 6, 79–80
 experiences of, 9, 52, 61–63, 65, 80–81

external, 62–66
forgiveness and, 68, 130–31
freedom from, 163–64, 166
healing from, need for, 85–86
heightened, from atonement metaphor, 79–80, 82, 85–87
as isolating, 152
original sin and, 66–70
punishment and, 82–83, 131–33
rituals and, 139
as sin, 85–86
See also blame
sharing, mutual, 163–66
Sheff, Nic, 28, 51–52, 125
Showings (Julian of Norwich), 134
sin
 addiction and, 50–51, 55, 68–69, 99–100, 99n38
 blame and, 36
 Calvin on, 41–44, 78–79, 84
 external conditions and, 42–44
 free will and, 40, 49–51, 99
 homosexuality and, 156
 vs. immorality, 99, 161
 origin of, 38
 recognition of, 160, 160n7
 salvation from (*see* salvation)
 See also original sin
sin-disease spectrum, of addiction, 36–37, 36i, 55
Sisters in the Wilderness (Williams), 76, 110
slavery. *See* enslavement
slips, in recovery. *See* relapses
sober reference points, 141
social drinkers vs. persons with addiction, 44–45
societal responsibility, for addiction, 67–68
societal view, on addiction, 14–15, 62–65
sovereignty of God, 47
Speaking in Parables (McFague), 108
spiritual transformations, Twelve-Step recovery and, 143–47
stages of change, 116–17
Stand Your Ground (Douglas), 109
Stash: My Life in Hiding (Robbins), 18, 26, 37, 116, 141–42
Steinberg, Neil, 127–28, 164–65
stereotypes, 14
stigmatizations, 14, 30, 32, 65, 113
Strung Out (Khar), 65, 80–81
Stump, Eleanore, 48–51, 92–93

substance use disorders (SUDs), 2, 2n1
substitution theory of metaphor, 73, 73n2, 92, 92n7, 93
suffering
   God's presence in, 170–73
   original sin and, 56
   seeing, importance of, 112–14 (*see also* seen (acknowledged in empathy))
   vs. sin, 161–62
suicide, 63, 105–6, 171–73
surrender, 145–46
surrogacy, in penal-substitutionary atonement, 76–77
survival needs, 25, 37, 46, 53
synaptic clefts, 22, 22i
systemic injustice, 13–14, 43, 54–55, 68, 94–95, 95n20, 97

Tabernacle, building of, 128
temporal vs. eternal desires, 38–39, 53. *See also* goodness, choosing
theology
   patriarchal language in, 76, 86
   literature and, 108 (*see also* exodus story, as extended metaphor)
   models, importance in, 91
   sin and blame in, 36
theories of addiction. *See* addiction models
Thirst (Nelson), 124
13th (M. Alexander), 94
Though the Fig Tree Does Not Blossom (Marshall), 173
tolerance, neuroscience of, 24
totalizing condition, sin as, 42–44
Tragic Vision and Divine Compassion (W. Farley), 71
training and practice, for sober living, 141–42
transtheoretical model, 116
trauma, 17–18, 59–60, 67
triggers, 26
trust, 134–35
Tweak (Sheff), 28, 51–52, 125
Tweaked: A Crystal Meth Memoir (Moore), 146–47
Twelve-Step groups (recovery groups)
   about, 3–4n7
   brokenness in, 159–63
   choices and, 16, 16n27
   Christian roots of, 126–27n49
   community of, 151–53, 159, 164–65
   God's role in (*see under* addiction: God's/church's role in)
   grace and love from, vs. church, 3–5, 7, 159, 165–66
   importance of, 150–51, 159
   meeting attendance at, 142
   "powerlessness" and, 52, 63n25, 117
   relationships in, as supportive, 3–4, 164–65
   sense of belonging in, 152
   sharing in, 163–66
   spiritual transformations and, 143–47
   vulnerability in, 166–69

unfaithfulness, punishment for, 131
unlovable, sense of being, 4–6, 155–57, 163–64, 171. *See also* penal-substitutionary atonement doctrine
Urge, The: Our History of Addiction (Fisher), 46

Vargas, Elizabeth, 9, 52, 127, 147
Victims and Sinners (Mercadante), 68–69, 99n38, 126n49, 159
violence, 93, 113, 131–32. *See also* child abuse
volition and compulsion. *See* compulsion-volition tension
volition orders of will, 48–50
vulnerability, 166–69

walk of honor, 171–73
Ward, Keith, 92
war on drugs
   blame and, 11
   ineffectiveness of, 96–97
   mass incarceration and, 13, 63–64, 94–97
   metaphorical use of, 93–95
   retributive justice and, 97–99
war veterans, redemption of guilt of, 66–68
Waters, Sonia, 13, 18, 88, 97–98, 100
Weaver, J. Denny, 93
will, bondage of
   about, 41–42
   addiction, sin and, 50–51
   addiction and, 37, 44–45, 53
   Calvin on, 41–48, 50
   church's responsibility to teach, 70–71
   goodness, choosing and, 50
   habits and, 117–18

metaphor of, 51–52, 51n56, 54, 56, 65–66, 69–71
models of addiction and, 53–57
original sin, without, 68
pastoral care and, 70–71
shame and, 65–66, 68–70
See also will, freedom of
will, freedom of
accountability and, 40
Alcoholics Anonymous on, 63n25
Augustine on, 38–41, 48–51, 54
Calvin on, 45–48, 47n42
vs. choice, 45–47 (*see also* choices)
good, choosing, 38–40, 39n15, 47–50, 47n42, 53, 55

habits and, 26–27, 54, 117–18, 122–25, 128
help, asking for, 48–49, 70, 111, 111n20
original sin and, 39–40
Pelagius on, 39–41, 48–49
Pharaoh's, 117–18
sin and, 40, 49–51, 99
Stump on Augustine's position on, 48–51
See also will, bondage of
Williams, Delores, 76–77, 101, 103, 110, 132
womanism, 76–77, 106–7
worldly vs. eternal desires, 38–39, 53. *See also* goodness, choosing

www.ingramcontent.com/pod-product-compliance
Lightning Source LLC
Chambersburg PA
CBHW070612070126
37807CB00001B/1